S0-CUG-942

Public Speaking

COLUMBIA JUNIOR COLLEGE
LIBRARY

Public Speaking

Today and Tomorrow

Ethel C. Glenn
University of North Carolina, Greensboro

Sandra H. Forman
University of North Carolina, Greensboro

SOUTH UNIVERSITY LIBRARY
COLUMBIA, SC 29203

PRENTICE HALL, Englewood Cliffs, NJ 07632

Library of Congress Cataloging-in-Publication Data

Glenn, Ethel C.
    Public speaking: today and tomorrow / Ethel C. Glenn and Sandra
H. Forman.
      p. cm.
    Bibliography: p.
    Includes index.
    ISBN 0-13-738915-9
    1. Public speaking. I. Forman, Sandra H. II. Title
PN4142.G5 1990   89-8768
    808.5'1—dc20   CIP

Editorial/production supervision and
  interior design: Jennifer Wenzel
Cover design: Wanda Lubelska Design
Manufacturing buyer: Ed O'Dougherty

 © 1990 by Prentice-Hall, Inc.
A Division of Simon & Schuster
Englewood Cliffs, New Jersey 07632

All rights reserved. No part of this book may be
reproduced, in any form or by any means,
without permission in writing from the publisher

Printed in the United States of America

10 9 8 7 6 5 4 3 2 1

ISBN   0-13-738915-9

Prentice-Hall International (UK) Limited, *London*
Prentice-Hall of Australia Pty. Limited, *Sydney*
Prentice-Hall Canada Inc., *Toronto*
Prentice-Hall Hispanoamericana, S.A., *Mexico*
Prentice-Hall of India Private Limited, *New Delhi*
Prentice-Hall of Japan, Inc., *Tokyo*
Simon & Schuster Asia Pte. Ltd., *Singapore*
Editora Prentice-Hall do Brasil, Ltda., *Rio de Janeiro*

Contents

Preface

Students and teachers alike may face a new textbook with some concerns. Will it be interesting? Will it cover the subject thoroughly without being overly long and tedious? Is the content testable? For many students, this is not only a new textbook but also a new content area, for they have had no formal coursework in public speaking. Some newer, younger instructors may be teaching public speaking for the first time. More experienced professors will be comparing this book with others they have used in the past.

Whichever your role, we hope that you will find this book to be clear, straightforward, current, and reasonably balanced between the extremes of simplicity and difficulty. The authors have taught public speaking for many years and have tried to combine their personal experience with research and observation.

A good public speaking textbook should offer both the *whys* and the *hows* of speech composition and delivery. Some authors have concentrated more heavily on the *whys,* the descriptive, theoretical approach. Others have focused on the *hows,* prescriptively offering time-tested guidelines for speech preparation and presentation. Most authors try to do some of both, recognizing that depth and specificity may be somewhat limited if we are to keep the book within a reasonable length.

In this book, we have often only alluded to a theory without explaining it in full, giving only one or two footnotes as to its source rather than a fully developed bibliography. Because our target audience is introductory-level classes, we feel that too much theory and research would be beyond the scope of the course. On the practical side, we have tried to offer many specific "tips" as well as examples. Doubtless we could provide many more examples to illustrate the points and could be even more prescriptive in telling you how to put together a speech. But concerns about the book's length discourage further illustration. And our belief that too much formularizing of the *how-to* kills student originality and imagination prevents us from giving you what is often called a "cookbook" approach to public speaking.

The other aspect of introductory public speaking that has been of special concern to us in our classes and that we have tried to address in this book, is the relationship between what you will learn in this class and how you will use that knowledge in nonclassroom settings. For lack of an adequate term to suggest life experiences other than those of students in classes, the phrase "real world" is used to differentiate. We grant you that it is a poor label, for it seems to imply that school is not real. We all know better. Nonetheless, if we can agree that "real world" carries a certain meaning, even if we object to its accuracy, we can talk about the similarities and differences between the world outside the classroom and an academic setting.

Some speech professors prefer not to address the differences. Some do not feel any real differences exist. Our viewpoint developed from the many comments and questions raised by our students about such issues as audience analysis and adaptation, speech purposes and their relationship to topic choices, and environmental factors of presentation settings (lecterns, platforms, microphones, and so forth). Our students sense some genuine differences between real world and classroom, not in the theory that underlies speech composition and delivery, but in the application of that theory. They want to know how to plan not just for the classroom, nor as an emulation of very famous speakers, but in the way that most people who work in business and industry and who do extensive volunteer work must plan for the speeches they routinely give.

We have tried to address this concern, both directly in our discussions and by using a mixture of examples from both classroom and "real world," "everyday" sorts of speakers. We explain our process for collecting these examples in the first chapter. We hope this approach will enable students not only to succeed in classroom speeches, but to take away with them the knowledge and skills that will prepare them for a lifetime of speaking to groups of people.

As to the structure of the text, it is divided into five major parts, each containing three chapters. Each part deals with a different major aspect of the speech making process, while the individual chapters offer guidelines for step-by-step speech preparation.

Part I, The Speaker and the Listener, sets the stage for all that will follow in the course. You will learn about the role of public speaking in today's world as well as the expectations for your public speaking classroom. You will study listeners and listening, for all speech making is planned and designed with listeners in mind.

Part II, The Speaker and the Selection Process, prepares you to select meaningful and interesting topics for your speeches and to learn the various purposes of speeches and how they can be related to the needs of the listeners. You will be shown how to find and use the illustrative and supporting material that makes speech topics come to life.

In Part III, The Speaker and the Development Process, you will learn to organize the materials that you have discovered—creating workable outlines and planning the beginnings and endings of your speeches as well as structuring the main body of ideas. One chapter is devoted to preparing and using visual aids that can help a speaker add clarity and interest to the speech.

Part IV, Development Patterns for Different Speech Purposes, deals with building informative, persuasive, or special occasion speeches. Each serves a unique purpose and has special guidelines for preparation and delivery.

Part V is devoted to The Speaker and the Delivery Process and covers the use of the voice and body, language, and several elements of the speaking situation, such as microphones, lecterns, and different types of rooms and auditoriums in which speeches are given.

Finally, a word about style. As we wrote this book, we thought constantly of talking to and with our own students, blending the informality of group discussion and question-and-answer sessions with the somewhat more formal professorial lecture. We tried to anticipate many of your questions and concerns and to talk with you about them. We hope that as you read you will put yourself in the role of listener as well as reader. We want to talk with you as we talk with our classes. We hope you will be an alert and interested listener and that you will learn the fundamentals of composing and presenting a speech. With your instructor's added lectures, class discussions, and your opportunities to deliver several speeches to the class, you should make real progress toward becoming an effective public speaker. That is our goal for you, and we hope it is your goal also.

Our special thanks goes to Professors Lois Einhorn, State University of New York, University Center at Binghamton; H. L. Goodall, University of Alabama in Huntsville; Edward Streb, Glassboro State College, Glassboro, New Jersey; Dan Mellinger, Cincinnati Technical College; and Nancy Goulden, Kansas State University, for reviewing our manuscript and offering helpful comments and suggestions.

Part I

The Speaker and the Listener

Part I gets you underway by overviewing the process of creating a speech and explains to you some of the techniques we used to find examples and illustrations of speeches in today's educational, business, and volunteer worlds. We then deal with listeners from two different perspectives: first, as audience members whom the speaker should come to know and understand and to whom the speaker needs to adapt the message; and second, as listeners to speeches, with emphasis on the many common problems listeners experience and some suggestions for becoming a more effective listener.

Chapter 1

Getting Underway

TODAY'S SPEECH MAKERS

In One Day Americans make 100,000 speeches. If they were all waiting their turn at the same soapbox, the speakers would form a line 28 miles long. It would take the last speaker nine hours just to walk to the podium.[1]

You will probably be one of those 100,000 speech makers some day. The college student of the 1990s looks ahead to a world in which the ability to be an effective communicator is a primary requirement for a wide variety of jobs, hobbies, and service activities.

Speaking in public is one of the most ancient and respected but often terrifying and misunderstood acts of human society. As far back as 2500 B.C. in Egypt[2] and 500 B.C. in Greece,[3] authors have written books of instruction on becoming an effective public speaker. Today, numbers of teachers and trainers offer courses and workshops designed to help people handle the speaking obligations that fall to many of us during our lifetimes. Indeed, the ability to speak effectively and to some degree eloquently is one of the major marks of the educated man or woman. It is an essential for many careers. "Public speaking is

2

the best method of presenting yourself as a polished professional,"[4] one astute observer has noted.

This book is designed to provide you with an understanding of the basic techniques that help speakers prepare sound, clear, and interesting, hence more effective, speeches. Throughout the book, you will be given examples of speech settings, occasions, audiences, topics, topic development, and delivery techniques that your authors collected especially to illustrate speech making in today's business and social world.

The research technique used by John Naisbitt in his best-seller *Megatrends*[5] gave us the guideline for discovering what is taking place with public speakers today. Like Naisbitt, we went to newspapers, in our case to locate the kinds of speeches being given in American cities on a daily basis. We examined the papers from 20 different areas for a two-week period for every mention of anyone giving a speech. Most local newspapers give fairly comprehensive listings of area clubs and organizations that hold regular meetings. Newspapers also provide good coverage of events in which politicians and public figures speak.

What does not appear in the daily papers are the hundreds of speeches given across this nation each day in corporate and business settings. Presentations to corporate boards, management teams, or special groups such as sales or advertising task forces take place behind closed doors and are not open to a general audience. Yet they are speeches that you might be called upon to give some day.

Traditionally we associated public speaking primarily with lawyers, ministers, politicians, and teachers. Today, speaking opportunities are much more widespread, and people from many different professions are called upon to speak in public. To take another cue from Naisbitt, we have shifted from the industrial age to the information age, just as surely as the nineteenth century shifted from an agrarian society to an industrial society. Rapid advances in communication technology as well as major shifts in the world economy have brought us to the time and place in history where the gathering, sorting, interpreting, and disseminating of information involves an increasing number of persons with each passing year. While much of this information is communicated through the technology (computers and satellites, for example), we also have experienced growth in the number of opportunities for face-to-face communication. Not only do we have more business and social organizations than ever before in history, but we also have professionals, such as public relations practitioners and organizational communicators, who use speech making as well as print or other media to get across their messages. The Association of Communication Administration has suggested that by the year 2000, 35 percent of all persons employed in the United States will be in some way connected with communication and information.

This major shift in focus moves us from a world in which public speeches were given by a relatively limited number of people to a world in which a majority of those in the work and social arena will be called upon to communicate in public. With this in mind, we also set out to find what demands are being made on everyday people in their everyday jobs for some form of public communication. To accomplish this, we did an intensive study of the speech making in our own community over a period of several months. Here is a small sampling of the different jobs in which we found people giving speeches.

Some Jobs in Which People Give Speeches

architect
artist
banker
biologist
doctor
engineer
geologist
horticulturist
lawyer
librarian
pharmacist

politician
psychologist
fashion buyer
insurance underwriter
personnel manager
public administrator
real estate agent
recreational supervisor
sales executive
sports figure
stockbroker

The authors have the distinction of living in a mid-sized city (about 180,000 population) that has recently been cited as the most ideal place to live in the United States![6] Part of that rating might have been influenced by the types of people who live here—warm, open, friendly folks who were more than willing to let us come to their club meetings, staff conferences, board or team sessions, anyplace where we might hear someone speaking to a group of people. We use examples from these many speeches and speech settings to try to help you understand the speech making process.

These local speeches were made mostly by "plain folks," not famous politicians and paid public speakers. We believe these examples will be meaningful to you, for it is our assumption that most of you will not be President of the United States, nor even senators or congressmen. What we hope you will be is involved, active members of a large or small business or company, a governmental agency, a major corporation, or any organization that will provide you a means for making a living and building your career.

Probably many of you are already employed, for today's college population includes a generous percentage of students who have not gone straight from high school to college. As returning students who have already experienced the workaday world or the demands of volunteerism, you may have sought out a course in public speaking.

Whether you are a new or returning student, self-motivated or required to take this course, you are beginning an area of study that will profit you in a very practical way as you prepare yourself for a career that will in all probability call for you to give public presentations some day. While this course will also help you to become a better consumer of public messages by learning about speech making techniques and practices (see Chapter 3, "The Audience as Listeners"), the major emphasis is to prepare you for the role of speaker.

A PUBLIC, NOT AN INTERPERSONAL OR SMALL GROUP SETTING

The phrase *public speaking* implies an occasion with several people, invited or coming voluntarily, in attendance. While some speech settings might be private in that they are open only to members of an organization or special group, they still require the format of public speaking. That format generally suggests that one person will do most of the talking, while several other people do most of the listening. More often than not, the speaker knows in advance that he or she will speak and has prepared something to say.

Numerous other types of communication settings exist in business and service situations. Jobholders often find themselves in one-to-one conversations or interviews with colleagues or persons from other businesses. Telephone calls dominate much of the working day for many secretaries, receptionists, salespersons, managers—indeed, almost any level of employment. Your authors tend to view these situations as basically *interpersonal* in nature, therefore not the subject of a book on public speaking in careers.

In addition to these one-to-one occasions, working persons often find themselves in situations in which they talk with a few fellow employees in a *small group* setting. Committee or staff meetings and board or cabinet meetings may be designed so that all members interact freely and equally. No one person takes the floor to speak for a prolonged period of time while the others sit and listen. Again, we do not view talking informally in group meetings as truly comparable to the formal speech.

A panel discussion or symposium may combine the two—panelists may give a speech first, then discuss the issue based on the speeches each member has given. This differs from the committee meeting in that the formal panel has an audience, namely a group of people who sit quietly during the speeches and who may remain silent during the discussion unless a specific question-and-answer period is included. Speakers in a symposium will follow the same rules of good public speaking that anyone preparing to speak in a single-speaker setting will follow.

We see interpersonal and small group communication as distinctly different from public speaking. The number of participants, the level of participation, the balance between the roles of speaker and listener, the degree of formality, the type of preparation, and many elements of delivery ranging from posture to projection all change as we move from chairs in a circle to chairs lined up to face a podium.

Many of the principles you learn in public speaking can serve you well in the more private settings, especially such techniques as audience adaptation, the fundamentals of persuasion, or the need to provide support for your ideas.

The focus of this book, however, is on the speaker who addresses an audience in a one-to-many relationship.

RELATING BEYOND THE CLASSROOM

Beginning speech students face something of a dilemma. You must give speeches in a classroom setting before an audience made up of other students and the instructor. In most cases, your speeches will be graded, with those speech evaluations averaged together with written tests, outlines, and term paper grades to earn an overall course grade.

Yet much of the content of the course deals with speech making in far different settings. Learning to analyze audiences, to adjust topics and supporting materials to different groups of listeners, and to vary delivery techniques according to factors such as the size of the room or the formality of the occasion all presuppose "real world" rather than classroom situations.

In addition, speech students are usually asked to apply the principles of speech making not only to themselves as they prepare and deliver speeches, but also as a foundation for evaluating other speakers. This may be providing written or oral critiques to the other students in the class or may include assignments to go into the community and listen to and evaluate public speakers.

The course content, therefore, needs to be applied in at least three different ways:

1. as a guide to giving speeches in the classroom;
2. as a basis for evaluating classroom and other speeches heard during the course; and
3. as a preparation for listening to and making speeches in the future.

To aid in this application, each chapter of this book will conclude by giving you a discussion question relating the material in that chapter to one or more of the following three different perspectives:

1. for this immediate class in a college, university, or workshop;
2. for the career and social world at large;
3. by projecting you personally into some future time in your life.

For this introductory chapter, for example, you might discuss the question "Where might I be asked to speak in public?" Relating your reply to the first perspective, you might answer that you will speak in class because it is an inherent part of the course itself. You will not find public speaking courses listed in correspondence or extension catalogues! You must practice speaking in order to learn how to speak.

For an answer to the second step of the perspective, you might look at the demands for speakers in social and career settings in your city or state. Read newspapers or follow announcements in bulletins from clubs, churches, or other organizations where speakers are featured. Examine the following list of speech situations that are probably rather typical. This is by no means an exhaustive list—you can add to it as your training progresses.

SPEECH OCCASIONS AND PLACES

ROTARY CLUB (weekly meeting)	Restaurant (medium-sized private dining room)
PROFESSIONAL SECRETARIES (monthly meeting)	YMCA (large dining room)
KIWANIS CLUB (weekly meeting)	Elks Club (large dining room)
WOMEN'S HISTORY MONTH (special meeting)	College Student Union (lounge)
AMERICAN CANCER SOCIETY (monthly meeting)	Hospital (small conference room)
DELTA KAPPA GAMMA (study group)	Member's living room
MENTAL HEALTH ASSOCIATION	Church Parlor
COUNTY PRICINCT MEETING	Elementary School Lobby
AMERICAN FRIENDS SERVICE (committee meeting)	Public Lirbary (auditorium)
NATIONAL COUNCIL OF JEWISH WOMEN	President's Home
EMERGENCY NURSES ASSO.	Hospital (conference room)
HUMANE SOCIETY	Large College Auditorium
NATIONAL ASSOCIATION OF BLACK ACCOUNTANTS	Restaurant (small dining room)
DELTA KAPPA GAMMA (quarterly meeting)	Board of Education (conference room)

For the third step, think about the career you want for yourself. If you could choose anything—an ideal job or an ideal volunteer opportunity, what would it be? Even though you may not have settled on a college major and a concrete career goal as yet, you can still imagine yourself a few years from now. You can talk with professors or practitioners who can give you concrete suggestions as to where you might be or what kinds of speeches might be expected of you in a particular occupation. You can make this classroom more meaningful if you envision your own future possibilities as a speech maker.

STEPS FOR DEVELOPING A SPEECH

Another dilemma confronts beginning speech students. In order to prepare and deliver classroom speeches to the best of your ability, you need to have read, studied, and absorbed all the principles and guidelines of effective public speaking. Yet if you waited to give your first speech until you had mastered this textbook, heard all the lectures, and taken all the written tests, the course might be nearly over before you got on your feet.

You will need to begin giving speeches before you have learned all the speech making principles. As the class moves forward, you will add to your knowledge about the process by giving and hearing speeches, listening to lectures, and discussing speech making techniques. Yet in the beginning, you may feel unsure of what is expected of you.

To help you with those early speeches, the following list of 10 steps in preparing a speech may be useful:

1. Understand exactly the required assignment—
   a. Are you to introduce, inform, persuade, or give a special-occasion speech?
   b. Are you allowed to use notes, an outline, or a manuscript?
   c. Are you to use outside references?
   d. Is there a time limit?
2. Choose a topic that comes from some area you already know about or in which you are highly interested and somewhat familiar. As you make the choice, think about the other students who will be listening to you. What might interest them?
3. Spend time in the library, gather other pertinent written information (brochures, pamphlets, newsletters), or plan to interview knowledgeable individuals.
4. Put notes on paper that combine what you already know about the subject with the information you are gathering.
5. Formulate a specific topic statement that moves you from a general idea level to a clear-cut specific subject that can be covered in the allotted time.
6. Organize your ideas about the topic and your illustrative material—explanations, examples, or quotations—so that you feel you have backed up your ideas and made them clear.
7. Locate or make any visual materials you feel will be helpful—posters, charts, graphs, models, or real objects. Plan how and when you will use the visual material.

8. Plan exactly how you want to arrange the speech—how will you begin? Can you create an interesting closing thought that seems to tie the speech together?

9. Practice *out loud*, checking the timing of your speech with a watch or clock. Add to or take away from the content to make it fit the assigned time.

10. Rehearse out loud several times until you know how you sound. If your instructor has limited you to notes or an outline rather than a full manuscript, practicing aloud will help you as you enlarge and amplify notes into fully developed thoughts and sentences. Practicing aloud also helps you gain confidence.

Use this 10-step guide as you plan your first speech. Following each step carefully will help you handle speech assignments before you have completed your study of the textbook and supplementary materials on the principles of speech making.

DEALING WITH FEAR UP FRONT

Performance anxiety or stage fright concerns many if not most speech students. Performance anxiety is primarily connected to *delivering* the speech rather than the preparation process, yet the fear is so pervasive that some students begin to worry about it from the first meeting of the class. Dealing with it early on will not make the anxiety go away but can help you put it in perspective.

The word "cure" is often used by people who seek out special help for their performance anxiety. It is almost as if they felt they had a disease and were looking for a magic formula for a remedy. Stage fright is not a disease; rather, it is a natural physical reaction to a stressful situation. Few things that we are called upon to do put us under the figurative spotlight more intensely than standing before a group of people who are all looking at us, listening to us, expecting us to say something significant and to say it well. Numerous studies have found that a majority of people list speaking in public as one of their greatest fears.[7] And this fear is by no means limited to amateur or beginning speakers. "Even professionals aren't immune. Some of our most successful politicians, evangelists, and entertainers suffer extreme stage fright,"[8] one observer notes.

Researchers have identified two types of performance apprehension—*state* and *trait*.[9] *State* communication apprehension occurs when a certain situation places the speaker under stress, such as an appraisal interview with an employer, a tax audit by the IRS, or giving a speech in front of a group of people. *Trait* apprehension describes a speaker who is anxious or fearful in a number of different communication situations, even those that most people would not consider stressful.

The person who suffers from trait anxiety is referred to as a *communication apprehensive,* or CA. These people are far fewer in number than those who experience various levels of state apprehension. A true CA will experience difficulty in talking in social situations and may withdraw from conversation groups or even avoid attending parties or social gatherings. Any minor confrontation can upset the CA, who may avoid calling a cashier's attention to incorrect change or fail to question shoddy merchandise or poor services.

The CA needs special help and attention. Desensitizing programs are available in some universities, either through speech departments or in clinics operated by psychology or mental health units. Biofeedback has been useful in relieving the stressful symptoms such as excessive perspiration, uncontrollable shaking of hands or knees, or shortness of breath.

If you and your instructor determine that you have a severe problem, we hope you will seek out help. Our concern here, however, is directed toward that far larger number of students who experience state apprehension before giving classroom speeches but are otherwise relatively comfortable in communicating at parties or in confronting the mechanic who failed to make the proper automobile repairs. The term *performance anxiety* or the more familiar term *stage fright* refers to this state apprehension that many speakers experience.

Stage fright can be beneficial if the speaker can learn to channel and direct the nervous energy into a positive force that will add liveliness and animation. This added energy is useful if a speaker will work with it instead of against it. Performance anxiety causes additional hormones from the adrenal gland to be secreted into the system. This is part of the body's mechanism for handling danger or emergencies, for the secretion brings quick extra energy, added muscular strength, and better eyesight through constriction of the blood vessels. Working with the energy means using it productively instead of fighting it or blocking its flow. For example, intentional body movement can be substituted for immobile rigidity, while vigorous volume and vocal inflection can replace subdued monopitches. The mental energy required to generate or create new sentence structures is more helpful than the passive act of reading from a manuscript; hence, the speaker who refuses to depend solely on reading may be able to use nervous energy more readily.

Using stage fright productively so that you control it requires that you first of all put the speech act in its proper perspective. Think through answers to the following questions. If you tried to give a speech in your classroom but were not able to finish it because of your nervousness, what would happen? Would it mean an automatic F? Or would your instructor in all likelihood give you the opportunity to try again at the next class meeting? The last option is the most common one.

If you could not finish the speech, would the rest of the class laugh at you? Or think you are a failure? Or would they be sympathetic, with a high level of empathy, and anxious to help you master your problem? Again, the last option is the one we can guarantee you dominates in most classrooms. Friendly, encouraging audiences are the norm in speech classes. Furthermore, your classmates experience a similar discomfort when they give their speeches, so they understand what you are going through.

Accept the fact that stage fright is normal and natural. Your symptoms are not nearly so evident to the rest of the class as they are to you. Often audience members are surprised to find out after the speech that the speaker was genuinely uncomfortable, since the obvious signs could not be detected. You will grow more comfortable as the course progresses and you gain more experience before the class. In addition to this personal pep talk that helps put your speech making in the proper perspective, carry out the following suggestions for some things you can do both before and during your speech to help reduce the anxiety.

Before the Speech

1. *Be well prepared.* Most of us are more comfortable when we know that our material is thoroughly and carefully researched and organized and that we have practiced the speech out loud. Knowing that your topic is suited to you and the audience and that you have provided ample interesting supporting material helps you to feel confident that you have done what is expected of you. Good preparation can enable you to use an extemporaneous style rather than memorizing or reading your speech. Extemporaneous style is more spontaneous and avoids the danger of forgetting the words or losing your place in the manuscript.

2. *Be well rested.* If you are tired from lack of sleep the night before, you are less able to control the stress on your body. Never leave the preparation of your speech until the night before you are to give it. If you stay up late, you combine loss of sleep with lack of thorough preparation for a double dose of trouble.

3. *Be well fed.* One of the parts of the body that stage fright tends to hit the worst is the stomach. Under stress, the stomach secretes excess acid, and if you have no food in your stomach for the acid to act on, it can increase your feeling of discomfort. However, do not overeat before a speech, for an overly full stomach can press on the diaphragm, a major muscle used in the breathing process. Most banquet or after-dinner speakers learn to eat lightly, for the overly full feeling can be a distraction when you are talking.

4. *Be neat and trim.* All of us have certain standards about our own appearances, certain clothes in which we feel better because we believe we look better, and certain preferred hair styles, makeup, beards or mustaches, or any feature of our outward self. The more secure you are that you look good, the more confident you will be.

During the Speech

1. *Focus on the audience, not yourself.* Think about the people you are talking to, not yourself. Try to actually look at different people in the audience—catch someone's eye for a few seconds. Some time ago an erroneous idea was circulated that looking over the heads of the audience would help to make a speaker less nervous. This is inaccurate, for it is only when you make genuine contact with members of the audience, talking *with* them instead of *at* them or *to* them, that you can begin to relax. As Michael Motley reminds us, "A more useful and accurate orientation is to view speeches as communication rather than performance. The speakers' role is to share ideas with an audience more interested in hearing what they have to say than in analyzing or criticizing how they say it."[10]

2. *Think about the topic, not yourself.* You should have a genuine interest in your subject and a belief that what you have to say is important. Focus on the content of your speech so that you can take your mind off yourself.

3. *Make use of your nervous energy.* Gestures, facial expressions, and movements of the torso are helpful in freeing tension. You can move your entire body by stepping forward or back or from side to side, even if you are limited by a lectern or microphone. Locking your knees and standing rigid makes the situation worse.

Talking with good volume and animation also helps. Breathing deep from your diaphragm, with a conscious focus on full expansion of the triangular area below the bottom of the lower ribs and just above the waistline, will be of real aid in controlling the physical symptoms of stage fright.

4. *Use pauses to catch up.* Do not be afraid of pausing between sentences or major ideas. Pauses usually seem much longer to the speaker than to the listener. Use the pause time to take a deep breath and think through your next sentence or idea. This gives you time to exert control over your thoughts and your body.

A degree of performance anxiety will always be with you. Think in terms of learning to *control* rather than *overcome* your stage fright. As with many fears, dreading in advance that you will be afraid and will be unable to handle it is usually worse than the actual anxiety experience. Approached with a positive attitude and using the suggestions offered here, your speech performance will grow easier and you will become more confident as the course progresses.

KEY POINTS

- Public speaking training in the 1990s needs to prepare students for a large number of business, social, and service settings in which they may some-day speak.
- A national newspaper search and an intensive series of visits in the Greensboro, North Carolina, area have provided the authors with numer-

ous illustrations and examples of the types of speeches being heard routinely in the United States today.

- *Public speaking* implies a unique audience-speaker relationship and makes different demands on the speaker than does interpersonal or small group communication.
- Speech occasions should be examined from both a classroom and real world—current and future—orientation.
- Beginning speech students can use a series of steps to prepare speech assignments before all the techniques for speech making have been presented. Each of these steps will be covered in detail in later chapters.
- Finally, performance anxiety is a natural response that all speakers experience. Four specific steps can be taken before the speech and four steps during the speech to help a speaker reduce the severity of the symptoms and control—not eliminate—stage fright.

QUESTION FOR DISCUSSION

What are the kinds of speeches that you are going to be asked to give during this speech course? How do those speeches relate to the speeches that you have heard in the past year? How do you think they relate to the speeches that you might be required to give some day as a part of your chosen profession?

ACTIVITIES

1. Attend a speech somewhere in your community. Report back on the title of the speech, nature of the occasion, and your general impression of the speaker.
2. To help you understand the pervasiveness of public speaking, add to the list in Chapter 1 with other jobs, volunteer opportunities, and situations and occasions in which you think people might give a speech.
3. Start an index file in which you list topics that you feel qualified to talk about or topics that you would like to know more about. Collect materials on each topic by jotting down information you discover in newspaper/magazine articles, on television/radio programs, in books, and so forth. (Be sure to annotate each file card for future use.)
4. If your instructor agrees, a few rounds of impromptu speeches during the first two or three weeks may help you gain confidence in standing before the class and thinking on your feet. Impromptu speeches are done on the spur of the moment and without preparation. Some impromptu topics might include unusual experiences, travel or vacation adventures, or favorite books/movies/television programs. For

those of you who work, describe the interior of your office or store, relate an incident when dealing with the public, or explain the responsibilities of your present or past job.

5. In order to help you control your nervousness, locate the triangle formed by your lower two ribs as they move downward and outward toward your sides and by your waistline across the bottom. This is the triangle where the center of deep breathing is located. Practice feeling it expand and contract as you inhale and exhale. Then, purposely tighten the muscles in the triangle area until you feel a firmness and control. Practice this several times until you are sure you know how to do it. The next time you feel frightened when you get up to give a speech, tighten and release the triangle several times as you breathe to speak.

REFERENCES

[1]Tom Parker, *In One Day* (Boston: Houghton Mifflin, 1984), 31.

[2]Karl F. Robinson and E. J. Kerikas, *Teaching Speech: Methods and Materials* (New York: David McKay, 1963), 21.

[3]First textbook attributed to Corax and his pupil Tisias. See Lester Thonssen, A. Craig Baird, and Waldo W. Braden, *Speech Criticism*, 2nd ed. (New York: The Ronald Press, 1970), 40–42.

[4]Sandra Ralston, as cited in "Smart Talk for Careers," *Black Enterprise*, January 1988, 25.

[5]John Naisbitt, *Megatrends: Ten New Directions Transforming Our Lives* (New York: Warner Books, 1984).

[6]Robert M. Tierce, Paper given at the Association of American Geographers, Washington, D.C., April 1984. As reported in the *Greensboro News and Record*, April 24, 1984, A-1.

[7]Frank E. X. Dance and Carl E. Larson, *Speech Communication: Concepts and Behavior* (New York: Holt, Rinehart & Winston, 1972), 155–56.

[8]Michael T. Motley, "Talking the Terror Out of Talk," *Psychology Today*, January 1988, 46.

[9]See either James H. Geer, "The Development of a Scale to Measure Fear," *Behavior Research and Therapy* 3 (August 1965): 45–53; Peter Taggart, Malcolm Carruthers, and Walter Somerville, "Electrocardiogram, Plasma Catecholamines and Lipids, and Their Modification by Oxprenolol When Speaking Before an Audience," *The Lancet* [#7825 Vol. II for 1973 (August 18, 1973)]: 341.

[10]Motley, "Talking the Terror Out of Talk," 48.

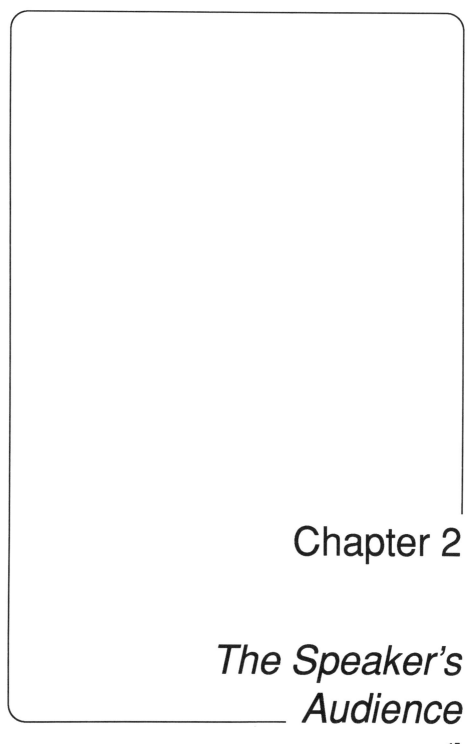

Chapter 2

The Speaker's Audience

AUDIENCE ADAPTATION

Think for a moment of the various ways you respond when your telephone rings at home. As you first answer it, you have a moment of no reaction while you say "Hello" and wait to find out who the caller is. Once you know who is on the other end of the line, your next statement may be anywhere from a restrained "Yes, sir" if it is your boss, to a happy shout if it is an unexpected old friend. You may say a disgusted "What do you want?" to a person you find annoying or a cold "I'm just not interested" to a salesperson or solicitor.

What you have done without even thinking about it is to adapt or adjust to your listener. As Bert Bradley clarifies, "Audience adaptation may be defined as the actions taken as a result of audience analysis to develop the maximum aura of credibility."[1] We make both broad and subtle distinctions in what we say and in how we say it based on the judgments we make about the person or persons we are talking to. These distinctions appear in all the elements of oral communication—the topic we select to talk about, the words we choose to express our ideas, the examples we pick, the rate of speaking, tone of voice, degree of animation, use of gestures, postures—any factor may change as we adapt to our listeners.

As you prepare yourself to speak in a public setting, you need to consider your audience so that you can make similar adjustments. The major difference is that, for a public speaker, much of the analysis can be made in advance, rather than only at the moment, and the process is conscious and intentional rather than the subconscious response of the casual interpersonal speaker. In many business and service-speaking situations, you will already be familiar with the members of your audience—they may be people you work with daily or affiliates in a club, church, or organization. Yet in other situations you may speak to an audience of total strangers.

You can use a number of strategies to get the information you need to analyze the audience. For a local branch of a well-known national organization, such as the Lions Club or the Parent-Teacher Association, you can find reference materials in the library that will describe the group. If you have friends who are members, talk with them. Katharine Bruce suggests that you find other people who have spoken to the same group and talk to them about the type of audience you will be facing.[2] Finally, speak to the person who asked you to give the speech; ask specific questions about the group and the occasion.

The information you need about the audience falls under two major headings—demographic and relational/attitudinal. The term *demographic* refers to the vital statistics or facts about a group of people, such as age, gender, occupation, or religious affiliation. Demographic information will give you the specifics about the group and is usually the easiest information to find. Although some audiences will be so heterogenous that all ages, sexes, or occupations may be included, many more will tend to be homogenous, grouping around men or women, young or old, or particular business and social interests.

The relational/attitudinal elements are often more difficult to determine, for they involve what the audience members think and feel about you and what they think and feel about your topic. If we had the luxury of administering an attitude questionnaire to our listeners before we began to prepare a speech, we might be able to put together a fairly accurate portrait of the values and opinions these listeners hold. But in the absence of such specific data, speakers must do the best they can to find out about a group before going to speak to that group.

ANALYZING AUDIENCES BY DEMOGRAPHICS

Obtaining the following specific facts about your audience can help you select the best examples to use, the best lines of argument to present, and can suggest something of the overall tone of the speech—lighthearted, serious, humorous, inspirational, factual, alarming, challenging, or a host of other general modes a speaker can use.

Age. While some organizations may limit membership to specific age groups so that members will not vary more than a year or two from each other, most adult groups span several years if not decades. In general, speakers would probably be safe to think in terms of about four major age groupings: teen-agers, young adults, 30- to 60-year-olds, and retirees or senior citizens. On some occasions you may know that the group is primarily 25 to 35 years old, as with Junior Leaguers or Jaycees, for example, or that all members are past 65, as in certain retirement centers or groups like the Gray Panthers or RSVP (Retired Senior Volunteers Program). That will allow you to be even more exact in your adaptation.

Seldom would you be asked to give a formal speech to a group younger than high school or perhaps junior high school students. Below that age, youngsters would be more likely to respond to story telling or a dramatized presentation of the information. During the middle years, the 30- to 60- or 65-year-old bracket, audience members are less likely to be concerned with age-specific references than the very young or the very old would be. The young adults or middle group may have their similarity in other demographic variables, especially occupations and interests.

In adapting for age, consider such features as interest levels, a sense of history and knowledge of past events, the likelihood of tomorrows, and physical capabilities. You cannot depend upon young people to relate to examples from 30 or 40 years ago; you cannot depend on senior citizens to endorse long-range plans that will not develop for many years; security means more to the middle group; adventure probably means more to the young adults or possibly the teen-agers; death and its accompanying fears and preparations are more immediate to senior citizens and persons 50 years and upwards than to young adults; and getting and holding a job would most likely concern the teen and young adult groups.

When possible, topic choice and topic development should be made with the target age group in mind.

Gender. The women's movement of the past two decades has done much to call attention to topic separation on strictly male-female grounds. Prior to an awakened concern for full equality for women, we thought many subjects were either masculine or feminine. War and weapons, hunting, athletics, politics, and automobile mechanics were considered masculine subjects. Cooking, sewing, raising children, flowers and gardening, and personal grooming and clothes were thought to be of interest only to women. Interests today, however, transcend gender lines far more often than in the past.

Many clubs and volunteer organizations have memberships mostly of one sex: Lions Club, Rotary, Kiwanis, and various lodges such as the Elks or Moose are predominantly male. A number of daytime garden clubs, book and study clubs, and service organizations such as hospital volunteers have mostly female members. Recent litigation has caused some organizations such as the Jaycees to open up their membership to both sexes. Doubtless we will see more integration of the sexes in such organizations in the years ahead.

History suggests that people enjoy some subgroupings with only those of their same sex; hence, tradition continues to govern membership norms. College fraternities and sororities still retain sex sameness in their membership, as do a number of professional and educational organizations (Delta Kappa Gamma International Honorary Society for Women Educators or Zeta Phi Eta, National Professional Honorary Organization for Women in Communication Arts and Sciences, for example.) A few groups, such as the National Organization for Women (NOW) or Turning Point (RAPE Line and Family Abuse), were formed to serve the needs of women, but they do not limit their participation to women either as volunteers or clients.

Business settings are far less likely to produce audiences of all one sex, for in the working world fewer businesses are organized solely around a single sex. However, many jobs and professions continue to be dominated by one sex— nursing, elementary school teaching, and secretarial positions are still filled mostly by women. Welders, carpenters, automobile mechanics, and a host of physical-labor jobs are handled mainly by men.

Changing attitudes toward women make it difficult to suggest specific adaptive techniques. Speakers must be careful to avoid stereotypical assumptions such as women being motivated more by home and family, or that men are more likely to respond to appeals related to work or politics. To some degree this probably remains true, but it is changing rapidly. Perhaps the best advice is that you be more sensitive to the other demographic variables than to gender alone as a guideline—common interests or occupations will perhaps be a better base for adaptation than simply whether the audience has men or women in it.

Occupation.   Much of the speaking you will do in a business setting will have occupation as the most important common denominator for the audience members. Three different settings suggest three different types of occupation-related speaking. First, people come together to share concerns when they are practitioners of the same profession but work for different companies or in different locations—accountants, attorneys, architects, doctors, dentists, dancers, teachers, truckers, and typesetters. These people and many more have occupationally related organizations that meet to share matters of common interest and come to know each other both socially and professionally. The following are but a few of the hundreds of professional organizations in the United States.

Second, public speaking also takes place within a single business or corporation when the speaker must make a sales report, present a budget to the board of trustees, train employees in a new procedure or use of a new piece of equipment, try to gain support to institute a new organizational structure, or urge fellow workers to join in a protest or antimanagement action.

The third major arena for business-related speaking finds speakers taking messages from their companies or businesses to schools, clubs, or other groups who have some reason to want information about the business or some aspect of it. In many instances this falls under the heading of public relations and is considered a significant and necessary function by most major businesses. For

PROFESSIONAL ASSOCIATIONS

American Association of Critical Care Nurses
American Association of University Women
American Bar Association
American Business Women's Association
American Chemical Society
American Federation of Teachers
American Institute of Architects
American Medical Association
American Society for Quality Control
Association for Systems Management
Association of Certified Public Accountants
Association of Educators
Association of Life Underwriters
Association of Nurserymen
Association of Periodontists
Automobile Dealers Association
Barbers Association
Board of Realtors, Inc.
Data Processing Management Association
Federal Executive Association
Innkeepers Association
Legal Secretaries Association
Merchants Association
Ministers Fellowship
National Alliance of Postal and Federal Employees
National Association of Accountants
National Association of Women in Construction
Plumbing and Heating Association
Society of Real Estate Appraisers

example, insurance companies often send representatives to colleges and universities to explain the benefits of various medical and life insurance policies to graduating seniors. Certain investment firms have brokers available to speak on tax shelters, mutual funds, or a variety of other financial concerns.

When you speak to people who share a common profession, you can make assumptions about their understanding of the intricacies and demands of jobs within that profession. A level of common understanding probably exists and may provide a unique rallying point when that understanding is not shared by persons outside the profession. For instance, public school teachers and college professors suffer repeated criticism from those outside the profession that teachers in general do not work long hours because their time in the classroom may be limited. But within the ranks, all members have a common understanding of the many hours outside the classroom required to handle the job. Doctors understand what other doctors do, just as coal miners know about the work of other coal miners, or actors comprehend the demands made of other actors.

When speaking to people in your own profession, you may often cut short introductory explanatory steps that would be required for outsiders. You may use jargon and special technical or idiomatic language. "In-jokes" or special references that only insiders would understand are useful for establishing close identity between the speaker and the listener.

If you are speaking within a particular firm, corporation, or business establishment, the need for developing a general background to provide common understanding will be less important than the need to offer details of an immediate proposal or report. Listeners know the company, its goals and purposes, and why they are attending the session at which you are speaking. If you were speaking outside the organization, you would need to build a bridge to the listener in your introductory remarks based on a broad, general understanding of the organization you represented—what it was, what it did, and why it had a value or relationship to the audience members. When you speak within an organization, background of the *issue* that is the topic for your speech becomes the substance of your bridge building.

Finally, if you are speaking for your organization but to an outside group, you should probably assume that the listeners know nothing about your profession or the work your group or firm does. Often that may be the reason you have been asked to speak—to share knowledge about your job or some particular aspect of the job with those from another group. For example, a college or university club invites the personnel director of a large firm to talk to club members about job-hunting procedures; a businessmen's luncheon group has someone from a local television station tell members how the evening news programming is done; or a PTA wants a speaker from a Hot Line or Rape Crisis Headquarters to share information about the operation of telephone centers.

In all these cases, occupation is the major variable that speaker and audience members have—either by sharing the same occupation, or by the listeners having expressed an interest in learning something about the speaker's occupation.

Common Interests. Having common interests is similar to occupation as an important factor in considering who your listeners are when you are preparing a speech. The only real difference is that common interests would tend to be more avocational than vocational. Hobbies, pastimes, and spare-time activities would be included, as would many dimensions of volunteerism.

Again, the major question to ask yourself is: How much do my listeners already know about the hobby, activity, or volunteer organization that I am representing? You may find yourself speaking at a convention of model railroaders, a statewide conference of Big Brothers, or the final awards banquet following a regatta of sailing enthusiasts. If you are a model railroader, a Big Brother, or a sailor, you will share such a solid base of common information with your colleagues that little orienting material would be needed.

Or, you may speak within a local chapter at a meeting of a doll collector's club, an awards ceremony for a bowling league, or a training session for United Way volunteers. These listeners would have more immediate knowledge about and interest in the organizations than would outsiders.

Also, you might be a representative from your club or service organization going out into the community to speak before some totally different group, usually to share information about your society or chapter and the work it does or the opportunities afforded to members. Service organizations such as the Boy

Scouts, Girl Scouts, Friends of the Library, League of Women Voters, or the National Conference of Christians and Jews usually have speakers bureaus made up of volunteers who are willing to speak to other organizations. Audiences in this situation would probably know little about you and your group, but they are potentially open to learning.

Race and religion.   Just as with using sex as the prevailing variable for designing audience adaptive techniques, using race or religion is probably less apt to shape your design than is occupation or common interests, but it is nonetheless an important aspect of your prospective audience for you to analyze. Unless you someday become a member of the Ku Klux Klan or the American Nazi Party, we cannot imagine that you would ever include any assumptions, inferences, or examples that would in any way denigrate persons of particular racial or religious groups. However, some speakers may inadvertently choose speech elements that overlook or ignore minority members of the audience. A large Kiwanis Club reported that it had to come to grips with the numbers of guest ministers who included Jesus Christ in the invocations or blessings at their meetings—Jewish members objected. A high school girls' club complained that the woman who came to speak to members about makeup and hair styles talked about and had samples and examples of only those products useful for white teen-agers, although the club had almost one-third black membership. This woman failed to do her homework in finding out about her audience in advance. Although she tried to make a few adjustive remarks during the speech, it was obvious to all that she did not realize she would be speaking to black students as well as white students.

In some instances, race or religion may in fact be the distinctive element that binds the members of an audience. Obviously church or synagogue meetings would bring together a group of people whose major shared interest was religion. Nonsectarian groups such as the National Conference of Christians and Jews or the Urban Ministry, while not related to a specific institution, are formed along religious foundations. Race may be the unifying bond in groups such as the National Association for the Advancement of Colored People or the Council of Negro Women. Race and religion may be important predictors of an audience's attitudes toward a topic or even toward a person quoted in a speech, such as Catholics and the abortion issue or blacks and affirmative action programs. If you are taking a message from your business or volunteer organization to one of these groups, you will surely consider the constituency of the audience as you prepare your speech.

Other demographic factors.   Several other demographic factors can and should help you form a mental picture of your audience while you are doing your advanced planning. The educational level of the audience members, their income level, their political affiliation, their geographic ties such as certain parts of a city or state—all these and more may aid you in thinking through the facts about the people you are going to speak to. While the basic topic of your speech may remain the same in a wide variety of speech settings and before vastly different audiences, the development of the topic should change considerably when you devote serious time and study to audience analysis.

ANALYZING AND ADAPTING TO AUDIENCES BY RELATIONAL/ATTITUDINAL FACTORS

The other major aspect of the audience that you should think through and try to determine before planning your speech revolves around the relationship the listeners hold to you and the prevailing attitudes they might have about your topic.

If you are speaking within your own business or club, the audience members probably already know you. If so, you will not need to devote as much time in the introductory remarks to capturing attention and orienting the listeners to your voice and appearance. When you are speaking to a group of strangers, you will need to be much more careful to establish a rapport or connection.

Also, when you are already on friendly terms with your listeners, you can afford to be somewhat less formal than you could be with strangers. Occasional slang or particular in-group jargon can be effective, but might be lost on outsiders. References to other employees or club members can often build goodwill and tie into one of several techniques for holding attention—the use of the familiar.

Consider these two examples. "I saw Tom Talley in the hall on the way to this meeting and was reminded all over again of Tom's repeated efforts to be the number-one salesman of the year, a goal that took him fifteen years to accomplish." Or, "We all know how many deals have been signed sitting around Sam's backyard swimming pool with clients full of sirloin and Schlitz!"

Both these examples would work well in business settings where listeners know each other and know Tom and Sam, but both would be totally useless if audience members did not share that familiarity. And the second example could prove tactless if several audience members object to drinking.

If the audience does not know you, the person who introduces you can be of help in bridging the gap. In Chapter 12 we will offer some specific suggestions for building a speech of introduction, aimed for your use in those situations in which you must do the introducing. You can, however, use the same information to build a fact sheet or even a short manuscript speech to be used when you are the speaker. We find that program chairpersons and others assigned the responsibility of introducing a speaker are usually delighted to be given the information already prepared.

Again, compare the type of adjustment you make in the speaking situation to the type of adjustment you made in a social or interpersonal setting. If you go to a party or an open house and find that you know most of the people there, you relax, become more informal, smile and laugh more, use more familiar topics of conversation, first names and often nicknames, and in general "settle in" with a sense of comfort that you are on a safe ground—you know how these people will react to you. Yet if you arrive to find almost all strangers, you are more alert to remain somewhat formal, avoid excessive slang and personal references, and in general stay somewhat on guard as you feel your way along for the right level of communicative interaction. The same sense of searching the audience for the appropriate stylistic adjustment guides public speakers in new and different situations.

In addition to your relationship to the audience members, you need to try to find out what they know and think about the topic of your speech. Again, that may be very difficult to do when your speech takes you to a strange situation and a new group of listeners. Try first to determine why the audience members will be at the occasion where you will speak. Generally people attend a speech *voluntarily* or though some form of *coercion.*

Voluntary attendance suggests that persons wanted to be at the particular occasion, knew who the speaker was to be, and had some advanced interest in either the speaker or the announced speech topic. Voluntary attendance also suggests that a listener had the opportunity to stay away if he or she chose.

Coercion suggests some kind of force exerted to demand or require that listeners hear the speech. This may range from an almost mandatory attendance, such as chapel or convocation in a church-related school to a far more subtle pressure, such as a club that drops members from the roles unless they attend at least some of the monthly meetings each year. Whether a requirement, an obligation, a compulsory attendance, or an out-and-out force is used to get the audience members to attend, they are there for some reason other than spontaneous free will.

Audiences usually hold one of three attitudes toward you and your topics—*friendly, passive,* or *hostile.* Most of your speech making will be done to one of the first two—friendly or passive. Friendly audiences like you, want to listen to you, and have no serious problem in accepting your topic. That does not mean they must agree completely with what you say, but your material is not deeply offensive or in opposition to the basic value system of the listeners.

Passive audience members usually do not care. They neither like nor dislike you; they neither support nor oppose your proposition. Passive listeners may be in the audience because their jobs require them to be there or because they felt obligated through group membership. Listeners whose attendance was compulsory may have no real interest in being at the occasion; hence, they are apathetic about the speaker and the speech topic. For instance, retail merchants frequently schedule weekly briefing meetings with the floor personnel to update their knowledge of the merchandise. A temporary salesperson may view these meetings with indifference since the person does not plan to stay in the job for long.

Hostile audiences are those who seriously oppose the speaker or the ideas the speaker hopes to convey. When union members in a shop or factory are on strike, they might be hostile toward a representative from management who tries to talk to them at a meeting. Employees who have been laid off might be highly belligerent. Advocates of a woman's right to have an abortion might resent it if a speaker tried to use an occasion such as a devotional or inspirational talk to infuse antiabortion sentiments.

While you probably will not speak to many audiences who are outright hostile to you and who might yell, heckle, or even throw things at you, you may find yourself many times talking to people who are polite and who respect you as an individual but who oppose your proposition or topic. Much political speaking finds candidate pitted against candidate, party member against party member, and legislative proposals with clear-cut pro and anti factions. The nature of our political system allows and encourages the public sharing of opposing viewpoints.

In the business world, a carefully detailed advertising campaign may meet total rejection when offered to clients or agency management. A scientist who gives a convention paper announcing a new drug may find strong resistance from the medical community. Or an efficiency expert may encounter massive opposition from the accounting department staff members in a large corporation when he or she talks about a proposed totally new accounting system.

Volunteer, friendly audiences make your job as a speaker easier, especially in the beginning. You have less need to convince them you are worth tuning in. You do not have to cool them down or turn them off before you can turn them on. Beware, however, that you do not presume upon their friendly interest by anything less than your best preparation and best delivery, for they can easily become disenchanted if you do not measure up to expectations.

Passive audiences coerced in some manner, even if only a mild degree of obligation, require more ingenuity on your part. They can be won over, but many carry on "okay, show me" attitude like a chip on the shoulder, just asking to be knocked off. The use of humor and the familiar (examples, illustrations, and personal references that are well known to the listeners) can be helpful (see Chapter 15). Spend more time in the introduction trying to find a common ground or means of identification between you and the audience. Be enthusiastic and vital, but not gushy or phony. Remember that your major proposition or main piece of information that you are trying to impart may not win or get across if you have not paved the way by stimulating your apathetic listeners.

The hostile audience, most often found in persuasive speaking situations, requires the most skillful handling of all. You must overcome resistance to your proposal in order to win approval for it. You need to understand the opposing arguments carefully and be prepared to refute or in some way deal with them. You need to build a strong case for the favorableness of your plan through careful and thorough documentation and through constructing sound lines of argument.[3]

The relationship and the attitudes of the audience toward you and toward the topic of your speech are factors of audience analysis that you should not take for granted or leave to chance. Plan what you are going to say by picturing your listeners from the demographic analysis and your understanding of their attitudes. You have an infinite variety of approaches to any one given topic, and audience analysis can help you choose the approach that will gain the most effective response from that particular group of people.

HONESTY AND AUDIENCE ADAPTATION

We have had a few students who, after reading about and discussing audience adaptation, have asked us if we did not think that changing messages to suit different audiences was somehow dishonest. We hope you will not misconstrue the advice that you use a careful analysis of the audience as a tool to aid in adapting your message to mean that you are to be anything less than truthful.

An example can illustrate the difference between adaptation and dishonesty. Suppose you are asked by your college to become a part of its recruitment speakers' bureau. You will be sent to different groups to talk about the college and encourage support and attendance. In your speech to a group of high school students, you might stress the social and sporting events on campus, and you could focus on the many degree tracks that lead to excellent career opportunities. Why? Because high school students are deeply concerned about preparing themselves for future jobs, but they also would like to enjoy their college days.

Your second speaking engagement is to a group of parents of high school students who are presently helping their teenagers make a decision about which college to attend. You might stress the care the college takes to make sure its freshmen develop good health and study habits, for most parents worry about a child who is leaving home for the first time. You would certainly want to talk about the costs involved in attending your college, comparing them with other institutions in the same geographic area, since paying for their children's education is a major expense for most parents.

Finally, you speak to a group of alumni from your college. You may appeal to them to help you recruit by recommending the college to their friends who have adolescent children. You may want to stress some of the changes in the college campus and curriculum but also reassure the listeners that the basic values of the institution are intact. Alumni must be convinced that yours is still the best college to choose.

What you have done is to analyze the audience, then to choose the approach that your experience and intuition led you to believe would be the most effective with a certain group. Such adaptive strategies are part of the communication system that we all develop. Children from kindergarten through twelfth grade operate on a personal or intuitive judgment of other people as they form arguments and counterarguments. As children grow and learn more about others as well as more about themselves, their strategies and ability to adjust their communication to the listener become more sophisticated and complex.[4]

This capacity to adapt is inherent in the adjustive nature of communication. Our language and its accompanying paralanguage (voice tones and inflection) offer us a wide range of choices in the way we frame and form a message. Learning to select from that range the option that will gain the most favorable response is what is meant by a "rhetorical strategy" in the classic sense of the word *rhetoric*. This becomes dishonest only if the speaker's motive is devious, or if in planning one's adaptive strategy the speaker lies, purposely misleads, or short-circuits logic and truth. If in giving your recruiting speeches, you lied about the number of students or types of social activities, failed to present all the extra costs to parents, or in any way deliberately falsified the supporting material, then you would not have been truthful and honest. Wayne Minnick describes unethical behaviors as falsifying or fabricating, distorting evidence, consciously using specious reasoning, or deceiving the audience about the speaker's intent.[5]

Adjustive strategies can be used to flatter excessively, to deceive, to cheat, to entrap, or a host of other fraudulent purposes. But the blame for such misuse lies in the intent of the speaker, not in the process of adapting or in the adaptive strategy itself. For adaptive strategies can also serve a number of admirable purposes—to exhibit tact, to pacify, to comfort, or to take the sting out of bitter realities. Adjustment of speaker to audience is a noble goal, for it brings us closer together in human understanding. Only dishonest speakers make the process dishonest.

KEY POINTS

- Audience adaptation is the process of adjusting the message so that it will be most effectively received by a given group of listeners.
- Audience demographic factors such as age, sex, occupation, common interests, race or religion, educational level, political affiliation, and geographic ties should be obtained by the speaker before he or she prepares the speech.
- Speakers need to assess their potential relationship to the audience and the attitudes those audience members hold toward the speech topic.
- Whether audience members attend the speech voluntarily or through some form of coercion will affect their attitude toward the speaker.
- Audiences may be friendly, passive, or hostile toward either the speaker or the topic.
- Considerations of honesty require that audience adaptation be made for the purpose of improving communicative effectiveness, not for manipulation of the listeners nor distortion of the truth.

QUESTION FOR DISCUSSION

What can you determine about the demographic features of the audience in your classroom? What about their attitudes and opinions? How might those be both similar to and different from the demographics and attitudes of audiences you might address some day in your career or volunteer activities?

ACTIVITIES

1. Take a single topic, such as "Why You Should Own a Home Computer," and outline the arguments you might make and list the examples you might use if you were going to give it before three different groups:
   a. a high school National Honor Society meeting
   b. a business and professional women's association
   c. association of real estate brokers
2. Make a list of clubs and organizations that you and your family belong to. What speech topics do you think would be of interest to the members of those groups?
3. Look up and define to your satisfaction the following terms:
   a. demagogue   d. agitator   g. motivator
   b. propagandist   e. firebrand   h. instigator
   c. persuader   f. rabble-rouser   i. stimulator

   Which terms suggest an honest or dishonest speaker?
4. Carefully observe all the classes you attend. Would you classify your classmates as passive or friendly listeners? Do any of them ever seem hostile?
5. Write out a list of questions you could ask class members about your topic to determine their interest and attitudes toward your speech purpose.

REFERENCES

[1]Bert E. Bradley, *Fundamentals of Speech Communication: The Credibility of Ideas*, 4th ed. (Dubuque, Iowa: Wm. C. Brown, 1984), 103.

[2]Deborah Churchman, "The Art of Giving a Briefing: How to Sell Your Message," *The Dallas Times Herald*, 21 March, 1984, C13.

[3]Robert C. Jeffrey and Owen Peterson, *Speech: A Basic Text*, 2nd ed. (New York: Harper & Row, 1983), 214–16.

[4]Jesse G. Delia and Ruth Anne Clark, "Cognitive Complexity, Social Perception, and the Development of Listener-Adapted Communication in Six-, Eight-, Ten-, and Twelve-Year-Old Boys," *Communication Monographs* 44 (1977): 326–45; Barbara J. O'Keefe and Jesse G. Delia, "Construct Comprehensiveness and Cognitive Complexity as Predictors of the Number and Strategic Adaptation of Arguments and Appeals in the Persuasive Message," *Communication Monographs* 46 (1979): 231–40; Jesse G. Delia, Susan L. Kline, and Brant B. Burleson, "The Development of Persuasive Communication Strategies in Kindergarteners Through Twelfth-Graders," *Communication Monographs* 46 (1979): 241–56.

[5]Wayne C. Minnick, *The Art of Persuasion* (Boston: Houghton Mifflin, 1957), 283–84. See also Charles U. Larson, *Persuasion: Reception and Responsibility*, 2nd ed. (Belmont, Calif.: Wadsworth Publishing Co., 1979), 254–57.

Chapter 3

The Audience as Listeners

At the beginning of the first chapter you read a quotation that offered an educated guess that 100,000 speeches are given in the United States each day. Audiences for those speeches might range from a handful up to several hundred people who may come together to hear a particular speaker. Suppose we chose an arbitrary average figure of 50 listeners per speech, a conservative guess when we think of the number of speeches given in large auditoriums to as many as 2,000 to 3,000 listeners at a time. An average of 50 listeners multiplied by our 100,000 speakers suggests that 5 million Americans hear a speech each day! This does not include the huge audience that listens to speeches given by politicians on television and radio at the state and national level.

The majority of you will give some speeches sometime in the future. All of you will listen to many, many speeches throughout your careers and in your leisure time pursuits. This chapter offers suggestions for making you a better listener, a more effective "consumer" of public messages. It will also help you to understand what is going on in the minds of your audience as they listen to you. First you need to understand a basic definition of listening and then to examine some of the problems that cause most of us to listen at less than peak efficiency.

LISTENING DEFINED

Listening is one of those terms that we all know, yet getting a precise definition that satisfies teachers and researchers alike is not so simple. We prefer the definition of listening offered by Wolvin and Coakley: " . . . receiving, attending to, and assigning meaning to aural stimuli."[1] An examination of this definition will help you understand and limit the dimensions of listening.

Aural stimuli are inputs of sound that you receive through your ear, where sound wave vibrations strike the eardrum, move through the small bones in the middle ear, the cochlea in the inner ear, and finally through the auditory nerve into the brain. Hearing is the act of receiving the aural stimuli. Without first hearing the sounds, we would be unable to listen to them.

The second part of the Wolvin and Coakley definition hinges on the words *attending to*. We do not have to listen to everything we hear. In fact, we often choose to ignore certain sounds, to filter them out and to pay no heed to them. For hearing to become listening, we must want to do more than just receive sounds. We must be motivated to concentrate on those sounds and to be purposely mindful of what we hear. This is the process of paying attention or *attending to* aural stimuli that is an essential component of listening.

The final part of the definition states that we must *assign meaning* to the sounds before the listening act can be complete. You may hear a garbled mixture of sounds, but unless your brain can find a way to associate those sounds with something that makes sense to you, you will not be able to listen. You might hear a foreign language that you do not understand, but you cannot truly listen because you are unable to assign meaning to what the speaker says.

Two other elements are often associated with listening, but like Wolvin and Coakley, we do not believe they are essential ingredients of the listening definition. These are the elements of *memory* and *response.*

Memory.   The first of these associated elements is memory. We have a common tendency to criticize people who do not remember something at a later time as having not listened in the beginning. But this may not be the case. We may listen carefully at the time, then simply forget later on. The mind does not retain every detail of every message that is put into it.

On the other hand, we have almost no way to test listening comprehension except through memory. For me to know that you have understood me, you must repeat what I have said or answer questions about my message. This requires that you remember, at least temporarily, what you have heard.

We hold an item in memory only a very brief period of time unless we transfer it to long-term memory. This transference is aided by processes such as repetition, rehearsal, active attempts at recall, and association with other memories.[2] You probably remember very little about the last speech or lecture that you heard. Yet does that mean you did not listen at the time? Not necessarily. You simply may have failed to engage in the active transference process needed to retain the speech for recall purposes. To become a better consumer of public speeches, you will want to work to improve your memory as well as your listening ability. They are closely entwined, yet distinct mental processes.

Response.   The second element that is often associated with listening is response. How do I know whether or not you have heard me accurately unless you respond to me overtly, either verbally or nonverbally? But does lack of response mean that no listening took place? Like memory, response is difficult to disassociate from listening, yet two distinct processes seem to be at work. While they often go hand in hand, they do not necessarily depend on one another.

Another misassumption about response is that lack of agreement on the listener's part results from poor listening. Perhaps you have had someone say to you after an argument, "You did not listen to a word I said," when the truth was that you listened carefully and could repeat each of the speaker's major points. What you did not do was to agree with or be persuaded by those points. Clearly a difference exists between listening and a response of agreement.

An overt response, verbal or nonverbal, is one of the most helpful ways that a listener can reinforce a speaker's confidence that he or she has been heard. But the absence of response does not mean that no listening has taken place. In fact, faking response with vigorous head nodding and frequent "uh-huhs" might be a listener's trick to hide inattention and poor listening.

The essential steps in listening are, then, the receiving, attending to, and assigning meaning to aural stimuli. Memory and overt response usually go along with listening and are the chief tools by which we assess the listener's skill. Yet neither response nor memory is a necessary listening component. Improving memory focuses on a set of skills that are similar but not identical to the skills that we seek to perfect in order to improve our listening ability. With this definition of listening in mind, some of the barriers to effective listening can be identified and classified.

BARRIERS TO EFFECTIVE LISTENING

Some barriers can be found in the *receiving* part of the listening process. If the speaker does not talk loud enough or enunciate clearly, or if outside noises or distractions overpower the speaker's sound waves, you may be unable to receive the signals. At this level, we would probably say you could not *hear* rather than you did not listen.

Some barriers also exist in the third level of the listening process, the level of *assigning meaning.* If someone speaks to you in a foreign language, uses a dialect of English with many vernacular word meanings that you do not know, or talks to you in a professional or technical jargon that is unfamiliar, you will have genuine difficulty in assigning meaning. Those words have no previously stored referents in your brain—that is, no past experiences associated with them that enable you to understand them. Similarly, if someone speaks about events or occurrences that you have never been through, while you may share in them vicariously to some extent, the depth and sense of actuality of the speaker's meaning may elude you.

Most of the barriers, however, fall in the second step in the definition of listening given by Wolvin and Coakley, the part of the process called *attending to.* For a variety of reasons, we may not concentrate or focus our attention on the speaker's message; hence, we lose the opportunity to assign meaning or understand what has been said.

One reason why it is so easy for us to lose concentration comes from the interesting difference between the time required to speak and the time required to listen. The average speaker says around 140 to 150 words per minute. Anything over 200 words per minute would sound fast to you. Yet you can, for at least short periods of time, listen to and process upwards of 400 words per minute. You are actually capable of listening fully twice as fast as most people speak.[3]

This differential leaves you with a generous portion of *listening spare time.* Because your brain can handle the listening task in about half the time, your tendency to use the other half, the spare time, for thoughts of your own may set up a competitive mental activity. Your own thoughts may become more interesting and absorbing, and soon you have left the speaker behind, tuning out the words completely. You are lost in thought, preoccupied or daydreaming, the result of letting the listening spare time become a distraction rather than using it to enhance your listening effectiveness.

Specific barriers that result may be labeled failure to concentrate or failure to filter out distractions, whether external or internal. Noises or competing activities create external distractions. Internal sources can be personal problems, boredom, or lack of physical movement to stimulate the body. Material that is excessively complex and hard to follow or poorly organized and randomly presented may contribute to mind wandering. Another internal distraction may be the listener's dislike of the speaker or negative attitude about the speaker's topic.

Other barriers to effective listening may arise when we begin to compose messages in our minds that contradict those of the speaker. If we react too quickly, often without hearing the speaker's full thought, if we seriously disagree with the speaker's premise, or if we are overly prone to evaluate everything we hear as right or wrong, we will probably be guilty of poor listening.

Lack of attention may come from poor motivation. The listener may have no real desire or reason to listen—he or she sees no potential reward or profit. A person may be so self-centered, so egocentric that the person cannot fulfill the more giving, less active role of a listener. Or inattention may be the result of a lifetime of poor habits and a total lack of exposure to any instruction in good listening techniques.

Whatever the cause or reason, ridding ourselves of possible obstacles that may get in the way of effective listening will contribute significantly to our becoming more successful communicators and consumers of public speeches.

FIVE P's FOR BETTER LISTENING

We have organized the suggestions for improving your listening skills under five headings, using words that begin with the letter *p* to help you remember. This illustrates one of the most useful of the mnemonic devices or techniques to assist memory, that of grouping ideas under key words that are alliterative (begin with the same first letter) or words whose first letters can be formed into an acronym (such as MADD, for Mothers Against Drunk Drivers, and SADD, for Students Against Drunk Drivers). We can more readily recall when lists or sequences are given a pattern or an association. How many of you who took music as a child still remember that "every good boy does fine" identifies the ascending order of the musical staff lines—e, g, b, d, and f? Remember that listening and memory are closely related, so "tricks" that help you remember also help you to be a better listener. The five *p*'s for better listening are:

1. *Prepare and Preview.* You will listen more effectively if you do some advance preparation. If your supervisor announces that he or she will talk to you and your fellow employees about a new process for handling accounting procedures, make sure you check your knowledge of existing procedures so you will have a solid basis for comparison. If your club sends out a notice that the speaker for the next meeting will be from a nearby cancer research clinic, do a little study on the clinic or the person who will speak.

Find out well in advance exactly where and when the meeting will be so that you do not rush in flustered at the last minute, giving you no opportunity to ready yourself to listen. When possible, get a seat where you can see the speaker easily. Clear sight lines may help your listening, for you can add your interpretation of visual cues, such as the speaker's facial expression, gestures, and body movements, to the words you hear. Avoid sitting near open doors or windows where outside noises can easily distract you.

2. *Perspire and Persist.* You are not expected to actually perspire as you strain to listen! We use the word metaphorically, much as you would say "sweat it out" when you have to wait a long time for something important or "in a sweat" meaning impatient. The word *perspire* is associated with hard work, persistence, and a high level of drive and energy.

Good listening requires just that—hard work, energy, and an activeness that is deceptive because it is internal rather than external and visible. Nothing has to show to an observer when you listen. Speakers must use their voices and move their mouths, but the energy required for listening is mostly mental.

Several visible indicators of mental alertness—erect posture, direct eye contact, frowns or smiles, and shaking or nodding heads—serve the highly useful function of reinforcing the speaker's constant concern that he or she is "getting through" to the audience. As the speaker grows secure that the circular or transactional process of communication is indeed taking place, that confidence enhances the relationship between speaker and listener, and both can profit from the improvement. Outward physical signs of listening are helpful, but they are not necessarily accurate representations of true mental energy.

To improve your listening, you need not only to exert constant mental energy and alertness but also to persist throughout the length of the speech. This is not always easy if speakers are dull or talk overly long. But if you truly want to be a better listener, expending effort to stick with even boring or difficult speakers will help you gain added skill.

3. *Pick Primary Points.* Too often when hearing speeches we get hung up in a pattern of listening to details so carefully that we somehow let the main points escape us. Perhaps this comes from a classroom focus on test taking that often emphasizes detail over general understanding. Also, particular items may be colorful and attention getting—an unusual word, a novel phrase, an unexpected metaphor, an astonishing statistic, an apt quotation, or a graphic description. These are factors that we encourage speakers to use in order to increase listener attention. As a listener you should enjoy such interesting details, but only for the moment. Dwelling on them, keeping them too long in conscious thought, can cause you to lose a main idea.

See if you agree with us on the three main points of the following hypothetical news release:

> The nation's public colleges and universities reeled today under a Congressional budget decision to do away with all federal direct grants and loans to students in state-supported institutions. The move, labeled by its opponents as the "private school supremacy" measure, will make federal funding available only to students who attend privately owned colleges and universities. Designed to prevent the imminent collapse of all but a few of the larger, more well-endowed private institutions, the measure assumes that large sums of state tax money used to support public colleges should be balanced by a federal tax infusion into the private schools, lest the closure of many private schools cause an overflow of students into public institutions.
>
> The National Council of Institutes of Higher Learning has fought the measure bitterly, arguing that it directly opposes the basic concept of public education. Several state colleges and universities fear they may go under if large numbers of students transfer to private schools in order to obtain grants-in-aid. The full impact will be felt in the fall of next year when the measure goes into effect.

Main Points

1. Federal grants and loans to students eliminated in public institutions.
2. Designed to balance state funding of public institutions by support of private institutions.
3. Student transfers to private institutions may force closing of many public institutions.

Moment-to-moment listening may keep us from perceiving a total speech unity. It may be likened to looking at a painting from one foot away, examining each square inch separately, and never stepping back to take in the whole picture. The moment-to-moment listener may delight in a humorous or touching anecdote or illustration yet be unable to restate the speaker's theme or identify the topic.

Your listening spare time is the most important tool you have in extracting main ideas or major substance from what you hear. Use that spare time to paraphrase and restate to yourself, to review periodically, to summarize, to draw connections between various subpoints of the main topic, to test the relationship of pieces of evidence to your inclination to accept the speaker's assertions, to rehearse into memory special highlights that you want to keep, or any of a number of mental operations that pull all of the "corners of your mind" into the single-purpose act of listening to, finding, and retaining the essence of the speaker's message. This further emphasizes our argument that effective listening is hard work.

4. *Ply Pencil and Paper.* Many of the speeches we attend, especially those connected with our jobs, require that we retain the details for a later time. Announcements are often made in group meetings, and audience members need the specifics from those announcements for future reference. Times, dates, places, names of key persons, citations of reference materials, and quotations are just some of the specific details that we may hear from a speaker and wish to keep for a later time.

Learn to take a pencil or pen and paper with you to all speech occasions from which you may need to retain isolated facts. Write those facts quickly in an abbreviated fashion by leaving out syntax function and connecting words (*a, the, of, by, and, but,* etc.) and by recording only a few key words that will help you recall the point. As soon as the meeting is over, go back and fill out your notes so that the ideas are complete and legible.

We took the brief notes listed below the following announcement to help us remember:

> Local union 2218 will have a barbeque supper on Saturday, July 10th, from 5 p.m. until 7:30 p.m. The barbeque can be bought either chopped or sliced, and will be served with a plate of cole slaw, corn bread, and iced tea. The adult plate is $3.50, while a child's plate is just $2.00, with free refills included. Take-out orders are also available. The supper will be held at Union Hall at the crossroads and is open to the general public. Proceeds will to to the building of a new high school auditorium.

Our Notes

BAR-B-Q, Sat.,7/10, 5–7:30, $3.50/2.00, Union Hall.

You may find that a similar key-word approach can help you outline a speech or lecture on those occasions when it is essential that you have an accurate record of the main ideas as well as some of the significant details. Trying to force a speech into outline form, however, can confuse the listening note-taker if the speaker presents ideas in a random rather than structured manner.

Do you agree with our outline of the following short speech of explanation?

> Respiration impacts on the human voice in at least three distinct ways. Some people breathe deeply habitually, and certain speakers make more skilled use of expelled air for voice production than do others. A well-controlled, strong breath supply can enable a speaker to have a louder voice. Since air striking the vocal folds is the beginning of vocal sound, the stronger the striking process, the better the resultant vibration. In addition, fully expanded lungs allow the speaker to take in more breath, so that if he or she can also control the exhalation, then longer passages of sustained speech can be produced. Although most modern prose can be read in relatively short phrases, sometimes the ability to sustain long phrases or sentences is useful. Finally, controlled exhalation improves a speaker's voice quality, for such respiration-related problems as breathiness or huskiness may be avoided if the vocal folds are struck with a clear breath supply. Controlled deep breathing is an asset to acquiring a better voice.

Our Outline

> Respiration helps voice:
> a. to be louder
> b. to be held or sustained longer
> c. to have clearer tone, free from quality problems

In general, pencil and paper are best for keeping details, while using your listening spare time to review and rehearse is best for grasping overall thematic intent.

5. *Postpone Protests and Praises.* Suppose your instructor comes in at the beginning of class and says, "I am going to give you a test. . . ." Groans and accusations of "not fair, you did not announce a test" fill the pause before the instructor completes the idea—"over the material in chapter three, and I think we should be ready for that test by next Friday." Big sighs of relief spread across the classroom as you and the other students realize that you jumped to a faulty conclusion after hearing less than half the sentence.

This example of replying too quickly illustrates the problem that the fifth and final *p* is designed to offset. If we let emotional listening and response patterns dominate our receptive communication, we will probably make errors in interpretation and judgment. A friend of ours coined the expression "jumping to concussions" that she substituted for "jumping to conclusions" because she said that overly hasty response was as damaging as a serious blow to the head!

Postpone your judgment until you have heard a speaker out. Do not begin to formulate objections and arguments before the speaker has presented the main points and primary evidence. On the other side, some speakers may lull you into complete agreement early in the speech, only to turn in a different direction midway through. You could commit your support too early, causing you to fail to hear the latter part of the speech critically.

For example, suppose a student begins a speech in your classroom with a rousing plea to get all the class to join him tomorrow in a march on the university president's house as part of a major demonstration. "No way," you say to yourself. "I'm no troublemaker. He could never talk me into joining in a protest movement. I will not even listen to the rest of this speech; I'll read my book." You tune out the speaker, only to find out later that he explained that tomorrow is the president's birthday, and students were organizing an enormous surprise party as a tribute and recognition.

On the other hand, suppose that a classroom speaker began by asking if you would like to make better grades. Certainly you would. And furthermore, the speaker continues, you could earn those better grades easily, painlessly, and in less time than you presently devote to studying. With these as well-developed, well-supported first and second main points, you may have real trouble processing the speaker's final point—that you join him in illegally accessing the university's academic computer and changing the recorded grades! Many listeners have been led astray by just such a deceptive arrangement of ideas in the parts of a speech.

Be critical of what you hear and evaluate the speaker's assertions and evidence. But withhold finalizing your overall response until the speaker has completed his or her ideas and drawn subpoints and support material into a conclusion that reflects the total speech, not merely certain aspects of it.

Practicing the techniques of the five p's can help you become a more effective listener, a more informed and intelligent consumer of public messages.

KEY POINTS

- Another goal of this course is to help you become a better listener to speeches.
- The Wolvin and Coakley definition of listening identifies three steps in the process: receiving, attending to, and assigning meaning to aural stimuli.
- The process of *memory* and the act of *response* are closely related but not necessary components of listening.
- Barriers to effective listening can be found in all three steps in the listening process, but are most common in the second or *attention* step.
- The five p's for better listening are:
    prepare and preview

        perspire and persist
        pick primary points
        ply pencil and paper
        postpone protests and praises

QUESTION FOR DISCUSSION

How can this speech class help you to become a better listener? What can you do to ensure improvement in listening, not just in this class, but in all your courses and other situations where you need to listen?

ACTIVITIES

1. Have someone read aloud to you a newspaper or magazine article and make an outline or a set of notes by reducing each paragraph to a few key words.
2. Have someone read aloud to you and experiment with your listening spare time. See if you can write a shopping list, a list of errands you need to run, or a list of small jobs you need to do. While writing, keep up with the reader's main ideas.
3. Make a content outline of the speeches you hear in the classroom.
4. Listen carefully as your classmates give their speeches, but take no notes. Following each speech, write a one-paragraph summary or make a list of key points.
5. For the next two weeks as you walk across the campus or drive along the streets, instead of letting yourself become lost in your own thoughts, try listening to all the sounds around you. Hear human or animal sounds, sounds in nature, the sounds of machines and mechanical devices—try actively listening and processing all that you hear.

REFERENCES

[1] Andrew D. Wolvin and Carolyn G. Coakley, *Listening*, 2nd ed. (Dubuque, Iowa: Wm. C. Brown, 1985), 74.

[2] Lyman K. Steil, Larry L. Barker, and Kittie W. Watson, *Effective Listening: Key to Your Success* (Reading, Mass.: Addison-Wesley Publishing Co., 1983), 80–81.

[3] Florence I. Wolff, Nadine C. Marsnik, William S. Tacey, and Ralph G. Nichols, *Perceptive Listening* (New York: Holt, Rinehart & Winston, 1983), 154–55.

PART II

The Speaker
and the Selection
Process

In Part I, you studied the process of analyzing an audience and learned some techniques for becoming a better listener. In Part II, we will focus on the three major areas in which you must make significant choices as you begin to prepare your speeches: selecting a topic, formulating both a general and a specific purpose, and finding the supporting material to be used in the speech. Some guidelines on using the library, a major source for finding supporting material, are offered.

Chapter 4

Topic Selection

41

One of the concerns our speech students voice most frequently is, "I don't know what to talk about." In most business and service organizations, we usually start from the speaker's area of expertise as the basis for choosing the subject matter of the speech. People are asked to speak because they already know something about that particular organization or process, issue, event, or activity related to their work or volunteer efforts. Some professional speakers may be given free rein in topic selection, but far more often they are asked to speak about a subject they are given in advance.

In the classroom, however, speech purposes, the subject of Chapter 5, may come first. Assignments are often organized around a purpose framework. You may be asked to prepare an informative speech, a persuasive speech, a ceremonial speech, or some other general aim rather than being assigned a specific topic or subject. This is a major difference between classroom and "real world" speaking. The first two of the following suggestions, then, will be more applicable to your immediate work in this class. Career speakers will have already fulfilled them, merely by being who, what, and where they are in their professions or avocations.

SPEAKER INTEREST AND RESOURCES

1. *Choose a topic in which you are interested.* You will spend a considerable amount of time in planning, preparing, and practicing each of your speeches.

Why spend that time with anything less than a subject in which you are interested? The more the subject appeals to you, the more enthusiastically you are likely to approach it. Speaker enthusiasm is contagious—audience members usually catch it! And because in the classroom your audience is made up primarily of your peers, you may assume with some degree of safety that what interests you will also interest your listeners. This assumption is based on what you have learned in Chapter 2 about shared demographic features as a fairly reliable predictor of interest. Analyze your class along the lines of age, common occupation, and common interests.

Do not be overly critical in predetermining that the listeners will not be interested in you or your proposed speech. Many students who tell us they are unable to find a topic have in fact thought of many topics, but have dismissed them all as uninteresting and hence unsuitable.

As you move through the remaining chapters of this book, we hope you will become convinced that interest level has more to do with the way a topic is

SELECTED TOPICS

Book Banning: A Threat to Freedom
Why Gun Control Does Not Reduce Crime
Why Home Audio Taping Should Be Banned
Why You Should Join a Sorority (or Fraternity)
The Importance of Knowing C.P.R.
De-criminalizing Marijuana
Pro-Life vs. Pro-Choice
Banning of Medical Experimentation on Prisoners
Decreasing Military Aid to El Salvador
Why the State Constitution Should be Revised
National Health Insurance
Sexual Abuse of Children
Racial Discrimination on Campus
Reasons to Give the Gift of Life: Be a Blood Donor
Adopting a Pet
Nuclear Weapons: To Freeze or Not to Freeze
Drinking and Driving: They Don't Mix
The Works of Andrew Lloyd Webber and Tim Rice
Techniques of Brainstorming
Regulations of Soccer
Medieval Sports and Games
History and Techniques of Yoga
Hair Styles Through the Ages
What Constitutes Corporal Punishment
Rules of Etiquette
Analysis of Different Types of Arson
Why We Should Like John McEnroe
Why Pregnant Women Should Not Smoke
Young Republicans and the Grand Old Party

developed rather than the topic itself. The topics listed on page 43 are only a few of the many topic areas we have found to be of interest to student audiences and speakers.

2. *Choose a topic you know something about.* The same scene has been repeated in so many plays and movies that is has become a cliché—the young aspiring writer approaches the established author with a story that shows writing talent, but is on some far-fetched subject matter. The older, wiser author advises the aspirant to go back and "write what you know." Langston Hughes said it best when he wrote:

> Go home and write a page tonight,
> And let it come out of you,
> Then it will be true.[1]

The cliché provides excellent, highly useful advice for the speaker as well as the writer.

As you begin, make an inventory of your own background—jobs, hobbies, volunteer service, travel, unusual family situations—as suggested in the first activity at the end of this chapter. Place an asterisk by those subjects that are the most interesting to you. If you have chosen a topic that truly interests you, then you probably already know something about that topic.

This does not mean that you must know everything about the subject before you begin. Research will doubtless be needed to add to what you know, to fill in a few gaps, and to provide you with credible sources for quotations and illustrations. But adding to existing knowledge is a very different process from starting to research a totally new topic.

As you finalize your topic choice, you need also to consider the availability of additional research material. More than one student has written away for necessary pamphlets and brochures, only to have them arrive after the assigned date for the speech. Given the wealth of library resources available to most college students today, you should be able to locate needed material on almost any topic. In Chapter 6, we will offer some specific techniques for researching speech topics.

Any list of student-speaker interests is bound to exclude some of the class members. Many returning students are not in the traditional 18- to 22-year-old group, many students are married and have children, some working students take only one or two courses and cannot participate in campus activities, and no group of 20 to 25 people, however well matched demographically, will share interests totally. Compare our list in Activity 3 at the end of this chapter with your own campus.

LISTENER EXPECTATIONS AND READINESS

The first two suggestions for choosing a topic were geared primarily to student speakers in the classroom, where topic choice is less tied to professional or avocational interests. The next two suggestions are useful and important in both classroom and nonclassroom settings. Again, use the process of analyzing audiences by demographic and attitudinal characteristics to help you comply with these next two listener-related suggestions.

3. *Choose a topic the listeners can grasp and understand.* Most speakers who talk over the heads of their listeners do so because of the development of the topic, rather than basic topic choice. Any subject can be developed many different ways, depending upon the organizational pattern, supporting material, and vocabulary choice. But while development may be the primary problem, caution is still necessary in choosing a topic, for audience members may lack the background or scope of knowledge to follow the speaker without the inclusion of far more explanation than is feasible in the short time allotted most speeches.

For example, suppose you are a chemistry major who has become interested in qualitative organic analysis and decide you would like to speak to the class on tests for detecting olefins, those compounds containing carbon-carbon double bonds! Most of your listeners lack the knowledge needed to understand the subject without extensive background development. And since such background would use up most of your allotted speech time, you might do well to choose some other topic for your speech.

Or perhaps you want to persuade for or against the MX missile. Can you, in the five to seven minutes most often allowed for a classroom speech, give your listeners what they need to know about the missile itself—its payload of warheads, its range, its destructive power, its offensive and defensive potential—and still have time to develop a series of persuasive arguments? You must try to determine whether your listeners already have a basic knowledge of your subject and how much you can assume without explanation.

Even as seemingly simple a subject as exploring the fine points of a screen pass in football can go right over listeners' heads if they do not know the basics of the game. Following an actual speech on this subject, well illustrated with a series of blackboard drawings, some of the classroom audience members wanted to know what all the X's and O's were for. The speaker had mistakenly believed that everyone knew that the members of two football teams are represented by X's and O's in diagramming the movement in particular plays.

Narrowing from a broad subject area to a specific speech topic needs to be done with the audience clearly in mind. Thinking about your listeners' readiness level instead of simply choosing from your own interests may prevent you from talking over their heads. The opposite is possible, of course—that you choose a subject that is so simplistic that the listeners are bored. This has happened less frequently in our own classrooms than the overly complex speech. And even the most simplistic of topics can be enjoyable when interestingly developed. Careful consideration of the listener will help you avoid either extreme.

4. *Choose a topic your listeners will be interested in.* Just as with the consideration of your listeners' knowledge level, the issue of their potential interest should also impact on your topic selection. Again, while we believe that almost any subject can be made interesting with the right development, certain topics still may be more appropriate for some audiences than for others. We know that both age and sex factors influence interest level. Young people feel less direct concern with the physical problems of aging or the choice of the right retirement center, whereas older people may not care much about the latest dance steps or finding a part-time job while in college!

We suggested earlier that in the classroom you may safely assume that your classmates will share some of your own interests, provided those interests are not too narrow or too unorthodox or "far out." Before finalizing a topic choice in nonclassroom situations, talk with a few members of the group for whom you will be speaking. Get to know something about them. Perhaps your instructor will let some of you design a questionnaire that would provide both demographic information and clues to listener interests on a few popular topics such as politics, drugs, career choices, or marital life styles. (See Activities 5 and 6.) These techniques will help you discover areas where your interests overlap the rest of the class.

CONSIDERATIONS OF TIME AND SPACE

The final two suggestions for helping you select speech topics are applicable for either classroom or career settings. Failure to adhere to time allocations has ruined many a well-planned program and thrown many a speech instructor behind in finishing a round of speeches. The speech teacher has the power to interrupt and stop a long-winded student. Program heads will seldom risk embarrassing or offending a speaker by asking him or her to stop because the time has gone by. Failure to consider the space or area in which the speech is to be given has caused problems with everything from the degree of formality in style and language to the uselessness of preplanned visual aids that cannot be seen.

5. *Choose a topic that can be handled in the allotted time.* Most beginning speech students seem afraid they will not have enough to say. However, many classroom speeches run too long as run too short. The problem is usually that the topic was too broad or complex for the assigned time. As a rule of thumb, it is far better to develop one aspect of a topic thoroughly than to give superficial treatment to a broader view of the same subject.

Many speakers—even those with a great deal of experience—seem to lose all sense of time when they begin to speak. Some go on and on. Perhaps the assigned time was 15 minutes—some speakers may talk for 30 and be shocked and incredulous afterwards to find out how long they had held forth. Some speakers, more often the less experienced, will think their speech has been six to eight minutes, when actually they were on their feet only two to three minutes. Something about the act of public speaking seems to interfere with our ability to perceive the passage of time!

Common courtesy demands that you do not intrude on the time given other parts of a program or class period by having your speech be too long. Many clubs and organizations have working members who attend meetings during lunch hours. They do not wish to be rude and walk out on overly verbose speakers, but they often must get back to the store or office at a set time. In the classroom, instructors carefully plan the number of speeches to be heard each day based upon the assigned length of those speeches. Many teachers include accurate timing as part of the student's grade on the speech.

The obvious solution is, of course, careful planning. Choose a topic that can be handled in the designated time. Know in advance what you are going to say and stay fairly close to your outline. In career settings, determine what else will be on the program. Find out from the chairperson how strictly you need to adhere to a designated length for your speech. If time is absolutely crucial, as it often is with speeches on radio and television, you will probably depend more heavily on a written manuscript rather than extemporizing from an outline. This helps you avoid wandering off into unplanned elaborations.

Careful planning is most often a matter of limiting to one or two aspects of the topic rather than covering the entire area. For example, you may identify a dozen reasons for joining a sorority or fraternity, but you will pick out only the best three to develop during your speech. Or, you could develop a case for national health insurance by comparing the United States to other nations or by presenting extensive illustrations and examples of tragedies for people without health insurance. You could build the case statistically by developing cost projections, or you could relate health insurance to a basic political philosophy and system of government. But you cannot take all these approaches in a single speech. You must narrow to a viewpoint that can be fully explained in the allocated time.

With a sufficiently limited subject and careful planning, you can learn to time your speeches so you can come within a minute or so of the exact time you were asked to fill. One word of caution about time concerns delivery of the speech rather than planning it, yet is important to mention here. Be subtle and minimize the use of your watch as a time guide. We find it distracting when a speaker removes a wrist watch, places it on the lectern, and stares at it frequently during the speech. This is often accompanied by meaningless interjections such as, "I can see I am about out of time," or worse still, "If time permitted, I would tell you about the interesting. . . ." Occasional glances at your watch or a nearby clock can help you shorten or lengthen your speech as needed. But a far better method of meeting the time requirement is skillful topic selection and development and careful rehearsal.

6. *Choose a topic that is appropriate for the size of the audience and the space in which you will speak.* Most speech students think of standing on a platform behind a lectern, perhaps with a wide sea of unlit faces in a dim and cavernous auditorium—a frightening prospect indeed! While this impression is sometimes the case, far more often you may find yourself in a small board or conference room, a church meeting hall, or someone's living room as you give your speech. Our research on the speech making in our community uncovered something interesting taking place in the settings for career speeches that we had not previously thought about. One-third of the speeches that we covered in depth were presented in lounge areas and the living rooms and dens of people's homes. Study the following list of speech occasions and places:

SPEECH OCCASIONS

(Meetings/Workshops/Lectures -- Size of Audience & Location)

SUNDAY	MONDAY	TUESDAY	WEDNESDAY	THURSDAY	FRIDAY	SATURDAY
1 Church Fellowship Night 75 Fellowship Hall	**2** Toastmasters Club 35 Hotel Small Ballroom	**3** Alpha Chi National Honor Society 35 YWCA	**4** American Friends Service 15 Public Library Meeting rm.	**5** American Marketing Assn. 20 Bank Board Room	**6** Assn. of Machinery Computing 25 Company Meeting Room	**7** Assn. of Women Students 60 Campus Classroom
8 Young Democrats 100 YMCA	**9** Career Placement Debate 150 School Auditorium	**10** Industrial Relations Club 25 College Union	**11** Historical Book Club 15 Member's Home	**12** Rotary Club Luncheon 40 YMCA Lunch Room	**13** YMCA Options for Living Lecture 35 YMCA Lecture Hall	**14** Young Republicans 75 Public Library Auditorium
15 Intern'l Assn. of Business Communicators 25 College Classroom	**16** English Club 35 Student Union	**17** District Dental Org. 75 Resturant meeting rm.	**18** Insurance Club 50 Library Meeting rm.	**19** Kiwanis Club Luncheon 40 YMCA	**20** Mary Kay Cosmetics Training 100 Hotel Ballroom	**21** RSVP Meeting 60 Library Auditorium
22 Delta Kappa Gamma 30 High School Lunch rm.	**23** Political Rally 500 Civic Auditorium	**24** Science Museum Lecture 60 Museum Planatarium	**25** American Bar Assn. 400 Hotel Ballroom	**26** Students Concerned for Central America 25 Classroom	**27** Political Science Club 20 College Lounge	**28** Community Theatre Lecture 80 Civic Center
29 Residential College Forum 25 Dormitory Living Room	**30** Young Lawyers Assn. 125 Hotel Meeting rm.-	**31** Symphony Guild 100 President's Home				

The size of the space limits and controls the number of people who will make up your audience. Meeting places are usually chosen because their seating capacity matches the size needs of the club or organization. Few situations are more difficult for a speaker than facing a handful of listeners in a very large auditorium when an anticipated crowd fails to develop.

When selecting your speech topic, audience size should be a part of your guideline. As a rule, topics and especially topic development must be kept more generalized for larger groups. Highly specific subjects are more suitable for smaller groups, where members are more likely to share common interests and knowledge level. For example, the subject of educational changes might be narrowed differently in the following settings, where in each case, both the size and similarity of interest of the different groups impact on the topic choice.

AUDIENCE	EXPECTED NUMBER	SPECIFIC TOPIC
1. All citizens of Glenville	2,000	Improving our public schools

(Topic must be kept broad and general since audience will be from all walks of life. Large group requires formal speech.)

2. PTA of Glenville High School	200	The parents' role in improving Glenville High School

(Topic can be narrowed to the high school, to what parents can do, and can be prepared and delivered more informally with the smaller crowd.)

3. Teaching meeting, Glenville High School	50	Implementing upcoming curricular changes

(The teachers need to understand how the change will impact on their day-to-day duties. Speech should be shorter to provide an extensive question-and-answer period.)

4. Student Assembly, Glenville High freshmen and sophomores	400	New course requirements for college entrance

(Students want to know if they are facing new graduation or college entrance requirements. Will likely be somewhat agitated if the news has leaked out that big changes are underway. Probably a large assembly in the high school auditorium.)

5. Glenville School Board	12	Funding to implement curricular changes

(The school board is responsible for finding the money. Might be a group discussion rather than a formal speech, although an opening presentation is probably necessary. May meet around a table in a board room.)

The size of the space for the meeting or program also directly affects the required formality of your speech style. A sliding rule can be applied—the larger the setting, the more formal you should be. "Formal" includes language features—less slang and vernacular language, a more academic or standardized language, and a more highly structured grammar and rule-bound syntax. "Formal" also suggests less use of personal names and references to individual audience members, less local color and in-group humor, and a sense of linguistic distance that is part of the basic definition of formal versus informal speech style.

Delivery features will change too, for the large auditorium requires the speaker to stand up, speak louder and clearer, and avoid asides or throwaway remarks that could not be picked up by all listeners. Gestures are usually larger, so they can be seen, but may also tend to become less spontaneous and natural. Chapters 13 and 14 will offer you several specific suggestions for adjusting delivery.

While the best speakers work hard to see that they do not become stiff, stilted, and remote in large, formal settings such as a major auditorium or church pulpit, both the added size and the actual distance between speaker and audience have decided impacts on the degree of communication formality.

Closely tied to the size of the area in which you will speak is the way the furniture is arranged. Large auditoriums will have platforms to elevate the speaker so he or she can be seen by more people. Some lecture halls elevate the audience at various levels, so listeners look down at the speaker. Different levels and increased distance add to the authority the speaker creates. In smaller meeting rooms, chairs may be around a large conference table, with the speaker standing at one end. Chairs may be arranged in a semicircle, with the speaker standing at the open part of the semicircle. These arrangements are less formal.

If possible, find out in advance what the layout of the space will be like. Try to picture yourself in that layout as you plan the speech. Because much of the adjustment to space is more a matter of delivering the speech rather than planning it, specific suggestions for using lecterns, microphones, conference or dinner tables, or any of the other furnishings that speakers encounter will be offered in Chapter 13. We believe, however, that both skillful topic selection and speech planning are best done when the speaker can know and visualize the space in which he or she will present the finished product.

KEY POINTS

The six rules for topic selection are organized under three subdivisions:

- *Speaker Interest and Resources*
    1. Choose a topic you are interested in.
    2. Choose a topic you know and can learn more about.

- *Listeners' Expectations and Readiness*
    3. Choose a topic the listeners can grasp and understand.
    4. Choose a topic your listeners will be interested in.
- *Considerations of Time/Space*
    5. Choose a topic that can be handled in the allotted time.
    6. Choose a topic that is appropriate for the size and layout of the space in which you will speak.

QUESTION FOR DISCUSSION

How do the criteria that govern the selection of topics for this speech course differ from the criteria that guide speakers that you hear in other settings? How do they differ from the guidelines that will dictate topic choice in your future career speeches?

ACTIVITIES

1. Using pencil and paper, make a list of your interests and activities—clubs, hobbies, special reading interests, jobs you have held, unusual friendships, travel, etc. Make the list as complete as possible.
2. From this list of activities and interests, select and narrow to four that you think would make good speech topics. Write a title and thesis statement for each.
3. Take each of the four speech topics and plan how you might change it if you were going to give the speech to
    a. this class
    b. a small club you belong to that will meet in a member's home
    c. a group of 100 to 200 strangers in a local community center or small civic auditorium
4. We took the lists that our students made in the first activity above and drew the following general areas identified as of interest as possible speech topics. How might these differ from a list compiled at your school?

Campus Politics	Study Habits
Graduate/Professional Schools	Physical Fitness
Sports	Dating
Relating to Parents or Children	Making Money
Consumer Information	Books
Drugs and Drinking	Hobbies
Theatre/Music/Dance	Travel
Animals (Pets)	Food

5. Distribute the following demographic analysis form to your classmates. Compile and share the results. Many other items could be added to complete the profile.

name	age	place of birth

where you lived most of your life	where employed	type of work

married?	how long?	children?	their ages

member of church/synagogue?	denomination

6. Distribute the following interest survey to your classmates. Compile and share the results. (Other students might do similar questionnaires, focusing on different topics.)

"I would be interested in hearing speeches on the following topics." (Indicate your level of interest by circling the appropriate number from 1 to 5):

   1 = no interest at all
   2 = vaguely interested
   3 = no opinion
   4 = somewhat interested
   5 = very interested

CAMPUS CLUBS AND ORGANIZATIONS	1	2	3	4	5
FAMOUS PEOPLE	1	2	3	4	5
PHYSICAL FITNESS	1	2	3	4	5
NATIONAL POLITICS	1	2	3	4	5
DRUGS	1	2	3	4	5
HOBBIES	1	2	3	4	5
WORLD PEACE	1	2	3	4	5
NUCLEAR ENERGY	1	2	3	4	5
THEATRE/MUSIC/DANCE	1	2	3	4	5

REFERENCES

[1]Langston Hughes, *Montage of a Dream Deferred* (New York: Henry Holt & Co., 1951), 39.

Chapter 5

Speech Purposes

In Chapter 4, we talked about selecting topics for speeches. In this chapter we will offer you guidelines for selecting both general and specific purposes for your speeches, as well as formulating thesis statements and titles. Having this material in two chapters may suggest to you that two related, but different steps, are taking place. In reality, the two steps occur simultaneously in most of our speech planning. Topic selection might come first, with thoughts of purposes and audience needs following after. Or as is often the case in the classroom, you may have been given a speech assignment by one of the types of general purposes. You would then work from that general purpose toward a specific purpose by tying in your particular topic. The two steps thus go hand in hand.

Public speaking has become a tradition-bound event in our society. Although some of the norms have changed over the years (the average speech length in the nineteenth century was an hour and a half to two hours, whereas today it is 20 to 30 minutes) we retain certain expectations that tie speaker, event, and occasion into a pattern. This pattern has developed as speakers have sought to satisfy the needs of the listeners, while at the same time accomplishing certain purposes of their own.

Some of the listener needs that may be met through hearing speeches include (1) the need for facts and information, (2) the need to understand opposing arguments as an aid to decision making, (3) the need to be motivated to be a participant rather than a spectator, (4) the need to laugh and relax, (5) the need for beauty and inspiration, and (6) the need to share a communal, ritualized experience with other listeners.

These listener needs can be blended with speaker purposes to guide in preparing the speech. As you, the speaker, target to fulfill your purpose, remember that audience members come to the speech occasion with a set of expectations and needs. The successful speaker is able to fulfill his or her purpose and satisfy the expectations of the audience.

GENERAL PURPOSES

The five major categories of general speech purposes will be discussed in this section. They are called *general* purposes because they are free from topic specificity. Regardless of your subject, you need also to be aware of what you want to take place in your listeners, and that becomes your general purpose. At least five general purposes and the accompanying needs of listeners are commonly recognized. If the goal is *to inform*, the speaker builds on the listeners' needs for information. If the aim is *to convince*, arguments must be offered that will help listeners make a decision. If the speaker wishes *to actuate* the audience, reasons for such action must be presented. The speech *to commemorate a special occasion* fills the listeners' need for inspiration and ceremony, while the speech *to entertain* gives audience members laughter and enjoyment.

Almost any subject could be developed to fulfill at least two or three of these general purposes, although certainly not at the same time. Some topics could develop to meet all five. For example, if your subject matter is *cats*, you could present *information* about breeds of cats or instructions for care and feeding. You could try to *convince* your audience that cats make the best domestic pets. Or you might decide to *actuate* the listeners to go out and buy a cat, or perhaps take home a charmer whom you just happen to have with you and who is in need of a place to live! A beautiful story of a devoted and faithful pet could serve as a focus of an *inspirational* speech on loyalty. And a cat lover could build an *entertaining* speech around feline antics.

The following discussion explains the five general purposes, relating them to the needs of the listener.

To Inform

The *general purpose* in the informative speech is primarily one of wanting to share facts and information. The speaker wants to help the listener know or understand something that he or she, the speaker, already knows. This purpose will most probably grow from an area of expertise already held by the speaker through job training, education, a hobby, or some other source of building a body of knowledge. The speaker may be a professional who is paid to share this information or a volunteer who simply has a deep interest in the subject.

Some degree of persuasive intent is present in most informative speaking, for we hope the listeners will understand, accept, and perhaps do something with the information we give them. But the primary thrust of the speaker in overt persuasion is the development of good reasons why the proposition should be accepted. In informative speaking, the primary thrust is simply the presentation of the facts themselves.

The *listeners'* general needs in the informative setting center around our natural desire to want to learn something new, to expand and reinforce our previous learning, and to in some small way satisfy the very natural curiosity that we hold about the world around us and the objects and inhabitants that comprise that world. Knowledge is a form of power. Our society places a high premium on education, both formal and informal. The number of adults who flock to a variety of continuing education programs in everything from formal university course work to arts, crafts, and recreational training testify to our need and desire to continue to learn.

To Convince

Persuasive speaking can be divided into two general purposes. In the first, the *speaker's goal* is to convince the audience of the desirability of one side of a controversial issue over the other. The speaker has a belief or a vested interest in a social, political, moral, or personal issue where two or more different opinions exist. For personal or professional reasons, the speaker hopes to gain the listeners' support and advocacy of one particular position instead of the other.

The *listeners' need* arises from the drive we all have to formulate belief and attitude systems about the world in which we live. We build our belief systems throughout our lives, changing and altering them as we move through different experiences and take in new and stimulating thoughts and ideas. We make a number of major decisions at all stages of life. When speakers give us the advantages and disadvantages of particular plans and proposals, it helps us to make decisions in which we can feel more secure and comfortable, for we feel we have made those decisions based on solid information and reasoning.

To Actuate

The *speaker's purpose* in this second type of persuasive speech is to move listeners beyond just acceptance of a position by asking them to move toward a desired course of action. The speaker may need the support in the form of listeners' physical behavior in order to fulfill the speaker's long-range goal. The speaker might need listeners to vote for him or her, to buy a particular product, to join a group, sign a petition, march with other protesters, or take a number of other possible actions. John Makay and William Brown have defined the persuasive act as one in which a speaker seeks a goal that can only be mediated (met or satisfied) through the actions of someone other than the speaker. Oral communication is the primary means that we use to reach that goal when we do not consider coercion or force as acceptable motivators.[1]

The *listeners' needs* in the speech to actuate stem from our socialized need to take action, to do, to be a part of the life around us. One definition of mental illness in Western society includes the inability to ever take a position or to make a decision that requires follow-up action. Our society does not applaud indecisiveness, nor encourage long periods of inaction, as do some of the Asian cultures. We are buyers, talkers, doers, sometimes voters, and "movers and shakers" in a generally active life pattern. Listen to the pride with which your friends tell you that they purchased a "real bargain" after extensive shopping, or took out the "very best" life insurance policy or joined the club with the "biggest benefits package." Often after we have made a major purchase, such as an automobile, we seek out information that supports the choice we have made and reject any negative evidence about the make and model we have bought.[2] We need to believe that we have acted wisely. And the effective actuating speaker will help us develop or reinforce that belief.

This tying of belief system to behavior or action suggests that a speaker will seldom if ever focus only on either *convincing* or *actuating* the listeners. Obviously we must be convinced before we decide to act, so any speech designed to stimulate listener action must first provide the basis for belief. Conversely, if a speaker significantly alters your belief by convincing you of the value of one viewpoint over another, somewhere down the line you might behave in a different fashion. Earlier in this chapter we acknowledged that some degree of persuasive intent exists in informative speaking and that the need to inform is part of the act of persuading. Similarly, we recognize that what has been called the "conviction-action dichotomy," that is, separating the speech to convince from the speech to actuate, is actually impossible, for a constant overlap of the elements exists. Yet it is possible, for practice purposes and for learning to understand the concept of a general purpose, to target your speech toward either conviction or action. Your main goal would be to affect *belief* in the speech to convince and to affect *behavior* in the speech to actuate, although you recognize that these two outcomes are not mutually exclusive.

To Recognize Special Occasions

The *speaker's purpose* in a speech on a special occasion may be mainly one of inspiring, honoring, or paying tribute to other persons or institutions. Ceremonies have developed in and around certain gatherings, such as dedications, giving awards, saying formal farewells, or introducing other speakers. Many traditions surround these events, and as members of a society we often take part in these ceremonies, either as speakers or listeners.

The speaker has no great body of information to impart, but will certainly have to gather the pertinent set of facts about the person or the occasion. Seldom would the speaker wish to move the audience members to major outside action or to make any significant change in their belief systems. Rather, the speaker hopes to elevate the listeners' feelings and sensitivities toward the honoree or the event. These speeches pay respect, say thank-you for a job well done or for being a significant person, wish well to our friends and colleagues, honor major growth and development both physical and social, or in many other ways recognize the customs and traditions that have become a part of our heritage of ritual. The speaker, much like a gracious host or hostess, provides a link between listener and honoree or between listener and event.

The *listeners' needs* grow from ancient drama and ritual that has developed across the centuries as mankind has melded into well-knit social groupings. Just as we have ceremonies to initiate the newborn, to recognize coming of age, to celebrate marriage, to commemorate birthdays and great historic events, so we have ceremonies in which we accept certain oral messages as integral to the completion of the observance. Although we may at times complain about "too many long speeches," we would doubtless feel cheated if the annual Oscar, Emmy, or Tony awards simply showed a list of the nominees, the name of the winner, and his or her picture. How dull that would be! The sense of sharing and experiencing together comes through clearly if the event is a televised Academy Award presentation or a farewell dinner party for your boss in some hotel dining room or on your patio. Ceremony simply for the sake of ceremony and for the level of respect it suggests to our fellow beings is a sufficient drive among listeners to deserve having a significant speech purpose.

To Entertain

The *speaker's purpose* in this final category is perhaps more akin to the special-occasion speech, but it is geared toward *amusing* listeners rather than *inspiring* them. The successful entertaining speaker today must battle against strong images of wonderful professional comedians who use the stage, TV, and night clubs to punch out routines filled with jokes, anecdotes, and one-liners in a highly polished manner. Being entertaining is not easy—it takes hard work, long practice, and perhaps some innate talent.

Often the entertaining speaker is a professional rather than a career or volunteer speaker such as we anticipate that you will be. For this reason, many public-speaking teachers do not include rounds of speeches to entertain in introductory-level courses. You may be encouraged instead to put some fun and humor into your other speeches, but to keep your major purpose on one of the types discussed earlier.

This is not to imply that the speech to entertain cannot have a serious message or purpose, for often it does. The speaker may make a significant point or appeal, yet come at it obliquely by getting listeners in a relaxed, light-hearted vein.

The *listeners' need* is a part of the desire we have for amusement, entertainment, or something to break through the humdrum, boredom, and unhappiness that unfortunately characterizes many lives. Most of us love fun and enjoy sharing laughter with friends. The drive for entertainment is a healthy, normal one that can often be fulfilled by a skilled speaker, usually in a pleasant, partylike setting, such as a banquet, dinner, or other festive event.

GENERAL PURPOSE: SPEECH TYPES AND SITUATIONS

1. To Inform
   business progress report
   classroom or other lecture
   church school lesson
   travelogue
   demonstration (produce, appliance, craft)
   sermon (church history, biblical interpretation)
   commentary
   panel discussion

2. To Convince
   professional lobbyist
   sales or project presentation
   debate or filibuster in Congress
   sermon on leading a better life
   critic/reviewer

3. To Actuate
   employee motivation
   evangelical gathering
   sales talk pitch
   membership recruitment—club/organization
   military recruitment—Army, Navy, Marines
   courtroom
   sports lockerroom pep talk
   political campaign
   soap box agitator

4. To Inspire
   awards banquet
   Fourth of July
   commencement address/valedictory speech
   funeral
   initiation
   inaugural
   dedication (building, monument, bridge)
   pep rally
   keynote address
   welcoming address

   5. To Entertain
       banquet/dinner
       review/variety show
       club meeting
       roast

SPECIFIC PURPOSES/MAIN THEMES

Once you know what general purpose you want to achieve in your listeners'
mind—sharing information, convincing, actuating, ritualizing, or entertaining—you can make a link between that general purpose and the topic of your
proposed speech. That link becomes the *specific purpose,* a statement that applies
only to one particular speech rather than a whole category of speeches.

The specific purpose should begin with the two words that identify the
general purpose—*to inform, to convince,* and so forth. The specific purpose statement should then be completed with a single sentence overview of the main
thrust of the speech:

> to inform the audience about the new system of registration to be put into
> effect in the fall.
>
> to convince the audience that children of abusive parents are better off in
> foster homes.
>
> to actuate the audience to buy Calvin Klein jeans.

The statement of specific purpose is seldom if ever read to the audience in
this exact form. However, we advocate placing the specific purpose statement at
the top of your outline page. Refer back to it frequently as you prepare your
speech. All that you plan to say and do in the speech should reflect directly from
that purpose. But do not plan to say or read that statement to your listeners. Of
the many ways to begin a speech, perhaps the dullest and least imaginative is to
say, "Today I am going to talk to you about a new system of registration" or
"Today I want to get you to buy Calvin Klein jeans."

Then create a statement of main theme, sometimes called a *thesis* or *topic
statement.* This is a statement that phrases your specific purpose in a more
interesting manner, leaving out the two words that identify general purpose.
The statement of main theme is usually presented toward the end of the introduction of the speech, after you have gained the audience's attention and tried
to form a bond between you and your listeners. Communication consultant Jack
Franchetti asks you to remember that you must

> decide what your audience needs to know if you are to achieve your goal. What
> one thing do you want ringing in their ears as they leave? Share that message in a
> way that illustrates vividly why it is to their benefit to listen. Put it into a single
> sentence. This is your bottom line.[3]

If your speech is to be announced in advance through a brochure, poster, or newspaper story, you will also need to give it a *title*. A title contains the essence of the specific purpose and main theme, but in a shortened catchy manner. You may wish to leave the selection of a title until after you have completed your preparation so that you think of this speech as a whole, not its parts. Many speeches, especially those given in classrooms, never require titles.

We believe, however, that everytime you prepare a speech that you should put in writing all four of the ways in which we identify purpose.

general purpose
specific purpose
main theme
title

Notice in the following examples that we move from the general purpose—what, in a broad sense, you want to do with the audience—to the specific purpose. Here we tie the broad aim to the topic of this particular speech. Next we create a theme statement that offers the listeners a conversationally phrased complete sentence overview of the topic. Finally, the title should be short and snappy. Find just a few key words to convey the main idea.

1. *general purpose:* to inform
   specific purpose: to inform the audience about new job opportunities in our local area
   main theme: A number of jobs are open to college graduates in the (your city) area that you may not be aware of.
   title: Tomorrow's Jobs

2. *general purpose:* to inform
   specific purpose: to inform the audience about current research in muscular dystrophy
   main theme: New research discoveries offer hope that muscular dystrophy, a major crippler of children and young adults, may some day be prevented.
   title: A Brighter Future for Jerry's Kids

3. *general purpose:* to convince
   specific purpose: to convince the audience that deficit spending at the federal level encourages individuals to go into debt
   main theme: The federal government has established a norm that makes you and me believe it is okay to borrow rather than do without.
   title: Public and Private Borrowing

4. *general purpose:* to actuate
   specific purpose: to stir the audience members to action so they will sign a petition to keep the library open until midnight
   main theme: I want to urge you to add your name to the list of those

students who need access to the library between 10 and 12 each night.
title: We Need Later Library Hours

5. *general purpose:* to inspire
specific purpose: to inspire the audience to emulate the good works of Nancy Taylor as we dedicate this building to her
main theme: As we dedicate and officially open this magnificent new building, we think again of the many accomplishments of Nancy Taylor, for whom the Taylor Building becomes a memorial.
title: The Heritage of Nancy Taylor

6. *general purpose:* to honor
specific purpose: to honor Kevin Carstairs as he retires after 40 years of service
main theme: This special occasion gives us the opportunity to recognize Kevin Carstairs, not only for his 40 years of loyal service but also for having left us a legacy of challenging goals and creative approaches to problem solving.
title: To Kevin Carstairs, With Love

KEY POINTS

- The reasons or purposes behind public speeches have developed from a combination of listener and speaker needs.
- A speaker cannot accomplish his or her purpose unless some need exists in the listener that the speaker can tap or touch.
- General speech purposes are usually divided into five major categories:
    to inform
    to convince
    to actuate
    to recognize special occasions
    to entertain
- The specific purpose combines the general purpose with the topic of a particular speech.
- The statement of main theme is a well-phrased, "audience-ready" formulation of the specific purpose.
- A speech title is a shortened, catchy highlight of the specific purpose and main theme.
- Speakers should put on paper the four ways of expressing speaker purpose:
    general purpose
    specific purpose
    main theme
    title

QUESTION FOR DISCUSSION

Why is it important to identify general and specific purposes of a speech? What purposes will most probably govern the speaking that you will do some day in your profession?

ACTIVITIES

1. Attend a speech on your campus or in your community. Afterwards, write down what you believe to be the general and specific purposes. Did the speaker make them clear? If the speech had a title, do you think it was appropriate? Why?
2. Write a main theme sentence for each of the following specific purposes:
   a) to actuate the listeners to vote against a proposed bond referendum to build a new high school.
   b) to nominate William Andrews for president of the senior class.
   c) to inform the audience of the new video games available in the Student Union.
3. Write a title for each of the same three speeches in Activity 2.
4. Taking a broad topic such as "newspapers," write three entirely different specific purpose statements—one informative, one persuasive, and one entertaining.
5. Take the four topics you identified at the end of Chapter 4. Write a specific purpose and a main theme statement for each for an informative speech. Write a second set of statements with persuasion (either conviction or actuation) as the general purpose.

REFERENCES

[1]John J. Makay and William R. Brown, *The Rhetorical Dialogue: Contemporary Concepts and Cases* (Dubuque, Iowa: Wm. C. Brown, 1972), 66–68.

[2]Based on Consistency and Cognitive Dissonance Theories. See Leon Festinger, *A Theory of Cognitive Dissonance* (Stanford, Calif.: Stanford University Press, 1957); Fritz Heider, *The Psychology of Interpersonal Relations* (New York: John Wiley & Sons, 1958); as overviewed by Robert A. Wicklund and Jack W. Brehm, *Perspectives on Cognitive Dissonance* (New York: John Wiley & Sons, 1976, chapter 5).

[3]Jack Franchetti and George McCartney, "How to Wow 'em When You Speak," *Changing Times*, August 1988, 30.

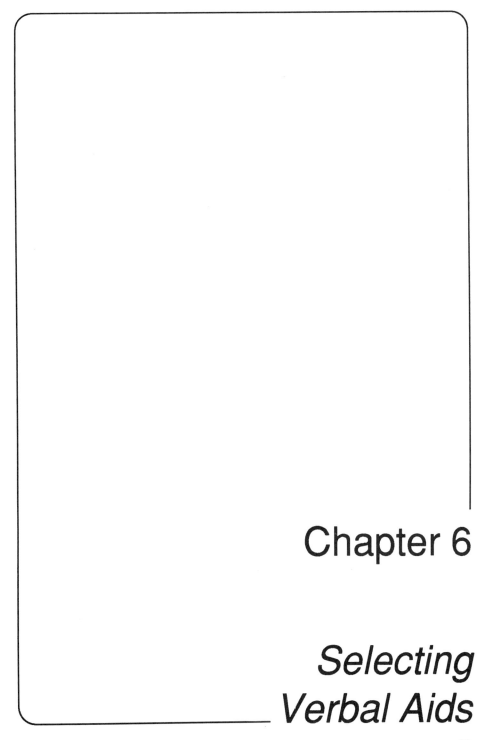

Chapter 6

Selecting
Verbal Aids

The final phase of the selection process is the discovery and choice of the supporting materials that you will use to clarify, illustrate, and expand your chosen topic. Up to this point, you have made a careful study of the people who will be your listeners, given serious consideration to your own knowledge and interests, thought through the general purpose that you hope your speech will accomplish, and finally selected and narrowed the specific purpose or topic of your speech. Now you must begin a careful search of your own memory, key source persons, and the wealth of written material available to you in the library as well as in daily newspapers and magazines.

Verbal supporting material is the heart of a speech. We could give an entire class the same topic, with the same specific purpose, yet come up with 20 different speeches, for each speaker would choose a different approach to develop the topic. The supporting material helps to build the explanation in an informative speech and to structure the argument in a persuasive speech. It helps to construct the good reasons why a listener should go along with the speaker's proposition.

The process of discovering interesting and useful materials to advance the argument or clarify the assertion you have made in a specific purpose statement is the beginning of the creative or artistic aspect of speech making. Most of this material will come from outside the personal experience of the speaker. Finding supporting materials is a constant and ongoing process for people who give speeches regularly, and many are always on the lookout as they read, watch television, or listen to other speakers. Some speakers keep files of anecdotes, stories, statistical information, and unusual quotations, sorted and cross-referenced by various subjects or topics.

The process of finding effective supporting material is often woven throughout the speech preparation period. You may find new and better stories, examples, or proof of any sort after your speech is outlined and in the polishing phase. Flexibility in inserting, deleting, or making any changes that improve the speech should be maintained right up to the final rehearsal period. While we suggest that you devote a significant amount of time at the beginning of the speech-building process to research aimed at uncovering as much useful supporting material as possible, this does not mean that the process stops here. After you are well into the outlining or even rehearsal stages, you may find a gap or weakness that sends you back to the reference sources for further help.

The term *verbal aids* is useful in thinking about supporting material. Most of you are familiar with *visual aids* to instruction or persuasion—charts, photographs, drawings, models, slides, filmstrips, transparencies, and a host of items designed to be perceived visually. They can add greatly to the clarity and inducement level of a message by supplementing sound with sight. Verbal aids are the spoken equivalents, those explanatory and motivational thoughts and ideas perceived aurally that can help listeners create mental images through language rather than through visual stimuli. Chapter 9 deals with the preparation and use of visual aids as helpful adjuncts for speakers.

Yet many speakers use no visual materials of any sort, depending entirely on their skills in painting with words to open the avenue by which they enter the listeners' minds. Verbal supporting material, when combined with unique arrangement and skilled utterance of the speaker's ideas, is the basis of proficiency, effectiveness, and even eloquence in speech making.

FORMS OF SUPPORTING MATERIALS

Explanation

The simplest and most used verbal aid is a basic *explanation*. If you want to tell us how to hang pictures, explain that we need picture hangers, which we will hammer into the wall at a preselected eye level, and upon which we will place the wire or metal hook attached to the back of the picture. Explanations should be as clear and accurate as possible, including necessary detail but omitting confusing evaluations or irrelevant side issues. If you want to place value judgments on paintings of landscapes as contrasted to still-life canvases, or want to detour into processes for refinishing old wooden frames, do it in another part of the speech (or in another speech), not during the explanation of how to hang a picture. Note the difference in clarity between the first statement and the second statement in the following examples of an explanation:

  a. To drop and add courses after the semester begins, you need good luck because most classes you want will be closed. Go to the appropriate drop department to have your card stamped, hoping you don't get a grouchy prof who would rather be out on the golf course. Take the stamped card to the Registrar's Office, where the lines are interminable, and wait to see if sections of courses you want have opened up, if you are lucky.

  b. Dropping and adding courses can be traumatic—desired sections are closed, professors become grouchy, and waiting lines may be interminable. The necessary steps are to go first to the appropriate academic department that controls the course you wish to drop and have your card stamped. Take the card to the Registrar's Office, where openings in other courses are posted as they become available.

Here are some other explanations, chosen from the speeches we observed in our community. Study them carefully to help you increase your own ability to explain in a clear and interesting manner.

A water task force was appointed. That came about because we had found ourselves getting involved in extending water and sewer lines from a city to an industrial site outside the county, where the counties involved would have to spend $300,000 to run water and sewer from the city limits. We made a decision based on an eighteen-month return on our investment, which you businessmen know is a good return. Since that time there have been two other businesses located along that line. We're actually now looking at a situation of a return on our investment of less than a year. So we feel it was justified.

> speaker EXPLAINS why water and sewer lines were run

Darrell Frye
"County Government"

Common reactions to a diagnosis of cancer—probably the big ones—are fear and anger and shock. I don't think that anyone should consider those to be a weakness of any type. Those are very real reactions that people have, not only to cancer, but to other problems that they experience in life. Those are very real, and a cancer patient should be able to have those feelings and to express them. We as personnel need to help them deal with that and to let them know that it is not a weakness—this is a real feeling of reaction, and to try to help them get through that time.

> speaker EXPLAINS common reaction to cancer diagnosis

Carolyn Rice
"Expressing Feelings"

Definition

Much informative speaking is in reality a major effort to define as well as to explain. In the speech on hanging pictures, you should probably define the difference between a picture *hanger* and a picture *hook*. The term *hanger* is used to identify the triangular metal support, usually held by a single nail, that is placed into the wall, and is sometimes called a *bulldog* hanger. The hook is either a rectangular corrugated piece or a circle of metal attached by a nail, brad, or staple to the back of the picture itself. The hook fastens over and into the outward extension of the triangular hanger. (A more detailed definition might include the brace or counterweight theory behind the hanger that enables a relatively small nail to support several pounds of picture weight.)

When speakers deal with more abstract subjects such as philosophies, social theories, psychological concepts, or political ideologies, definition of terms is essential. What is "an ethic"? what is "morality"? what is "poverty"? what is "prejudice"? what is "classical condition"? what is "reality therapy"? what is "democracy"? what is "fascism"? Whole speeches can be built around clarifying and defining one of these terms.

Definition is achieved in a number of different ways. Take a common table fork, for instance. It may be defined by *classifying* it: flatware—an implement used in eating and serving food. It may be defined by its *origin:* The ancient Romans used one- and two-tine skewers in food preparation, but only after the Renaissance did forks come into common table use. Defining by *purpose* is helpful: A fork is an implement for spearing, holding, and taking up of food, used in lieu of fingers for transfer of food from the plate to the mouth.

We often define by listing *synonyms:* spear, tine, prong, trident, or furcula (look it up!). *Operational definitions* are stated in terms that allow us to identify and repeat specific steps in a process: The table fork should be held in the right hand in America (in the left hand in England and many European countries). Solid food such as pieces of cut-up meat or chunks of vegetable should be speared on the tines, while smaller morsels or soft foods should be scooped onto the flat surface formed by the tines and then transferred to the mouth.

These are all useful approaches to the process of defining. Part of the speaker's art lies in the ability to prejudge all major terms on which the audience members will probably share similar prior meanings, then to define any other terms that may be confusing, unknown , or so open to a variety of interpretations that failure to define may leave listeners thinking some different meaning from the one the speaker intends.

The dictionary is only a beginning spot for finding definitions. Dictionary definitions are *denotative* in nature, for they are rather fixed notions of word meanings, devoid of the rich background of experience under which we learn language. *Connotative* definitions add layers of meaning from personal experience that enrich and color words for us. Two keys words that the federal government has repeatedly attempted to define, with only limited success, are *poverty* and *pornography*. Poverty is more than an arbitrary amount of money per family. In many ways it is an attitude toward life or an overall life style. And what is pornographic to one observer is enjoyable erotica to another. The connotations stirred up by these two words are varied and complex. In building your own definitions, you must go well beyond the dictionary and draw from your own experience as well as literary sources. Look at the way two speakers defined different terms in these examples:

> For those of you who want a definition of what hospice is, it is simply a frontier program that works with terminally ill people during approximately the last six months of their life. The program is licensed, medically directed, and confidential. We have volunteers and professionals who make visits in your home, to see your grandmother or grandfather or somebody in your family who is terminally ill. We help support your family.
>
> Kitty Boone
> "Hospice of the Piedmont"

speaker
DEFINES
"hospice"
program

> What is a budget? A budget is a systematic method of figuring out what you want to spend your money for based on how much money you make and how much money you owe.
>
> Elizabeth Madison
> "Money Survival"

speaker
DEFINES
"budget"

Description

Detailed description may be a form of supporting materials in itself or may be used to make illustrations more interesting. The dictionary defines description as "discourse intended to give a mental image of something experienced (as a scene, person, or sensation)."[1]

In describing, we choose language that best helps the listener imaginatively see the same picture that is in the speaker's mind. The listener's mind is like a piece of canvas; the speaker's words are the raw paints that, when skillfully blended and applied, will create a picture in the mind. Listening expert Florence Wolff believes that PIM (picturing in the mind) is a useful technique for speakers, and she offers it as a key to increased listening comprehension and improved memory.[2]

While you may possibly use quoted descriptive material from other speakers or literary sources in your speech, we encourage you to develop your own power of description. Much of the art of the storyteller is the ability to describe clearly and vividly. Careful observation of people and situations helps you to see colorful and interesting details that you might otherwise miss. Practice by writing character sketches about interesting people you have seen, by thinking through all the realistic details of the place you live or visit regularly, or by orally giving a graphic account of an event you have witnessed.

Description may vary in length from just a few words to full paragraphs. Narration is closely related to description. Narrative moves a story forward, whereas description may tend to freeze plot development for a moment to elaborate on specific details of the story's setting or the people involved. Yet the two processes are similar, as you can see in the following examples.

[Speaker has visited Nicaragua] I had seen the destruction from the day before. I saw an entire tobacco barn, which was just a corrugated tin building, that had been blown up by mortars, which was a loss of thousands of dollars of tobacco that had already been harvested. I went into a home that had been hit by mortars. I talked to the mother whose three kids were hit—I saw the kids' blood on the wall, their sandals in there—one of those kids died the week we were there.

> speaker DESCRIBES what he saw in Nicaragua

            Homer Yost
            "U.S. Intervention in Central America"

At 8:30, I walked across the street. I wanted to freshen up a bit before the exam—it was to be a four-hour exam. The building had at one time been a women's dormitory and they did not have men's restrooms. The only men's room in the building was in the basement. There were no students or other people around, so I went down to the men's room and washed my face and said a final prayer. I started to walk out and the door handle turned completely around in my hand. I pulled on the door handle—I turned it. I was in the basement—the chances of anybody finding me were very remote. A high window opened into a well with an iron railing. I climbed up and was trying to push the grate up. I thought I'm going to push and if I can't get it up, I will start to scream. Well, about that time some poor unsuspecting soul walked into the men's room. I don't know what he thought, because I came flying out the window yelling, "Don't shut that door!!!"

> speaker's DESCRIPTION of being locked in a restroom is also a humorous ANECDOTE

            John Young
            "Education in the Insurance Industry"

Examples and Factual Data

A fourth form of supporting material is an *example*, sometimes called a piece of factual data. In a speech to convince listeners that women's clothing and fashion design is as appealing a career choice for men as it is for women, a speaker might cite the names of Christian Dior, Calvin Klein, or Yves St. Laurent as examples of men who have been successful in the field. In a speech on the role of the quarterback in winning professional football teams, names such as John Elway, Joe Namath, or Joe Montana might be used as examples.

In arguing the merits of a college education in higher income potential, the speaker would probably list several sample salaries of jobs or professions for both college and noncollege employees. This would also be *comparison*, another form of supporting material, but as it is a comparison of factual data, we can call it both an example and a comparison. Some might say that because the speaker gives the salaries in numbers, in this case in dollar amounts, that *statistics* is also involved. While the use of statistics is certainly a valuable form of supporting material, we prefer to define statistics as some sort of interpretation of numbers and figures, not a mere listing of numbers as facts.

Examples tend to be brief in nature, for when they are expanded, they become illustrations or anecdotes. Examples should be thought of as particular facts, incidents, or samples that represent a larger group of people, ideas, events, or concepts. The use of an example often clarifies meaning to a listener when just an explanation or definition of the larger category would not be as clear. Suppose I urged you to eat more high-fiber foods in order to protect against hardening of the arteries. You might not disagree, but perhaps the large category "high fiber" lacks specificity in your mind. If I listed as examples whole wheat bread instead of white, cereals with *bran* in their names, and nuts for a snack, you would have some examples of high-fiber foods.

In choosing examples to use in your speeches, make sure they truly represent the larger category. An ice cream sundae is not high-fiber food, no matter how good it may be. Also be sure your examples can be recognized by your listeners. Choose examples based on the principle of audience adaptation. In the speech about football, if your audience is composed primarily of businessmen over 40, the names of Don Meredith, Sonny Jurgensen, and Norm van Brocklin would probably stir up meaningful associations. But if the audience is mostly college students, unless they are football historians, you might do better to use more contemporary names, such as John Elway, Jim McMahon, or Dan Marino.

Finally, be sure that you choose enough examples to make the point clearly. We suggest three or four. Do not go overboard; the use of 10 or 12 names or labels become boring.

> There are three types of spending. There are fixed expenses, which you cannot change, which you are always going to have, such as your tuition and car payment. Then you have flexible expenses which are somewhat variable and up to your discretion. These include food, clothing and health care. And then you have discretionary expenses, those that are totally under your control. That would include entertainment or gifts. Those are the three types of spending.
>
> Elizabeth Madison
> "Money Survival"

> speaker gives
> EXAMPLES
> of fixed,
> flexible,
> discretionary
> expenses

Nontraditional occupations for women are those occupations in which men predominate, such as medicine
or the law. Moderately traditional occupations are
those in which the distribution of the sexes is approxi-
mately equal. Examples might vary from place to
place, but would include psychologists and social
workers. The highly traditional occupations are self-
explanatory—nurses and secretaries.

> speaker gives
> EXAMPLES of
> nontraditional
> and traditional
> jobs for
> women

Maude Alston
"Suicide Among Women"

Illustrations and Anecdotes

Many times a speaker may wish not merely to list unelaborated examples but
also to use either factual or fictional story-type material to help clarify, expand,
and add interest to the topic. The fine-line difference between a somewhat
lengthy example and an illustration is not especially important, and we often
hear the terms used interchangeably. We might say that the list of Dior, Klein,
and St. Laurent *illustrated* the point that men can succeed in the fashion industry, while a story about a person who lowered high blood pressure by adopting
a high-fiber diet might be identified as an *example* of what a diet can do.

Generally we think of illustrations as longer and more storylike than
examples. In addition, illustrations do not have to be factual, but may be pieces
of fiction. Illustrations are real, fictional, or anecdotal in nature. Anecdotes may
be based on either fact or fiction and differ mainly in that they tend to be more
amusing and told as narratives. Much of what friends exchange as jokes are
anecdotes with a funny punch line.

As with examples, illustrations help to clarify abstract ideas. But more
importantly, they bring words to life by creating scenes that listeners can picture
visually while the speaker discusses the idea. A good storyteller has a wonderful head start toward being an interesting speaker, for she or he can intersperse
attention-holding illustrations with statements of fact and assertions of arguments.

A factual illustration might help listeners understand the meaning and
purpose of the concept of *eminent domain*, defined as, "a right of a government
to take private property for public use by virtue of the superior dominion of the
sovereign power over all lands within its jurisdiction."[3] While this somewhat
wordy dictionary definition makes some sense to us, the concept can come to
life if the speaker will tell about an actual case in which an individual has tried
to block a major construction project such as a superhighway or airport. Thousands of people stand to be served by the project, but one person, pressing
personal ownership rights, tries to stop it. Eminent domain guarantees that the
rights of the individual cannot threaten the rights of larger groups of citizens.
The illustration clarifies the definition.

You could handle this illustration in one of two ways. You could cite a specific case, including names, places, and some reference to where you discovered the information. This lends the weight of authenticity to your illustration. Or, you could make up a story of your own, something that might have or could have happened. This is less authentic, hence potentially less convincing.

The fictional illustration is completely acceptable, provided you clearly identify it as fiction and not imply that it actually happened. Such identification is simple—begin the story with, "Suppose that there was a man living in a little house. . . ." Immediately your audience knows this is imaginative, not a real situation. Other phrases such as, "Let's imagine that . . ." or "What do you think might have happened if . . ." will help you establish your illustration as fictional. If you have selected the illustration from a literary source, a brief phrase such as "Mark Twain tells us about a man who . . ." or "In O. Henry's short story 'The Last Leaf' . . ." identify the source for your listeners.

Be on the lookout for dramatic or moving illustrations, as well as those that are funny. Collect good jokes, anecdotes, human-interest stories about people and their experiences, and add them to a file of other forms of supporting material you find in books, magazines, short stories, or newspapers. Note the way the use of illustration helps to make the point in these two speeches from our community.

> We are near an interstate here. The Federal Roads people will not let you touch anything. If somebody put a sign up there, they would put you in jail. Now—and this is a true story—we had very important visitors coming on one occasion. As a matter of fact, it was Hubert Humphrey. We wanted the park to look pretty. But the grass and weeds on the federal property was this high. So, I told our people to go cut it. And the next day, they descended on me. Said, "Who gave you permission to do that?" I said, "Nobody, it just needed mowing and I thought we'd help you out." And they said, "Under penalty, now, don't ever do this again." I said, "That's what you get for dealing with ignorance—I am sorry, but I didn't know the rules. But I promise you this—if you'll keep it mowed, we'll never mow it again!"
>
> Ned Hoffman
> "Research Triangle Park"

speaker **ILLUSTRATES** how initiative can be used to offset bureaucratic inaction

> I walked down the Champs Elysees in Paris on a beautiful evening, dark and quiet. It was a beautiful day; I was in short sleeves. As I got down to the end of the Champs Elysees, on a side street there was a little bar. I thought I would stop and have a little refreshment. I walked in, and I started to tell the bartender what I wanted to drink, but I didn't speak French and he didn't speak English. Years ago in high school I had

speaker **ILLUSTRATES** point that

some French somewhere, but I couldn't find it at my fingertips at that time. I turned around and almost bumped into a handsome young Frenchman. "You American?" he asked. "You join me and my wife—we talk English very good—we practice with you." I told him what I wanted and he ordered my drink. We went back to the table. There was a gorgeous French girl. He introduced me, and I sat down. Her first words were, "So sorry your country is in such bad shape."

mass media may create faulty impression of America

> Monty B. Pitner
> "Mass Media Missing the Mark"

Testimony

A primary method for adding believability to statements that we as individuals may make is to use statements made by other people who share a similar viewpoint to our own. Small children show that they have learned this pragmatic technique early on when they argue, "Susie's mama said she could go to the park if you'd let me go," or "I have to watch this TV show—my teacher said I would learn a lot from it." An assurance that I am not the only one who believes as I would have you believe strengthens my argument.

Testimony, then, is a direct quotation or a paraphrase that authenticates factual evidence. The degree to which an explanation can be clarified or an argument strengthened by adding outside backing depends on how believable that outside source is for any particular listener. Recognizable experts in given fields are preferable sources of support. If you want to explain how the National Aeronautics and Space Administration (NASA) views its role in dispensing information to the public about all phases of our space program, quoting a top NASA administrator or someone from the agency's public relations staff helps assure listeners that you know what you are talking about.

The further removed you are from the reality of your topic, the more you need to use expert opinion. Many career speakers who represent business or service organizations are their own experts. Nonetheless, they still frequently employ testimony in their speeches. As a student speaker, you may lack direct or firsthand knowledge of the speech topics you select, but you build that knowledge through research and investigation. You add support and credibility by quoting experts.

As you select testimony to use in your speeches, make sure that the person you quote is truly an expert in the field. Advertising often makes use of a persuasive strategy in which popular or famous individuals endorse products. The buyer is supposed to imitate the behavior of those well-known people and also buy the product. Entertainers such as Bill Cosby for JELL-O™ products, James Garner and Mariette Hartley for Polaroid™ camera, and Rosemary Clooney for Coronet™ paper products are examples. But these stars are not necessarily experts about the products: They are merely stating personal preference or, more likely, saying what they have been paid to say. Their statements should be viewed as *endorsements*, not testimony.

The public speaker needs to find testimony from genuinely qualified people whose credentials have been earned in the field for which they are referenced. Endorsement serves a purpose in certain limited speech situations. Listing well-known backers of a particular political candidate, public figures who identify with certain charitable organizations, or supporters of given propositions, bills, or proposed laws is a legitimate technique for building a *bandwagon* effect. The listener is asked to join a prestigious group by voting, giving, or ratifying in the same way that others have. For your classroom speeches, however, and for the majority of career speeches, endorsement is probably less useful than testimony. Testimony seeks not only a name value, but a name that can authentically be tied to verifiable data.

You can locate useful testimony either by interviewing experts yourself or by reading their remarks in print. Remarks are in print either because the expert has authored books or articles about his or her research or because a writer has interviewed the expert and followed through by quoting specific remarks. Both the quality and the reputation of the publication from which you take the testimony are general guides to its accuracy. *U.S. News and World Report* can be assumed to be a more reliable source than *The National Enquirer*. Always credit the source of your testimony, as in the following examples.

> What do you do with an uncooperative person? To begin with, we need to define it behaviorally. According to Skinner, you first state the behavior that you want in positive terms. Let's say you were working on someone who is a complainer. How would you turn that around? What is the opposite side of the coin to complaining?
>
> Dr. Dudley Shearborn
> "Organizational Behavior in the Marketplace"

> speaker CITES psychologist Skinner on shaping behavior

(*Note:* The speaker is probably correct in assuming that the members of the audience—upper division college students—know that he refers to behavioral psychologist B. F. Skinner.)

> On your table under your placemat is a handout that has a copy of Maslow's needs hierarchy and an organizational needs hierarchy. We will use this as a conceptual framework to discuss one of the dimensions of our community. In his research, Maslow found that in personal development there were basic needs that had to be met and satisfied before another level of needs could be fulfilled. Basically, a physical need has to be met before we can be concerned about safety needs, and those have to be met before we can think about belong-

> speaker USES Maslow's hierarchy of

ing needs, more emotional needs. Those of you who are familiar with the school system know that one of the reasons we have a breakfast program is because of a commitment to the idea that the hunger needs must be satisfied before we can get into satisfying intellectual needs. Then, belonging needs have to be satisfied before we can start addressing our self-esteem needs, and then of course the self-actualization—after all other needs are taken care of, we are then in a place to have those self-actualizing moments.

> Dr. Ernie Tompkins
> "Are We Doing It in Winston-Salem?"

needs to discuss community development

Quotation

Testimony is factual quotation. Another useful verbal aid is fictional or literary quotation. Many great authors have provided gems of wisdom, fun, and beauty in capsules of fine prose or poetry. Finding, keeping, and using appropriate literary quotations is another element of the public speaker's art.

While testimony adds primarily to the factual level of the speech to enhance the speaker's believability, the literary quotation serves more to add interest, color, and variety to the speaker's ideas. The quotation, usually from fiction, may add depth to the listener's understanding and appreciation of the topic rather than serve primarily as verification and authentication. No hard-and-fast rule separates the two forms of quotation, for testimony may be colorful and interesting, while a literary source may be used as a form of proof. The distinction suggests rather than dictates the difference.

Finding good quotations requires that public speakers be readers. A lifetime habit of reading novels, short stories, poetry, and plays provides opportunities to discover literary gems that can be added to the file of other forms of supporting material. Students might start by using a source such as Bartlett's *Familiar Quotations*,[4] then expand into literature and contemporary journalism for less commonly used quotations. Your ability to find good quotations will improve as you widen your range of reading material and as you get on the lookout for useful quotes.

George Bernard Shaw has always been a favorite playwright of mine—and in one of his plays, *Major Barbara*, a young woman declares, "I want to be an active verb!" That particular line has always struck me as one that would be worth embroidering on a sampler—or if I think about it, better yet—printed on a hundred thousand bumper stickers! "I want to be an active verb!" To wake up every morning and be able to say, "I can, I think, I feel, I wonder, I will, I serve."

> Sandy Hopper
> "Volunteerism in the 80s"

speaker uses QUOTATION from a great playwright

They'll have to be converted in their thinking. They'll have to think like God thinks. Isiah 55 says, "My ways are higher than your ways and my thoughts are higher than your thoughts." God just knows more than we do, did you know it? He knows more than we do. But then, on down a few verses, he says "So shall my word be that goes forth out of my mouth that it shall accomplish that for which it is sent." The word of God is given to us that we might learn to walk in God's ways and think his thoughts.

> speaker uses
> QUOTATION
> from the Old
> Testament

Gloria Stanwick
"Healing"

(*Note:* Ministers and church school teachers often use Scripture as both quotation and foundation for sermons and lessons. Note the interchange of "Isiah 55 says" and later "He says"—both acceptable uses of introducing scriptural quotations.)

"I'm so excited and I just can't hide it." The excitement that this Pointer Sisters' song refers to might not seem relevant to you as you prepare to begin your careers. Excitement, however, is vital not only in getting a job, but in advancing in your field as well. This excitement is also known as *motivation*.

> speaker uses
> QUOTATION
> from modern
> song

Roy Schwartzman
"The Importance of Motivation in Career Success"

Comparison and Contrast

The great language theorist I.A. Richards considered the metaphor to be the most useful of all language devices in its potential for eliminating human misunderstanding.[5] "For Richards, metaphor is more than a figure of speech that is used for stylistic effect in a speech or an essay. . . . . [it] is a major technique for facilitating comprehension."[6]

The term *metaphor* has two meanings. First, it is the specific figure of speech in which words or phrases are used to establish likeness between two objects or ideas but without use of the words *like* or *as* to suggest that relationship. Second, in a broader sense the word *metaphor* encompasses any kind of comparison, whether it is a simile, a factual or fictional comparison, a factual or fictional contrast, a literal or figurative analogy, or an allegory.

Modern-day scholar Michael Osborn works to classify metaphors and to try to understand how they operate on us.[7] On the simplest level, a comparison of any sort helps the listener understand a little-known concept by showing how it is like something better known. If you want an American audience to know about kindergartens in Japan, you might compare them to kindergartens in the United States. Both the similarities (comparison) and differences (contrast) may be pointed out. If I want to explain a pie graph that shows the federal budget, I might compare the wedges to personal budget categories such as food, housing, and transportation. The second is very familiar to you, while the first is less well known. I use the known to help you understand the unknown.

We have divided comparison and contrast from the analogy in much the same way that we divided examples from illustrations. We admit considerable overlap and possible problems of distinguishing a short comparison from a literal analogy. In the main, the difference is in factualness and length. Comparisons and contrasts are more often factual in nature and tend to be shorter, just as are examples. The analogy may be fact or fiction, but is often more expanded and more fully developed.

The difference between comparison and contrast is a simple one. Comparison looks for likeness or similarity between ideas or objects, while contrast tries to increase understanding by calling attention to the differences. Understanding what something is *not* may also be a useful way to try to learn what something *is*.

In choosing ideas for comparisons, make sure they are truly comparable. You have doubtless heard the expression "It's like comparing apples and elephants," a suggestion that the speaker has chosen two or more items that do not have true likeness or similarity. A faulty comparison may do more harm than good, for it can confuse the listener.

The concept of a just war is dead. There are civil casualties even in conventional war. In conventional war the civil casualties have come to outnumber the military casualties. The Russians lost six million men in the army, navy, and air force during the Second World War, and fourteen million civilian casualties, either direct military casualties or those who starved or gave in to famine, disease, and the like afterwards.

> John Grice
> "Obstacles to World Order"

speaker implies COMPARISON of modern warfare with that of the past

Do you want to grow old gracefully or wastefully? You grow old wastefully if you become resigned to tedium and indifference. An unknown writer says, "If you've left your dreams behind, if hope's grown cold, if you no longer look ahead, then sadly you are old." But on the other hand, if you have a positive outlook and a zest for living, then age is irrelevant and the poet's meaning is clear.

> Ila Johnson
> "Still in the Parade"

speaker CONTRASTS two styles of growing old (also includes a literary QUOTE)

Analogy: Figurative and Literal

Analogy is another method of using like elements in ideas or objects to lead listeners from the familiar into the unfamiliar or to dramatize and intensify thoughts through the technique of comparison. Analogies are usually more elaborated, longer, and more detailed than are simple comparisons.

Literal analogies are based on true situations. Persons active in present-day organizations such as Amnesty International or Americas Watch may compare the jailing of political prisoners in Turkey, Cuba, the Soviet Union, or many South and Central American countries today to the jailing of political prisoners during the Reign of Terror in the 1790s during the French Revolution. In both cases, individuals were incarcerated not because of criminal activities, but because they opposed the political philosophy of the ruling power. Today we share sympathetic understanding of the French revolutionaries, for we believe their cause was noble. By using the analogy, a speaker may try to motivate you to be likewise sympathetic with political prisoners around the world today.

A *figurative* analogy is drawn from a fictional or nonrealistic source or one in which the likeness is not readily apparent. If I want to help you understand the importance and the relationship of verbal aids to speech building, I may compare them to the branches of a tree in that they can be said to fill out the trunk or central idea. Another workable analogy might be to call supporting material the paving stones in a walkway, for they are integral parts of the whole. Verbal aids are not literally either tree branches or bricks, but the analogy is useful.

The most creative metaphors are figurative analogies. Comparing one's love to a "red, red rose," as did the poet Robert Burns,[8] or comparing a restless monarch to "the lion in winter," as did playwright James Goldman,[9] while specifically a simile and a metaphor, are both figurative analogies. More complex relationships may become major metaphors for longer works, such as Ernest Hemingway's use of the sea as a symbol of the force that drives man to persist against all odds,[10] or George Orwell's *Animal Farm* as an allegory of a totalitarian society.[11]

The ability to discover and build novel and meaningful analogies is another skill of the creative speech maker. Analogies have a tendency to become trite when overused: "the ball's in your court," "he struck out," "lead the team across the goal line," or "drop back ten and punt" are some of the many sports analogies that are presently popular. "I am the Captain of my soul,"[12] "There is a tide in the affairs of men,"[13] "A community is like a ship; every one ought to be prepared to take the helm,"[14] and "The Ship of State"[15] are just a few of many sea metaphors that have abounded in literature.

Try to find new and interesting ideas or objects to compare so that you help the listener by connecting something well known to a lesser-known concept. See how the analogies help in the following two examples.

We can get out with thousands of people who believe in what we're doing and who love this state and care about our future. We can go to those people and talk to them and ask for their help. I believe they're going to respond. In the last several weeks, I have seen this democratic victory beginning to come in. It is like the tide—it starts coming in very gradually. You hardly notice it, but you see it a little better every day. It is getting a little higher. And, I think that is what's happening here.

> speaker draws ANALOGY between a political groundswell and the ocean's tide

James B. Hunt, Governor
"Precinct Appreciation"

On the wall my desk faces at the Crisis Control ministeries is a very large green frog hidden under an even larger brown coconut shell. Each morning my frog greets me and reminds me of the proverb it illustrates which states, "The frog beneath the coconut shell believes there is no other world." What do my frog and thousands of people who act like him hide? What is it that they don't want to see or hear? Perhaps, just maybe, it is the evils of this world of ours.

> speaker implies a frog hiding under a shell is ANALOGOUS to people who will not see what is going on around them

Rev. Ginny Britt
"Needs of the Poor"

Statistics

The final verbal aid to speech making is the use of statistical data to help explain the speaker's idea or back up his or her assertion. The term *statistics* is applied to a professional field that focuses on the techniques of analyzing data to assure that experimental or survey results adhere to the laws of probability—that is, they do not simply happen by chance or accident. The term is used more broadly here to suggest any quantitive data that may be gathered and interpreted.

If as a researcher I sense that blue-eyed people are more easily persuaded than are brown-eyed people, I can only validate my intuition by finding out the level of persuasibility of a significant number of people of both eye colors. Statistical formulas help me ensure that my group truly represents the population at large and that any differences I find are not just by chance or accident of fate. By comparing the number of people in each eye color category to a numerically based persuasibility scale, I hope to earn the right to state my intuition as a fact. In brief, this is the task of a professional statistician.

Other people may employ numerical data, and we often use the term *statistics* to describe that data. Demographers, for example, may do nothing to manipulate subjects or data, but may simply report facts in numbers. Reports that give income averages, numbers of people in various age brackets, percentages of buyers' choices, voter preferences, or the death rate for heart-attack victims may all be called statistical reports.

A speaker can use numerical or statistical data to explain ideas or processes. For example, in an informative speech on solar collectors, the speaker may talk of temperature potential in centigrade or Fahrenheit degrees, anticipated efficiency percentages, or dollars-and-cents comparison to other forms of energy. Assertions of persuasive speakers can offen be backed up and reinforced by supporting them with statistics. Television commercials that argue that nine out of ten doctors recommend aspirin, that Ivory Soap is 99 and 44/100 percent pure, or that McDonald's has sold over 50 billion hamburgers all use numbers to support their appeal.

The public speaker needs to do something meaningful with those figures rather than simply report them. Merely reporting numbers does not ensure their usefulness, unless the numbers themselves are especially startling. *Comparing* figures can be helpful—how many more people voted Democratic than Republican in 1948, 1960, 1964, and so on. *Relating* numbers to a more familiar group is a useful technique, as in the following:

> If you took 50 billion regular McDonald's hamburgers and laid them side by side, you could probably go to the moon and back 12 times. . . . . Or take your 50 billion hamburgers to the equator and start laying them side by side, and by the time you're done, you'll have gone around the world 118.84 times. If you put 50 billion hamburgers on one side of a scale, it would take 30 *Queen Elizabeth* passenger ships to balance them.[16]

Restating numbers in a smaller way that can be more easily grasped by the listener is helpful; for example, saying that two people in the immediate audience will die in automobile accidents in the next year is more meaningful and dramatic than saying that 50,000 people will be killed on highways. Large numbers should be rounded off, such as saying "around a million" when the actual number is 999,968.

As a speaker, you need to find accurate statistical data and include it when appropriate, when you feel it will be useful, and when you can verify to a reasonable degree that it is accurate, unbiased, and honestly gathered. Always give credit to the source of your information. A phrase such as "Statistics tell us that . . ." with no mention of source or authenticity weakens rather than strengthens your case.

Facts recently gathered by the National Institute of Alcohol Abuse and Alcoholism are both impressive and depressing. Some of the NIAAA findings are that alcoholism and alcohol abuse continue to occur at high incident rates in American society. The economic cost associated with the misuse of alcohol is estimated at sixty-one billion dollars a year. Also, in one-half of all the murders in the United States, either the killer or the

speaker presents
DATA in RATIOS
(1/2, 1/4) to

victim or both have been drinking. One-fourth of all suicides are found to have significantly high amounts of alcohol in their blood streams. People who abuse alcohol are seven times as likely to be separated or divorced as the general population. . . . . Each year over 50,000 Americans die in traffic accidents. About half those deaths, an estimated 25,000, involve drunk drivers and pedestrians.

> Mike Patton
> "S.A.D.D."

| help listeners understand it |

This is a fascinating statistic—in any one 24-hour period, between 70–85% of adult human beings in this society will take a prescription drug. That's fascinating—in any one 24-hour period—70–85%. If it's the low end, that means 7 out of 10 of us. In some ways that is hard to believe. We are taught to rely on something else, not ourselves. . . . . Mark Gold, a medical doctor and one of our foremost authorities on drug addiction, wrote a book called *1-800-COCAINE*, the cocaine hotline number. Dr. Gold states that one out of every 10 adult Americans has tried cocaine at least once. Five thousand people a day are becoming addicted to cocaine.

> Dr. Richard Blue
> "The Addictive Personality"

| speaker REDUCES annual FIGURES to 24-hour time frame. Note "7 of 10" and "1 of 10" to make NUMBERS meaningful |

FINDING SUPPORTING MATERIAL

Several resources are available to you for finding the various types of material with which you will support your ideas and develop your speech. Your own past and present *experience* may offer a major source, especially if you stick to those speech topics that are already familiar to you. *Careful observation* of events and situations can add to your store of knowledge. *Visiting* business or civic organizations and getting brochures, pamphlets, newsletters, leaflets, or promotional packets may be useful. Much information may come from interviews. For the classroom speaker, the primary source for finding supporting material is the library. The following guidelines for interviews and using the library, as well as a few tips on using mass media as a source, may be helpful.

Interviews

Interviews can be an excellent source for additional material, provided you plan the interview carefully and that you do not center your entire speech around the content of just one interview. Carefully choose persons whom you wish to interview, making sure they can provide you with the information you want.

Always call and make an appointment. Even if you plan to interview a college professor during his or her posted office hours, you should call and set up a specific appointment, letting the professor know why you want the interview.

Structure your questions carefully in advance of the interview. Know the different types of questions that you can ask and use them according to your informational purpose. *Closed-ended* questions are those that require only minimal response, since that response is structured by the question. *Open-ended* questions suggest a direction for the respondent, but do not limit or restrict the answer. Closed-ended questions are good for gathering specific facts, whereas open-ended questions are better for discovering the interviewee's thoughts and attitudes.[17]

If you were interviewing the head of a public relations firm in preparation for a speech on "Careers in Public Relations," you might want some closed-ended questions: "How many employees are with your firm?" "Do you serve a local, statewide, or national clientele?" "Do you anticipate adding other persons to your staff in the next three to five years, and if so, in what speciality areas?" These questions would give you facts for your speech.

Some open-ended questions that you might ask could include: "Where do you see the public relations field going in the next 15 to 20 years?" "How have client expectations of public relations services changed recently?" "What is the scope of public relations in comparison to advertising?"

A *summary* question is helpful in drawing the interview to a close and in leading the interviewee to give a concise restatement of his or her position. Example: "Given all that you have said about the future of your own firm and the public relations field in general, would you advise a young person to choose public relations as a career?"

During the interview, make such notes as are essential for you to remember the content of the comments. If you plan to quote exactly, write that particular statement out in full and read it back to the interviewee to check for accuracy. If you anticipate a need to use several statements as direct quotes, you might ask the interviewee for permission to take a portable tape recorder with you. Taping an interview can save time, for you do not need to stop and write. Copyright laws allow you to use only small portions of the interview without seeking additional written permission from the speaker, in much the same way that you can quote a paragraph from a book, but not an entire chapter.

When the interview has ended, thank the interviewee for his or her time and leave. Do not hang around just to chat after you have all your desired information. Respect the interviewee's time and depend upon the thoroughness with which you have prepared your questions.

The Library

The most useful source for classroom speeches is the library. Career speakers are less dependent on the library because they are more likely to have personal access to their own printed materials. They subscribe to more journals and magazines, buy more books other than textbooks, and work in offices that subscribe to a variety of publications. In addition, they have had experience in the field in which they work or the service organization they are representing. As a student speaker, you must supplement your lack of experience by turning to the library.

Most colleges and universities have good libraries of their own. Most cities of a reasonable size have a public library. Students having just left high school or having returned to college after a lengthy absence from formal education have different levels of skill in using the library. Some of you may be adept in finding what you want, while others feel totally lost and unsure where to begin.

Begin by talking with the reference librarian. Reference rooms are the heart of most libraries. Many offer guided tours or have videocassette programs that explain library usage. If several other students in your class feel insecure about their library skills, perhaps your instructor can arrange a tour for the entire class. The most useful library resources include various background materials (encyclopedias, yearbooks, and news summaries), periodical indexes, and the card catalogue.

Background knowledge sources.   Begin by checking your general background knowledge of the topic. Many general and subject-specific encyclopedias provide an overview of a topic. Textbooks also overview and may include bibliographies of books and periodical articles on your subject. Yearbooks, such as the *Annual Review of Psychology* or the *Annual Register of World Events*, offer current essays or reports of important events of the past year. Recent news events are summarized in publications such as *CQ Weekly Report* or *Facts on File*. By checking first with some of the general background sources, you can help focus your thinking, limit your topic, and begin to build a specific bibliography.

Periodicals.   Given the time pressures on the average college student, it is not realistic to think that you will be able to read eight or ten complete books on your topic for each speech. You can, however, read eight or ten essays or articles. Building a bibliography of periodical sources (newspapers, magazines, or journals) is essential to your research. A number of indexes are available to help you locate information on your topic. The *Reader's Guide to Periodical Literature* is the best known, for it indexes most popular magazines such as *Time*, *Life*, or *U.S. News and World Report*. Many specialized indexes, such as the *Social Science Index* or *Humanities Index*, concentrate more heavily on academic and scientific journals. The indexes are organized by topic, with subjects listed alphabetically. You may have to browse awhile to find the best key words to lead you in the right direction.

Entries will contain the article title, author's name, an abbreviation for the title of the periodical, and the volume, date, and page number. The abbreviations used are listed in the front of the index—study them carefully, for many academic journals have very similar names. Make a list of several essays or articles you would like to examine, determine through the card catalogue or a journal listing computer printout whether or not your library subscribes to that particular journal, and get the call number so that you can find it in the stacks. Do not forget to check current issues that have not yet been bound and indexed.

Public Speaking

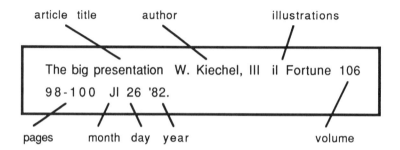

Books.   The card catalogue is a master listing of all the books in the library, cross-referenced by title, author, and subject. If you know an author's name or a book title, you can look it up by following the alphabetical order for the last name of the author or the first word of the title (excluding *a, an,* or *the*). You can also check the alphabetical listing of the subject for books that your library owns. A typical entry from the card catalogue looks like this:

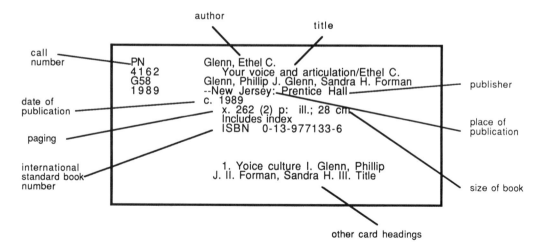

An increasing number of libraries are going "on line"—that is, computerizing the card catalogue. Rather than standing before cabinets with small drawers filled with index card entries, you will sit in front of a computer screen, where you can scan and browse in much the same way that you can with a traditional card catalogue.

In addition to on-line cataloguing, computerized searches for books and articles on particular topics are available in most large libraries. For a small fee, the user can tie into a large data base, using key words called *descriptors*, to secure a list of titles. Often the data base contains a short abstract of the article, enabling the reader to see whether or not the content would be useful. Talk with your reference librarian if you think a computer search might be of help to you.

Traditionally, note cards have been used to keep bibliographic citations [author's name(s), article title, book or journal title, volume number, date, and page number] as well as key ideas or quotations that might be wanted at a later time. Your authors remember copious stacks of note cards in our own undergraduate days. More recently, however, we see our students making extensive use of photocopying either in lieu of or in addition to note cards. Copyright laws allow limited student usage provided it is restricted to classroom preparation only. If you photocopy, make sure that the journal or book title and other citation information are on the copied page or that you add the details, especially page numbers, so that you can refer back accurately. A photocopied page or note card with the perfect quote or fact, but with no clue as to where it came from, is useless to you.

The keys to good library research are patience, persistence, and the willingness to ask questions and listen to the answers. Reference librarians are almost always friendly and more than willing to help you. Stick at it, learn your way around the library and how to use its many different sources, and you will be rewarded with an almost unbelievable quantity of information on an almost unlimited number of subjects!

Mass Media

A final source for finding good supporting material comes from the mass media, especially television. With a wealth of information on a wide array of topics, commercial stations, both networks and independents, and public television bring many opportunities to find resources that would be useful in building a speech.

Capturing the material can be a problem, however, unless you know in advance that a certain program is coming on and that you have access to a videocassette recorder (VCR) to tape the show. Many educational programs offer written transcripts for a small fee. Many college libraries buy videotapes of major educational programs. Copyright laws govern the length of time you can keep and reuse a recording, even for educational purposes. Material that comes from television must be credited just as written material is credited. Despite some problems in obtaining accurate quotations, television is a good source for speakers, for it has a high level of listener identification, especially when you reference popular programs and well-known television personalities.

Televised material is more readily available today than it has ever been and should continue to be even more accessible as the number of individually owned VCRs increases. And not every piece of supporting material that comes from television necessarily needs to be recorded. You might relate an anecdote or amusing situation that was on a popular show to help develop a point. One of our students gave a good speech on child rearing and used an effective illustration from *The Cosby Show*.

Attributing Sources of Supporting Material

Regardless of the source of your supporting material, you must give credit to the interviewee, book or article author, or television program from which it comes. A speaker does not cite sources in the same way that a writer does, for the writer must provide full bibliographic information, including title, author, publisher, and place and date of publication. While your instructor may require a full written bibliography for the sources you use to prepare your speeches, you need use only one or at most two of these key facts as you speak.

The following examples will help you determine a subtle, nonobtrusive, but effective way to let your listeners know the source of your material.

"National Geographic of April 1988 explained the difference clearly."	*explanation* (magazine)
"Webster's Collegiate Dictionary defines poverty as . . ."	*definition* (reference book)
"In *Tom Sawyer*, Mark Twain described the technique by which Tom whitewashed the fence . . ."	*description* (fiction)
"Michael Osborn writes that the metaphor is . . ."	*testimony* (journal article)
"A pamphlet published by Alcoholics Anonymous gives these frightening statistics about alcoholism . . ."	*statistics* (pamphlet)
"On *Nightline*, Ted Koppel compared elections in the United States to . . ."	*comparison* (TV source)
"The recent PBS series titled *The Mind* used an electrical wiring scheme as an analogy to the working of the human brain."	*analogy* (TV source)
"In a personal interview with Rod Thomas, President of the Greensboro Lions' Club, I learned that the Lions' annually give . . ."	*factual data* (interview)

KEY POINTS

- Supporting materials are verbal aids to the development of speech topics.
- The 10 forms of supporting material are:
  explanation
  definition
  description
  examples and factual data
  illustrations and anecdotes
  testimony
  quotation
  comparison and contrast
  analogy
  statistics
- Method of finding supporting materials include:
  personal experience
  observation
  visits
  interviews
  library research
  mass media
- Sources of supporting material should be briefly mentioned.

QUESTION FOR DISCUSSION

What are the differences in the ways that student speakers discover supporting materials from the sources available to the professional or service agency speaker? How can you, as a college student, gain access to the sources used by professionals?

ACTIVITIES

1. In Chapter 1, we asked that you begin a clipping or note file of possible speech topics. Add anecdotes, stories, jokes, personal experiences, or ideas from your reading that can illustrate these topics.
2. If you are a churchgoer, listen for the minister's use of illustrations. Most sermons depend heavily on illustrations to dramatize major points. Compare this to the types of illustrations and examples used by your professors in classroom lectures. How do these work as verbal aids?

3. Rewrite the following explanation to make it clearer for a visitor to a large factory.

> The Shipping Department is over there around the corner—you know, down there past where the water fountain is—it's on the same floor, but not on this same hall. It's on the hall around to the right, but after you go through the lobby out front. You know the lobby—out where you passed the water fountain—then there' another hall—around to the right—well, you go down there and I think that is where you'll find the Shipping Department—if it isn't there, try the left.

4. Rewrite the following description to make it more colorful and attention-holding for your classroom audience.

> We went to the beach. It was a nice day. The sun shone and it was hot but the breeze blew. We had chairs and an umbrella. Birds were flying. We felt good—we like the beach—it is so pretty. And especially on such a pretty day with the sun and the birds and everything.

5. As you prepare your classroom speeches, clip newspaper and magazine articles that include statistics related to your topic. How might those statistics be worked into speeches and how would they work as verbal aids?

6. Make a trip to your campus or local library. Find the card catalogue and look up at least five books on your next speech topic. Find at least five references in magazine and periodical indexes on the same subject.

REFERENCES

[1] *Webster's Ninth New Collegiate Dictionary*, (Springfield, Mass.: Merriam-Webster, Inc., 1984), 343.

[2] Florence I. Wolff, "Listening With Pictures in Mind: A Cognitive and Pedagogical Approach to Aural Visualization," Sixth Annual Convention, International Listening Association, Orlando, Florida, March 15, 1985.

[3] *Webster's*, p. 407.

[4] John Bartlett, *Familiar Quotations* (Boston: Little Brown, 1980).

[5] I.A. Richards, *The Philosophy of Rhetoric* (New York: Oxford University Press, 1936, 1950, 1965), 89–112.

[6] Sonja K. Foss, Karen A. Foss, and Robert Trapp, *Contemporary Perspectives on Rhetoric* (Prospect Heights, Ill.: Waveland Press, 1985), 33.

[7] Michael Osborn, "Archetypal Metaphor in Rhetoric: The Light-Dark Family," *Quarterly Journal of Speech* 53 (1967):115–126; "The Evolution of the Archetypal Sea in Rhetorical and Poetic," *Quarterly Journal of Speech* 63 (1977):347–363.

[8] Robert Burns, "A Red, Red Rose," *The Complete Works of Robert Burns* (Philadelphia: Gebbie & Co., 1886).

[9] James Goldman, *The Lion in Winter* (New York: Samuel French, Inc., 1966).

[10] Ernest Hemingway *The Old Man and the Sea* (New York: Charles Scribner's Sons, 1952).

[11] George Orwell, *Animal Farm*, Acting ed. (New York: Samuel French, Inc., 1964).

[12] William Ernest Henley, "Invictus," *Poems by William Ernest Henley* (New York: Charles Scribner's Sons, 1922).

[13]William Shakespeare, *Julius Caesar*, Act IV, Scene 3, *William Shakespeare: The Complete Works* (New York: Random House, 1952).

[14]Henrik Ibsen, *An Enemy of the People*, Acting ed. (New York: Dramatist Play Service, 1951).

[15]Henry Wadsworth Longfellow, "The Building of the Ship," *Poems* (Boston: Houghton, Mifflin & Co., 1883).

[16]"Just How Much Is 50 Billion, Anyway?" *Greensboro News and Record*, 20 November, 1984, A9.

[17]Donovan J. Ochs and Anthony C. Winkler, *A Brief Introduction to Speech*, 2nd ed. (New York: Harcourt Brace Jovanovich, 1979), 70–71.

THE SPEAKER AND THE DEVELOPMENT PROCESS

When the selection process has neared completion, with the purpose delineated, the topic chosen and narrowed, and the supporting material discovered and cataloged, the speaker is ready to begin the actual construction of the speech. In Part III, we offer guidelines for developing and arranging the thoughts and materials you have gathered and describe some of the visual aids that you may wish to include as you further refine and perfect your speech

Chapter 7

Organizing the Speech Ideas

PATTERNS OF ORGANIZATION

While any speech should be built around a single strong, central thesis statement, almost all speeches explore that statement by dividing the topic into several main points. Your goal may be as simple as to communicate information about an upcoming social event to your fellow club members or classmates, yet you will break that information into units—what, when, and where at a minimum, and maybe also who, why, and how much. If your single purpose is to convince fellow students to vote for your candidate for student body president, you will offer three or four good reasons why your candidate deserves the office; the reasons become the points of your argument.

The major points of a central idea can be arranged in a number of patterns, each suited to different types of subject matter. After we examine some of the most frequently used patterns, we will talk about the advantages of orderly arrangement, for both the speaker and the listener.

Chronological Pattern

We spend much of our lives in a series of steps that are points in time. History moves from past to present, the day moves from morning to night, and most of the concrete operations we perform—making up a bed, writing a term paper, or

94

constructing a building—are done in a pattern of first step, second step, third step, and so on. We call this sequence *chronological*, for it follows a time line.

Many speech topics are easily divided chronologically. Among the categories that best fit this pattern are historical tracings, biographies, speeches on how to make or build any concrete object, or any informative message whose components occur in a series. In the following examples, note the logic of the sequence of main points.

1. Specific purpose: to discuss women in the workplace since 1900
   I. 1900s: primarily primary and secondary teachers
   II. 1920s: secretarial positions
   III. 1940s: factory workers, replacing men at war
   IV. 1960s: management opportunities
   V. 1980s: CEOs
2. Specific purpose: to trace America's struggle for independence.
   I. Declaration of Independence
   II. Revolutionary War
   III. Constitution of the United States of America.
3. Specific purpose: to demonstrate the use of automatic bank tellers
   I. Insert pass card as directed.
   II. Punch in personal identification code.
   III. Conduct transaction as directed on screen.
   IV. Remove money, acknowledgment slip and card.

Spatial Pattern

Another method of dividing main points is by their arrangement in space. Topics ranging from unemployment to speech dialects to the weather might be arranged geographically by talking first about the northeastern United States, then the southeastern, and so on across the nation. While a day at Disney World could be described chronologically by what the speaker did first, second, and third, a more interesting pattern might be developed by taking the listener through the various areas of the park—Fantasyland, Frontierland, and Tomorrowland.

If you were to describe your home or apartment, you would probably do it room by room. The use of space as a dividing motif is both logical and interesting for certain topics, as in the following examples:

1. Specific purpose: To acquaint students with the campus library
   I. Main entrance
   II. Reference Room
   III. Card Catalogue
   IV. Reserve Room
   V. Checkout Counter

2. Specific purpose: to inform the audience about the Capitol Building
   I. The Rotunda
   II. The House of Representatives
   III. The Senate
3. Specific purpose: to explain communication "space"
   I. Intimate Space
   II. Casual-Personal Space
   III. Social-Consultative Space
   IV. Public Space

Topical Pattern

The most frequently used pattern is one in which the main points are divided by topics. Topics may be parts of a whole, as in a speech about the agencies encompassed in The United Way. Topics may be components of an abstract idea, such as the method of governance and the means of control of the economy as the two major components in explaining forms of government. Or topics may be elements of a structure, such as departments in a university or divisions of a large corporation. Almost any speech subject could be divided into subpoints through a topical arrangement. Study the following examples.

1. Specific purpose: to inform students about financial aid
   I. State and Government Grants
   II. Loans
   III. Work-Study
   IV. Specialized Awards
2. Specific purpose: to encourage students to join the "Greeks"
   I. You will make new social acquaintances.
   II. You may receive academic help and advice.
   III. You will become involved in community projects
3. Specific purpose: to explore hiking locations in the United States
   I. National Parks
      A. Yellowstone
      B. Grand Canyon
   II. State Parks
      A. Pisgah
      B. Fairystone
   III. Nature Trails
      A. local parks
      B. private clubs

Cause-and-Effect Pattern

A useful design, especially for persuasive speaking, is to develop a problem by first exploring the causes of that problem, then examining the effects that problem has created. For example, a retailer may need to convince workers that new display techniques must be adopted. This might be approached by discussing changes in the neighborhood, new or renovated competitive stores, or other causes for a drop in sales and increased criticism from customers. The changes were the cause, lowered sales and complaints the effect; the speaker may then present a plan to deal with this problem. Or the problem may be a need to get students to accept a year-long upheaval of the campus cafeteria service procedure: the cause, facilities that have not been renovated in over 30 years; the effect, inadequate and poorly equipped kitchen space that results in unappetizing food and shabby eating areas that make meals less enjoyable. Presented with a careful analysis of the *cause* and its *effects*, students are much more likely to tolerate a year of disruption while rebuilding is underway.

In using a cause-and-effect pattern, you must make sure you truly know and understand the causes. Careful research will help you avoid the mistake made in one of our classes; the student blamed an overprotective, parental attitude of the administration for lack of availability of personal telephones in dormitory rooms. Further research discovered that the administration had tried for years to get the phones, but the local telephone company had determined it was not cost-effective to make the expensive installation in older buildings. Careful research is necessary, for causality is not always easy to establish.

1. Specific purpose: To examine the decline in student activism
   I. The causes of the decline in student activism are
      A. Rise in tuition costs
      B. Time limitation—school and work
   II. The effects of the decline are
      A. Student organizations suffering
      B. Diminished student morale

2. Specific purpose: to heighten audience awareness to the dangers of environmental pollution
   I. The causes of environmental pollution are
      A. Dumping of toxic waste
      B. Proliferation of vehicle exhaust fumes
   II. The effects of pollution are
      A. Destruction of the ozone layer surrounding the earth
      B. Life, as we know it, may cease to exist

3. Specific purpose: to examine the increasing "fear of flying"
   I. An increasing number of people refuse to fly because
      A. Relaxation of government standards and regulations
      B. Airlines experiencing major increases in fatalities
   II. The effects of this "fear" are
      A. An increase in ticket prices
      B. Revitalization of other forms of transportation
         1. buses
         2. trains

Problem-and-Solution Pattern

Closely related to the cause-and-effect pattern is the *problem-and-solution* pattern. In the beginning, a speaker discusses and analyzes a problem; its causes may be included if the speaker knows them, but more importantly, the problem is clearly defined and its ramifications explored. For instance, many people today are concerned about the relatively poor performance of our public schools in giving students a solid educational foundation. Exact causality has not been determined. Yet a speaker could describe the problem with facts, figures, and examples, using this discussion as a base for presenting a specific proposal for improvement. Rather than cause-and-effect, the speech would have a problem-and-solution format.

This is a frequently used pattern when a speaker wants to move a group to action. Members of Congress advocating new legislation, or a group of stenographers asking a corporate board of directors to purchase new word-processing equipment, might make use of a problem-solution approach to present their case. The following are examples of this pattern.

1. Specific purpose: to offer a solution to poor public education
   I. The quality of public education is on the decline
      A. Low salaries do not attract promising teachers
      B. Lack of parental involvement
   II. The solution to this problem is
      A. Increase merit pay
      B. Creation of parent-teacher networking system
2. Specific purpose: to justify the use of capital punishment
   I. State prisons are overcrowded and expensive.
      A. The majority of inmates are repeat offenders.
      B. Imprisonment is not a deterrent to violent crime
   II. Capital punishment offers a viable solution
3. Specific purpose: to explain the need for public-speaking courses
   I. Students get few opportunities to interact with live audiences.
      A. Most classwork and homework is done "alone"
      B. Many professions demand proficiency at presentational speaking
   II. Public speaking courses offer students a forum to work on their individual skills in a guided environment.

VALUES OF ORGANIZATION

The work that you will do to find the most effective pattern for organizing the main points of your speech will be useful to you and to your listeners. While you are still in the preparation process, a well-founded pattern helps you think through the substance of your speech more carefully. It enables you to identify the logical relationships among the content items. And you may see obvious gaps or omissions. You may have left out a step in a chronological pattern or omitted one area if your organization is by space. Think of how much more useful a list of tasks and chores for the day would be if it were grouped by (1) home, (2) shopping center, and (3) on campus, rather that a random list of 14 or 15 things to do. And writing "shopping center" rather than incidental grocery, drug, or dime store items might help you note that you also need to pick up a suit at the cleaners, for you would picture the shopping center and the stores in it, not just miscellaneous items.

In addition to clarifying information and spotting possible gaps, clear organization is a useful tool for improving memory. Three or four main points that are grouped by design are much easier to recall than unstructured items. Which of these two lists could you memorize more quickly?

UNSTRUCTURED	STRUCTURED
broccoli	(fruits)
allspice	apples
cinnamon	bananas
bananas	cherries
carrots	(vegetables)
bay leaf	asparagus
apples	broccoli
asparagus	carrots
cherries	(condiments)
	allspice
	bay leaf
	cinnamon

Memorizing the main points of your speech is a far safer technique than trying to memorize the entire speech. You can easily forget the words of a sentence, but structured points that bear a logical relationship to each other will stick with you and can be recalled more readily.

Just as the structure helps you think clearly, see the logic of relationships, and remember the most significant ideas, your listeners are similarly benefitted. We listen more comfortably and with more relaxation when we can follow the flow of ideas through a sound and plausible pattern. Unstructured information is hard to follow, and we are more likely to let our attention wander away from the speaker. And we find it simpler to remember three or four clearly stated, rationally clustered main ideas than a series of ungrouped statements.

A pattern system helps you clarify your thinking, see relationships among subpoints, fill in missing gaps, and remember your speech. Your listeners will understand your premise and follow your arguments more easily and be more likely to remember what you have said after the speech is over.

OUTLINING THE SPEECH BODY

What we have talked about thus far in this chapter concerns the body or main portion of the speech. Most all speeches are divided into three parts—an introduction, a body, and a conclusion. The introduction sets listeners up for what they will be hearing, while the conclusion summarizes and draws together the content of the speech. We will talk about introductions and conclusions in Chapter 8, for most speakers find it more workable to prepare the body of the speech first, then go back and develop the introduction, and finally plan the conclusion. This is not a rigid method—sometimes a thought for a powerful closing might pop in your head while you are working on the speech body. But generally we will build the body first.

Main Heads and the Purpose Statement

In Chapter 4 we discussed formulating specific purpose statements. As you begin to structure the body of the speech, put your specific purpose statement at the top of the page. Refer back to it often, making sure that everything included in the body directly serves to fulfill that purpose. A helpful technique is to include in parentheses those words that connect the purpose to the main headings of the speech body. Study these examples:

1. Specific purpose: to inform the audience about Time Management (by describing the three steps that are)
    I. Formulating a weekly schedule
    II. Writing a daily "things to do " list
    III. Learning to say "no"
2. Specific purpose: to explain the concept of Reality Therapy (by giving its)
    I. History of Reality Therapy (by comparing it to)
    II. Other forms of therapy (by describing it)
    III. Techniques of Reality Therapy
3. Specific purpose: to convince the audience that aerobic exercise is beneficial (because it)
    I. Improves cardiovascular system
    II. Tones and firms muscles
    III. Controls appetite

The "because" linkage in persuasive speaking is especially important, for it leads you to focus on good reasons why the listeners should do or believe as you ask.

The parenthetical linkage is only for the planning stage of your speech. You would not repeat the connector aloud to your audience any more than you would begin a speech by stating the specific purpose. These are practice devices to help you organize and clarify.

Number of Main Points

While no rigid rule governs the number of main points that should be included in a speech, commonsense guidelines direct us. A one-point speech is just that—a speech built around a single argument rather than subdivided points. One-point speeches are usually short in length and deal with fairly simple topics.

Cause-and-effect or problem-and-solution speeches often have two main headings. The first would be the cause or problem, the second would be the effect or solution. Some topical divisions need only two main headings, for two subpoints describe the subject adequately.

Many speeches fall into the three-item division for short speeches (10 minutes or less) or four or five divisions for longer speeches. Three is a good number psychologically, for both the speaker and the listener. In motivational speeches in particular, three reasons why the listeners should do or believe as asked are more persuasive than one or two reasons yet are not as overly complex or hard to remember as four or five reasons might be. Let the content of your speech govern the number, but with this warning: If you have more than five main points, you have not found a useful method for subdividing the content, and you need to reexamine the structure.

Outline Format

When you have identified the main points of your speech, you are ready to begin constructing an outline. Even if you plan to write out a full manuscript of the speech eventually, you still should begin with an outline, for the outline is a visual representation of the organization pattern. We prefer that you learn to speak from the outline whenever possible, rather than read from a full manuscript, for it ensures more natural delivery.

Four principles govern the outline process: similarity, subordination, continuity, and inclusiveness. *Similarity* suggests that all items that are similar in weight (importance) should be assigned the same symbol in the outline. They are equally governed by the same subject and logically relevant to both the purpose statement and to each other. Main headings are given consecutive Roman numerals. To illustrate:

Specific purpose: to discuss the causes of crime
  I. Poverty
  II. Lack of Education
  III. Abusive Home Environments

You need to make sure that true similarity exists. In the list of foods that we outlined earlier (see p. 99), *fruit* is similar to *vegetables*, not to *apples*. Rearrange the scrambled outlines at the end of this chapter to make sure you understand the concept of similarity.

The second principle is *subordination,* which implies that when ideas are not of equal measure, the secondary point becomes a subset of the primary point in both layout on the page and the symbol system. In the following example, *a.* is subordinate to *1.,* which in turn is subordinate to *A.,* which is subordinate to *I.*

    I.
        A.
            1.
                a.

Each idea must occupy a different line on the page and must be indented. Again, the scrambled outlines at the end of this chapter provide you an opportunity to practice subordination.

The third principle, *continuity,* means that each head should lead logically to the next one. If the order is chronological, move from past to present or present to past, but do not jump around. If you choose a spatial pattern, move smoothly from area to area rather than hopping back and forth.

The final principle is *inclusiveness,* which means that all items in a pattern are present. A total description of a university "family" must include students, administrators, faculty, and staff. An inclusive development of the topic statement "Group hospitalization insurance is designed to spread the costs of hospitalization so as to benefit everyone" must include:

    I. the patient
    II. the physician
    III. the hospital
    IV. the community

Rules for Outlining

A few rules govern good outlining procedure.

1. The subordination principle demands that the interchange of letters and numbers must be consistent, with even indentation to the right for like symbols.

    I.
        A.
            1.
                a.
    II.
        A.
            1.
        B.
            1.

2. Never use but one symbol before a single item. *I. A.* on the same line would be incorrect.

3. Every item must have a symbol before it. Paragraph outlines may help in building introductions and conclusions, but they should be avoided in the body, since they are no longer truly outlines, but have become manuscript speeches.

4. Make the symbols stand out from the text.

INCORRECT	**CORRECT**
I. Clothes	I. Clothes
A. Jeans	A. jeans
B. shirts	B. shirts
II. toilet articles	II. Toilet articles
A. toothbrush	A. toothbrush
B. deodorant	B. deordorant

5. Outline main headings should be statements, not questions, for they are subdivisions of a major idea, not thought provokers for the audience.

While different speech subjects require different structures, in general we think of the body of an informative speech with main headings as steps in time, areas in space, or subtopics of the specific purpose. The subordinate material is the explanation, the illustration, or any of the verbal aids described in Chapter 6. In persuasive speaking, the main headings are usually assertions, with the subordinate ideas offering proof for these assertions. The assertions can take the form of reasons for supporting the speaker's proposition. We will offer further suggestions for developing the outline for an informative speech in Chapter 10 and for the persuasive speech in Chapter 11.

Types of Outlines

Outlines can be made with single words, phrases, or full sentences. A mixture of styles may be useful. We find that writing full sentences for the opening statement and for the main headings is helpful in finding the best wording for these crucial spots. Within the outline, however, a single word may be all you need to suggest that a particular piece of supporting material will fit in that spot. Some speakers use index cards with quotations or complex statistics written on them. The outline would indicate that a numbered card is to be used in the appropriate place.

The visual appearance of your outline makes a major difference in the success with which you use it. Scribbled, messy outlines with insertions and deletions are hard to follow. Outlines should be typewritten or neatly printed. Some of our students find that putting the outline onto cards is helpful, placing each main heading and each major subheading on a different card. Others have used their word processors with varying sizes and styles of type to differentiate main heads from subheads and supporting material. One of the business speakers we observed had prepared his outline using colored pencils to highlight the subsections.

Your instructor will offer guidelines for the particular type of outline that he or she prefers. After we have offered suggestions for preparing introductions and conclusions (in Chapter 8), we will give you a sample outline that we prefer. No single best way exists to outline, but the value of outlining is almost unquestioned. Develop the technique that works best for you and best suits the requirements of your course.

KEY POINTS

- Several patterns are useful in structuring the content of the body of a speech:
    chronological
    spatial
    topical
    cause-and-effect
    problem-and-solution
- Using a clearly structured organization helps the speaker clarify thinking, see relationships among ideas, fill in missing gaps, and remember the speech.
- Listeners can follow and remember the arguments more readily when the organization is clear.
- Main headings of the speech body should be linked parenthetically to the specific purpose statement.
- Topics are most often divided into three or four main headings.
- Learning the principles of similarity, subordination, continuity, and inclusiveness, with careful use of the outline symbol system, will help the speaker to construct useful speech outlines.

QUESTION FOR DISCUSSION

Why is an outline important in this course? What evidence do you see that other speakers outside the classroom have an outline?

ACTIVITIES

1. The title of your speech is "Our Campus: Its Buildings and Grounds." Devise three main headings if the speech were organized (a) chronologically, (b) spatially, and (c) topically.

2. The title of your speech is "Jack-o'-lanterns: Preparation, Design, and Display." Reorganize the following main headings into no more than three:
   You should buy a firm, well-shaped pumpkin
   You should buy candles.
   You need a sharp knife.
   Have plenty of old newspaper.
   Draw the design on paper.
   Transfer the design to the pumpkin.
   Cut off the top of the pumpkin.
   Clean out all the seeds and save for roasting.
   Carve the "face" on the pumpkin.
   Carve a small hole to hold the candle.
   Place in a window close to the front door.
   Light the candle at dusk.

3. Which of the following does *not* belong as a main heading because it lacks similarity?
   United States Presidents
   A. John Quincy Adams
   B. Samuel Adams
   C. Theodore Roosevelt
   D. Franklin Roosevelt

   Which of the following does *not* belong as a main heading because it lacks subordination?
   People in Charge of Other People
   A. Sergeant
      1. Private
   B. Employer
      1. Employee
   C. Student
      1. Teacher

4. In the following outlines, place the number from the statement into the appropriate blank to indicate the logical structure of the body of each speech.

(1)

Specific purpose: to inform the audience about some of the general cultural characteristics of the American Indians.

Central idea: While the numerous tribes of American Indians can be grouped with respect to their customs and language, certain typical traits could be found among the tribes, including especially religion, warring behaviors, and pastimes.

I. _____   1. Some spirits were thought to be especially powerful or active.
   A. _____   2. Among the Plains tribes, social position depended on military
   B. _____   exploits.
      1. _____   3. The active soul of the dead warrior was thought to exist in the
   C. _____   scalp.

II. _____

A. _____

B. _____
  1. _____
  2. _____

C. _____
  1. _____
  2. _____

III. _____

A. _____
  1. _____

B. _____

C. _____
  1. _____
  2. _____

4. Social dances, usually followed by feasting, were of great variety.

5. Playing ball was the chief athletic game everywhere east of the Plains.

6. the knife, the club, the bow and arrow

7. Nature was the source of Indian religion, with every animal, plant, and object of nature animated by a spirit.

8. Indian pastimes consisted of athletic contests, dances, and storytelling.

9. Musical instruments such as drums, whistles, and rattles often accompanied the singer or storyteller.

10. lacrosse, chunkey, netted stick ball, shinny

11. Some spirits were good; some were evil.

12. War and military exploits were more important to those tribes of Plains Indians and the regions east of the Mississippi.

13. farther south, they added the hatchet or tomahawk.

14. Color in nature had symbolic meaning.

15. Many of the myths were strikingly poetic.

16. Eastern and Plains tribes used many of the same weapons.

17. Song and story were handed down orally.

18. Scalps represented actual additions to fighting strength and size of family.

19. For example, the sun, fire, and water; the buffalo, eagle, and snake.

20. Scalping was an important ceremony of war.

(2)

Specific Purpose _____
I. _____
  A. _____
    1. _____
    2. _____
  B. _____
    1. _____
    2. _____
II. _____
  A. _____
    1. _____
    2. _____
    3. _____
  B. _____
    1. _____
    2. _____

1. Situation Comedies and Drama

2. Soap operas, talk shows, and game shows are popular favorites.

3. The major networks often run educational programs.

4. *Sesame Street*

5. Many educational programs appear regularly on the major networks and on PBS.

6. *L.A. Law* and *Miami Vice*

7. Both daytime and prime evening hours are filled with shows designed to entertain.

8. Oprah Winfrey and Phil Donahue

9. CBS's *Face the Nation* on Sunday mornings

10. *Bill Cosby* and *Family Ties*

11. ABC's *After-School Special*

12. *All My Children* and *Days of Our Lives*

13. PBS regularly schedules educational offerings for both children and adults.
14. *Wheel of Fortune* and *Family Feud*
15. *Nova*
16. Television has something for everyone.

Chapter 8

Beginning, Ending, and Connecting

THE INTRODUCTION OF THE SPEECH

With the body of the speech now outlined, you should begin constructing the introduction. The introduction requires the same careful discovery and arrangement of material, but since much of this material grows from the body itself, your introduction is well underway once the body is drafted.

The introduction serves several functions for the speaker. To begin with, it helps the speaker to capture the audience's attention and to shift the listeners' focus from themselves to the podium or front of the room. During the first few seconds or even minutes, listeners are still settling in their seats, adjusting their hearing to the speaker's voice, and absorbing the visual details of the speaker's appearance. They may miss the opening thought of the speech unless it is designed to grab attention quickly. This is also the reason why we almost never begin a speech by giving the first main heading as the opening remark—too many listeners might miss it.

A second function of the introduction is to orient the audience to the speaker, the speech, and the occasion, and to establish a bond between speaker and listener. We have stressed the need for you to adapt your speech to the audience. Listener-centered communication is far more effective than is a message in which the speaker puts forth his or her own ideas with no thought of the impact on the people who hear those ideas. In everything from topic choice to the selection of supporting material, you have been encouraged to keep your audience clearly in mind. The introduction gives you the opportunity to make the connection in a direct manner by letting the listeners know that you have something to say that may be meaningful to them. You are beginning the process of establishing credibility by giving the audience a reason for listening to you.

A third function of the introduction is to give a clear statement of the specific purpose, perhaps even previewing the main headings, so that the listeners know exactly what you plan to talk about. Nothing is more frustrating to an audience than a speaker who goes on for several minutes without letting audience members know what he or she is trying to accomplish.

Finally, the introduction gives the speaker the chance to express certain amenities, such as recognition of other important guests, acknowledgment of special ties to the group or one of its members, thanks for any special attention, or gratitude for having been invited to speak. Some of these traditional customs may be less important in informal settings or day-to-day business presentations and probably will not be necessary in your classroom speeches. For formal speech situations, however, these conventions are signs of a gracious and thoughtful attitude.

These functions can be fulfilled in three or four steps, each of which may be as simple as a single sentence or may be developed into several paragraphs. A good rule of thumb is that the introduction should not exceed one-fifth of the total length of the speech. If your classroom speech is limited to five to six minutes, the introduction should be no longer than one minute. A 30-minute address could have a five- or six-minute introduction. This is not a hard-and-fast rule, for the introduction must grow from the occasion and from the body of the speech. Some situations and some topics require a longer lead-in than do others.

The introduction can be outlined to show these steps, as follows:

I. Attention-getting material
II. Audience-orienting material
III. Statement of purpose and preview of main headings

Attention-Getting Material

Several rhetorical devices can be used to help gain audience attention. Many speakers begin with humor, by telling a joke, story, or personal anecdote. Humor is a good device not only for getting attention but also for establishing a bond between speaker and listeners. Laughing together tends to relax people and draw them closer. One important warning, however, about joke telling. The speaker who uses five or six jokes, then suddenly jumps into the heart of the speech without connecting the humor into the remainder of the introduction, will lose rather than gain audience attention. Listeners will think, "What did that have to do with this?" and their minds will stray away. Jokes or stories must have a direct relationship to the purpose of the speech. Furthermore, the speaker should establish that relationship for the listeners, just in case they miss it. For example,

> When I was asked to speak to you this evening, I was instructed to provide you with some substantive food for thought. However, I was also told that I should approach this occasion with a touch of humor. Therefore, before I begin, let me caution you to THINK and LAUGH at the appropriate moments.

> Victor Borge, the delightful comic pianist and after-dinner speaker, used to lament that the brain was a wonderful organ. It begins working the moment you are born and doesn't stop—until you get up to give a public speech.

Another warning: Off-color jokes may be funny at a party or in a night club, but they have no place in classroom or business-world speeches. And finally, practice telling jokes out loud. Many a good joke has been ruined in the retelling because the speaker leaves out an essential point or misstates the punch line.

Anecdotes do not necessarily have to be funny to make good introductory material. Sad or touching stories, real or fictional, can serve to arouse listener interest.

> Last summer I went to visit my great-aunt who lives on a farm in Oklahoma. In the corner of her living room I noticed an old violin. When I asked her if she played, she answered, "No. But there's a lot of pretty music in that old box just waiting for the right hands to bring it out." Her simple comment reminded me of the hidden talents and untapped resources within all of us.

> Albert Einstein was once invited to be guest of honor at a banquet. When he was called upon to speak, he said, "Ladies and gentlemen, I'm sorry, but I have nothing to say." Then he added, "But when I do, I'll come back." And he did—six months later. Wouldn't it be a better, less stressful world if all of us had the confidence to express our true feelings—and then act upon those feelings?

An opening statement that is *startling* in some way can serve as a good attention-getter.

> *Specific purpose:* to convince the listeners that AIDS patients should not be outcasts.

> In 1981, the first case of AIDS was diagnosed. Just seven years later, 39,000 people died of the dreaded new disease.

> *Specific purpose:* to convince the listeners to vote in national elections.

> If the same percentage turns out this year that showed up in the 1984 and 1988 Presidential elections, only 11 of the 20 of you sitting in this room will go to the polls in November.

A *quotation,* especially one from a famous person, a well-known work of literature, or a contemporary book or magazine, can help the speaker gain the listeners' ears. As with humor, the quotation needs to bear a direct relationship to the content of the speech that is to follow or to the relationship to the audience or occasion that the speaker is going to develop in the introductory remarks. Find a simple but clear way to credit the source of the quotation. For example:

> *Specific purpose:* to inform and demonstrate packing for traveling techniques.

> "Traveling Light is traveling smart," author Leah Felden tells us in her book *Traveling Light.* Today more of us are traveling than ever before.

> *Specific purpose:* to urge the listeners to improve their listening skills.

> Calvin Coolidge once said, "Nobody ever listened himself out of a job." In many cases, finding and holding a job is a direct result of good listening skills.

One other device that makes a good opening statement is a *rhetorical question.* This is a question you throw out for audience members to think about, but not for them to answer. In fact, a question that requires a show of hands or a verbal response from the audience has the tendency to refocus the attention from the speaker back to the listeners as they look around to see whose hand is up or to hear who speaks out. Rhetorical questions enable listeners to concentrate on the speaker's topic by silently formulating their own responses but without concern as to how other audience members react. Useful rhetorical questions might be:

> *Specific purpose:* to get students to volunteer to serve during freshman orientation week.

> Do you remember the first day you went to a new school—first grade, high school, or even college? Do you remember how nervous and apprehensive you were?"

A rhetorical question might be combined with a startling statement:

> *Specific purpose:* to present a program of study skills that ensures better grades.

> Are you confident that you are doing all the right things to pass this course? Well, snap out of your complacency, for the records kept on public speaking classes in this university over the past 10 years suggest that at least two of you in this room will fail this semester! Will it be you?

Audience-Orienting Material

In this step you need to create a goodwill bond between yourself and the audience and to find a way to connect the listeners to the speech you are about to give. Two devices will help you do this. First, tell the audience something that qualifies you to speak on the subject. Second, motivate your listeners by hinting at what they may gain from your speech.

Follow through three of the examples of different types of attention-getting statement from above as we add the second step:

Specific purpose: to convince the listeners to vote in national elections.

   I. If the same percentage turns out this year that showed up in the 1984 and 1988 Presidential elections, only 11 of the 20 of you sitting in this room will go to the polls in November.

  II. A. I voted for the first time in 1988, having had my 18th birthday a year earlier. I was so excited as I studied newspaper and magazine articles and listened to televised debates and speeches.

     B. Since many of you are about my same age, I expect you shared my excitement.

Specific purpose: to inform and demonstrate packing-for-traveling techniques.

   I. "Traveling Light is traveling smart," author Leah Felden tells us in her book *Traveling Light.* Today more of us are traveling than ever before.

  II. A. I made my first trip to Europe two years ago. I carried the two biggest suitcases I owned, crammed full with most of my wardrobe. I learned my lesson the hard way, lugging around all that weight and going back home with clean clothes I had never worn.

     B. When I made the trip again this past summer, I went with one medium-sized bag, polyester clothes, and a bottle of Woolite.

     C. Many of you are already planning trips abroad in the next year or two.

Specific purpose: to present a program of study skills that ensures better grades.

   I. Are you confident that you are doing all the right things to pass this course? Well, snap out of your complacency, for records kept on public speaking classes in this university over the past 10 years suggest that at least two of you in this room will fail this semester. Will it be you?

  II. A. I am going to make a good grade, but not because I'm that smart. I'm going to make a good grade because last year, my freshman year, I failed two courses the first semester.

     B. As an A and B student in high school, I was never so shocked or so devastated. I did not see the warning signs—I thought I was in great shape going into the last week of the semester with a 40 percent term paper in hand and a head full of facts for a 40 percent final exam.

    C. Many of you shared my experience. Some of you may be going through it right now.

    D. If I can help just one of you avoid failing just one course, I feel I will have fulfilled my purpose.

Note that in each of the three examples, the speaker has offered a brief explanation of his or her personal experience with the subject as a preliminary suggestion of qualification in this topic area. These three examples are from classroom speeches where time is short and where perceived speaker expertise may be nonexistent, especially early in the semester. In business and volunteer service settings, more credibility is probably established in advance. Audience members may know who a speaker is before the event, the speaker may have high status or prestige, and someone will most likely introduce the speaker, giving background information that will cause listeners to begin with a favorable attitude. In this case, the speaker's job is not just to capture listener respect but to build upon the preconception and hold the respect throughout the speech.

In each of the three classroom examples above, the speaker also made a simple statement that suggests what may be in the speech for the listeners.

1. Since many of you are about my same age, I expect you shared my excitement.

2. Many of you are already planning trips abroad in the next year or two.

3. Many of you shared my experience. Some of you may be going through it right now. If I can help just one of you avoid failing just one course, I feel I will have fulfilled my purpose.

These audience-orienting statements lead the speaker easily into the third section of the introduction, which we shall now discuss.

Statement of Purpose and Preview of Main Headings

A clear statement of what you hope to accomplish in your speech and how you intend to approach it is useful in putting audience members at ease and making them more receptive listeners.

Follow through the same three examples. (*Note:* We may be violating a premise of good outlining by showing you entire paragraphs in outline form. This is done so that you can understand the suggested full development of the idea and see where it would fit into the parts of the introduction.)

1.   III. I want to urge you to keep up that excitement by preparing yourself carefully, then by going to the polls in November and casting your vote. Voting takes only minimal time and effort. Casting your vote makes you feel good about yourself, knowing you are

an informed participant. And most important, you will be fulfilling your responsibility as a citizen.

2.   III. I'd like to share with you some tips I've discovered, through both
           research and personal experience. As an overview, these tips fall
           into three categories. First, begin planning well in advance so that
           you can reexamine your choices—last-minute packing is usually
           less efficient. Second, plan a mix-and-match wardrobe so that each
           outfit can be worn two or three times. And finally, do the actual
           packing—rolling clothes, using small insert bags, and making the
           most of suitcase space.

3.   III. My purpose today is to share with you some of the techniques that
           worked for me in the hope that they will work for you. I'll be
           talking with you about scheduling conferences with your profes-
           sors for progress discussions. I'll suggest ways to outline the text-
           book and highlight main points as you combine textbook and
           lecture note study. And I will encourage you to study with other
           students, for exams, by proofreading each other's papers, and by
           practicing your speeches aloud.

These examples are bare-boned skeletons of introduction outlines. Most
speakers would develop the three steps by elaborating on each point, adding
extra descriptive, explanatory, or anecdotal material. If the amenities mentioned
earlier are required, time must be allowed for them. Add to and expand, but do
not omit any of these three steps—all are essential to an effective introduction.

THE CONCLUSION OF THE SPEECH

A simple way to think of the conclusion is to see it as a reverse of the introduction. Just as step III of the introduction was a purpose statement and a preview
of main headings, step I of the conclusion should be a summary of those main
headings and a restatement of the purpose. The second step should again make
a direct tie between the listeners and the topic, and between speaker and
listeners when appropriate. Finally, a closing thought is much like the opening
attention-getting statement, and some of the same devices may be employed.
    The conclusion can be outlined to show these steps, as follows:

   I. Summary of main heads and restatement of the purpose.
  II. Audience-relating materials; final motivation.
 III. Closing thought.

The summary can be very short, often a simple sentence or two. Step II will
need more careful planning, for here you have the last opportunity to reinforce

the information you have shared or to call the listeners to action if your purpose has been to motivate.

Good closing thoughts, like good opening attention-getters, are often hard to find and call for speaker creativity in seeking them out. Most people who give speeches regularly keep files of interesting quotations, clever anecdotes and stories, short poems and literary references, and appropriate facts and statistics that might be helpful to them. Any of these can be used for closing thoughts. Listeners are left flat and unsatisfied if the speaker does not put a clear closure to the speech. Classroom speakers who suddenly stop, say, "Well, that's all I have to say," and walk awkwardly back to their seats cheat the audience and themselves of the final moment of completion of all the hard work that has gone into the speech. This usually happens when those speakers fail to devote sufficient time and effort to careful construction of the conclusion.

As with the introduction, we have given you a formula that is highly structured. As you become a more experienced speaker, you will find other outline methods that work well for you. But as a useful tool for the beginning speaker, we have found that the formula works quite well in structuring a solid speech and in helping you build your confidence by knowing that you have included the necessary components.

Follow through our same three examples as we suggest possible conclusions. Note the way the speakers mention both themselves and the listeners. Could you think of more appropriate or more effective closing thoughts?

Conclusions:

1.
   I. Remember, then, the major benefits you have to gain by voting—with only a minimal expenditure of time and energy, you will have the opportunity to feel good about being an informed participant and to do your civic duty as a responsible citizen.
   II. People in our age group are often quick to criticize the government, but are we as quick to let our voices be heard in the decisions made by our state and nation? You may become an active politician or party worker some day, but until that time, using your right to vote is the chief means you have of speaking out.
   III. In his Inaugural Address of 1885, Grover Cleveland said it clearly: "Your every voter, as surely as your chief magistrate, exercises a public trust." Let's don't violate that trust—go to the polls and vote.

2.
   I. So, you see, by beginning planning and actual packing well in advance, by taking a mix-and-match wardrobe, and by learning a few simple tips on suitcase use, you can make your trip to Europe or Hawaii or wherever you are going simpler and much more pleasant.
   II. Without heavy suitcases to carry, you can concentrate on soaking up the atmosphere and seeing the sights. The few minutes you

take each night in the hotel room to rinse out a shirt or some underwear is well worth the lightened load.

III. In closing, I turn again to Leah Feldon, who concludes her book *Traveling Light* by telling us, "Practice makes perfect. Soon you'll be able to call yourself the world-class traveler that every one of us can be. You can travel without worries—just try it and see! Here's to your success!"

3. I. In summarizing, then, remember to make an appointment to see your professor if you are unclear about assignments or unsure about your progress. Learn how to outline reading materials and pull your notes from various sources into a total picture. Finally, study with your classmates—help each other to speak, write, and think more effectively. These are not the only techniques for improving your grades, but they are three of the most helpful ones.

II. None of us want to fail—failure hurts. The blow to our egos is hard to overcome. I have used the blow I suffered last year, not as something to defeat me, but as motivation to learn to do better. It has worked for me—it can work for you.

III. I would like us to turn those statistics around—to let our instructor* and all the instructors of the other sections of public speaking know that we don't want a 10 percent failure rate—we want a 100 percent success rate. And we are ready to do our part to achieve it.

TRANSITIONS AND SIGNPOSTS

Listening to speeches is not easy. It takes concentration and focused mental effort. Distraction is a constant threat. Speakers need to help listeners as much as possible.

> Listeners become tired. Some even daydream a bit while you are speaking. Be helpful to these snoozers by planting signposts throughout your speech. Signposts are nothing more than key words and phrases which are repeated at various points, usually within the internal summary of each element of the speech.[1]

Furthermore, speakers do not always have an easy time staying on track and remembering the next point. Think of the times you have begun to tell something, only to find you have forgotten what you started to say! Using connectors and transitional markers helps the speaker and the listeners to stay on target, to keep the connection between ideas, and to move smoothly from one point to the next.

---

*Using the actual name of the instructor here would be a useful way to relate to the immediate audience.

Some words and phrases help us forecast or preview what is coming.

Later on, I am going to suggest to you the ways . . .

Then we will examine the issue of . . .

After analyzing the causes of this problem, I will propose several solutions.

Some words and phrases suggest that you are moving from one step to the next, such as "Turning to another dimension of the problem." The most complete transitions touch on both the preceding and subsequent points.

In addition to purchasing the best weight racket for you, you need to buy tennis balls suited to your own style.

Left-handed people not only have problems with desks, door handles, and scissors, they are also more accident prone and have more illnesses than do right-handed people.

A number of specific words mark movement through the speech outline. "Next," "following," "subsequently," "in addition," "furthermore," or "shifting to" all suggest that you are changing to another point in the speech. If the ensuing point differs only slightly, words such as "similarly," "related to," "closely connected to," or "linked" are useful in suggesting closeness. When you draw near the end of the speech, mark it with "finally," "then," "in summary," or "I'd like to conclude with."

Numbering main headings or items of supporting material is helpful. If you say *first, second,* and *third* as you give the main headings, clarity is increased. Examples such as "I want to tell you about three people who made it to the top despite physical handicaps" are kept orderly by saying, "The first man," "the second man," and "the third man." If you offer three reasons, say "One reason for believing . . . ," "another reason," and "the third and final reason . . . ."

Let your outline show through by including these brief verbal signposts. Your listeners will be better able to follow you and will appreciate your clear organization. And you will be far less likely to forget or to stray off the topic.

SAMPLE OUTLINE FORM

TITLE

Specific purpose: To explain . . . (complete this by a specific statement of your intention. For persuasive speeches, begin with "To convince" or "To motivate.")

(Place the specific purpose at the top of the page. You will not read it when you begin to speak. But it is a constant reminder of what you are trying to accomplish.)

Introduction:
   I. (Something that will catch attention)
  II. (Audience-orienting material)
 III. (State specific purpose and preview main headings)
Body:
   I. (First main heading—write as a complete sentence.)
       A. (Subhead or supporting material)
           1. (Supporting material or source of material)
           2. (Further support such as explanation, examples, and so forth)
       B. (Subhead)
           1. (Supporting material—verbal and visual aids)
           2. (etc.)
               a. (some explanations or descriptions may have sub-
                  components)
               b. (etc.)
  II. (Second main heading—complete sentence.)
       A. (Subhead—may be complete sentences, if needed, but may also be
          only a key word or a reference to a note card)
           1.
           2.
       B.
 III. (Third main heading)
       A. (Subhead: there may be no "B," for only one extended piece of
          supporting material may be needed to develop the main heading.)
Conclusion:
   I. (Summary of main headings)
  II. (Tie directly to audience)
 III. (Interesting or challenging closing thought)

KEY POINTS

- The speech introduction serves several functions:
    capturing audience attention
    orienting the audience to the speaker and the speech
    stating the speech purpose
    fulfilling necessary amenities
- Attention-getting material includes:
    humor
    anecdotes
    startling statements
    quotations
    rhetorical questions

- Audience-orienting material may be statements about the speaker that suggest his or her qualifications in the topic area and forecasts of what listeners may hope to gain from the speech.

- A clear statement of purpose is needed and may include a preview of the main headings of the speech.

- The conclusion of the speech summarizes the main headings and restates the purpose.

- The audience should be directly connected with a final explanation of topic relevance or motivation for future belief or action.

- Closing thoughts are some of the same devices used to gain attention in the introduction.

- Transitional and connecting words and phrases are signposts that help both speaker and listener know exactly where the speaker is in the organizational structure of the speech.

QUESTION FOR DISCUSSION

When listening to speeches outside the classroom, can you pick out a clearly formed introduction and conclusion? How might the introduction and conclusion for a speech inside a business organization differ from the ones you will prepare for this course?

ACTIVITIES

1. Make a list of the best jokes you have heard in the last six months. Are any of them possible openers for your speeches?
2. Take our examples of attention-getters and rewrite with another type of attention-getter to begin the same specific purpose.
3. What might you personally say to your listeners that would help them believe you have some experience with any of the following topics:
    a) selecting a college or university
    b) surviving registration
    c) advantages of living in a dormitory (or apartment)
    d) training dogs and cats
    e) playing winning poker (or bridge)
4. Find an interesting closing thought that might be used with each of the five topics in the preceding activity.

5. Make a list of the transition words listed in this chapter. How many more can you add? Where and how might they be used?

REFERENCES

[1]Ty Warren, "Championship Speechwriting," *Progressive Forensics* 1 (March 1984): 39.

Chapter 9

Selecting and Developing Visual Aids

We live in a visually oriented society. Television, movies, billboards, and brightly colored magazine advertisements have accustomed us to see as well as hear most of the messages that come to us. Business and industry have discovered the value in posters, brochures, direct-mail pieces, and newspaper ads to attract outsiders. Internally, they depend heavily on illustrated newsletters, handouts, presentation kits, and charts of all kinds to inform and persuade colleagues in daily transactions. The entire field of computer graphics underscores the emphasis we place on visual materials in our appeal to listeners.

Visual aids serve several purposes. We can clarify and explain by showing pictures and diagrams. We can substantiate by using visual items as a form of supporting material, thus combining verbal and visual aids. We can arouse listener interest as we appeal to both the eye and the ear, adding dimensions of reality to the abstractness of verbal description. And we can dramatize by using visual images, color, line, and design, thus lending support to the old adage that a picture is worth a thousand words.

Although as a classroom speaker you may be more restricted in choices of visual materials than you will be some day in the business world, you can nonetheless provide a number of eye-catching devices that will strengthen the impact of your speech on the listeners. Those of you who own your own computers or who have learned to use the computer laboratories that are now found on most college campuses can follow Christopher O'Malley's advice:

"The latest presentation software and hardware accessories enable any reasonably competent computer user to fashion paper graphs, overhead transparencies, color slides and even animated video shows that have all the earmarks of a professional job . . . . With these tools, you can do the almost impossible: produce a polished business presentation on demand—every time."[1]

Remember the list of possible speech topics for this course that you identified in Chapter 4. As you read about the various tyes of visual aids discussed in this chapter, think how you might use one or more of them in preparing any of those speeches.

CONCURRENT DRAWINGS

Most classrooms have chalkboards; most boardrooms or meeting rooms have flipcharts. Both offer speakers a chance to draw pictures or diagrams either in advance or as they speak. These are more like sketches than finished drawings, for they are done quickly and at the moment. Some speakers may use the chalkboard for little more than writing three or four key terms that listeners should remember, while others may place a series of quick drawings that explain or illustrate. For example, one of our students covered a large chalkboard with a dozen different drawings of a complex basketball play in action. The drawings enabled him to follow through the play as the team members moved to different positions on the court.

If you are going to write as you speak, plan in advance what you want to put on the chalkboard. Make sure you know how to draw what you want to show—how embarrassing if no one can tell that your sailboat is a sailboat, or if listeners think your dog is a horse! Make your drawings large enough and dark enough to be seen by everyone in the room. And most important, practice drawing with only quick glances at the board, spending most of your time looking at the audience. Concurrent drawings in no way relieve you of the responsibility to establish and maintain eye contact with the audience. Your speaking focus must be toward the audience, not away from them and toward the chalkboard. One of our former speech teachers was fond of saying "There is no expression in the back of your head or in your ear! The audience wants to see your face, and this is not easy when you are turned away drawing on a chalkboard or flipchart. Use these devices only when another visual aid cannot be prepared, and remember that when you do use them, keep your attention, face, and body directed toward the audience.

MODELS OR MOCK-UPS

A number of three-dimensional models can become useful visual aids. In our course that includes the human vocal mechanism, we have anatomical models of the larynx and the mouth that can be taken apart to show the different organs and muscle tissue. We use a mock-up model of the lungs, a bell jar with rubber stretched across the bottom to illustrate how the contraction of the diaphragm causes air to rush into the lung cavity. Similar models of the human heart, the ear, or a number of major organs can be used to illustrate a speech about some aspect of the human body.

Among the more interesting models that we have seen in our classrooms were toy furniture used to illustrate interior design principles, Tinkertoys® used to explain atoms and molecules, DNA in particular, and a light bulb with a dry-cell battery to show a fundamental principle of electric circuitry. A fascinating papier-mâché scale model helped us undertand the Battle of the Alamo, a home-rigged, battery-operated ticker was used to explain the Morse Code, and a toy sailboat illustrated the positioning of sails according to wind and desired direction.

Models have the advantage of being three-dimensional, enabling the listener to experience the depth more fully than with flat drawings. Models can also be moved around and shown from various directions. If you plan to use a model or mock-up, you must rehearse with it so that you can handle it easily. Some models have a number of pieces that are not easily taken apart and put back together again. Any model you choose must be large enough to be seen by everyone in the class. One of our students made a poor choice in selecting small model cars, which are only 2 to 3 inches long, to try to explain the differences in different models of automobiles—not even his classmates on the first row could see the tiny cars well enough to make out the differences.

When the model has several parts, you will need to point out those parts to the audience. Use a pencil or small pointer to indicate various subsections. Remember that as with chalkboard drawings, you must keep your eyes on the audience, not on your model. You need to know the model well enough that only an occasional glance at it on your part will be required. And in a short, formal speech, such as you will be giving in the classroom, never pass the model around for class members to look at. You may see your professor do this from time to time, but remember that your professor has several hours a week to lecture at a leisurely pace, allowing time to stop while students look at models or handouts. Your speech time is short and concentrated—you need to remain the focus of the listener's attention at all times, not displace that focus back out into the audience by passing objects or pictures around the room.

OBJECTS

Real objects have similar advantages to models or mock-ups and need similar care in their use. Over the years, our classrooms have seen a number of interesting processes demonstrated: bread dough mixed, kneaded, and shaped into loaves; ceramic pots thrown and painted; mortar troweled to lay a small brick wall on a board; plants repotted after major root and branch surgery! Large dummies have lain across the teacher's desk for mouth-to-mouth resuscitation, dressmaker mannequins have been draped with fabrics, and sacks full of everything from sneakers to coffee beans have been spread out as a visual tool to aid student speakers.

A clear distinction needs to be made between the speech in which a visual aid is a key piece of supporting material and the true demonstration presentation. If you have ever walked through a department store when someone was trying to sell kitchen appliances or cosmetics by showing customers how to use them, what you saw was a demonstration, not a formal, preplanned speech. The demonstrator might stop and start frequently, might engage in side conversations with customers, and have no definable introduction and conclusion. The task was to talk about a product as the speaker showed how that product should be used. Most public speaking teachers prefer that you think of the assignment not as a demonstration but as a speech that is illustrated by using a model or object. Your primary focus is on the speech itself—its construction, its main points, its supporting material—and on your method of delivering the speech. The object is an incidental item of focus rather than holding the spotlight. This distinction is an important one, for it enables you to remember that you are in front of the classroom to give a speech—the visual aid helps you but does not structure all that you say and do.

Just as with models, we would prefer that student speakers did not pass objects around the room. It clearly distracts the listeners. Of course, exceptions exist to every rule. One very effective attention-getter was used by a student who poured and passed around several small paper cups of water from a Thermos jug, only to proceed to tell the audience how many germs they had just ingested! Perhaps the fact that it was done as an attention-getter at the beginning of the speech made it work effectively. Not all speech teachers would agree that the device was effective, but not all speech teachers agree on all aspects of the use of visual aids.

As with any part of the process of preparing and delivering speeches, you need to keep your immediate audience constantly in mind as you choose visual aids. Matters of taste and good judgment must be considered. One student brought a very expensive camera as a visual aid, then told his listeners, "Most of you will probably never be able to own a camera this expensive." His credibility suffered from this insult to his classmates. On other occasions, some students have complained about objects brought to class by speakers, drug paraphernalia and explicit sexual material in particular. You must be sensitive to the mores of your particular institution, using them to guide your choices. If you have any question, ask your instructor in advance.

One final note of caution in choosing objects as visual aids: You yourself do not make a very useful object for demonstrating. If you try to show us how to shoot a basketball, drive a golf ball, or attach your skis, your body must become so actively involved that smooth speech delivery is almost impossible.

If you feel you need a human body to use as a visual aid, call on one of your classmates, leaving yourself free to concentrate on the thoughts and words of the speech.

CHARTS, DIAGRAMS, AND POSTERS

The ready availability of inexpensive poster board and portable easels have made charts, diagrams, and posters a favorite of the classroom speaker. A variety of visual approaches can be prepared in advance, leaving the speaker free merely to point and indicate rather than having to draw, write, or handle models or objects during the speech presentation. Well-done posters can add color, clarity, specificity, and interest level to the speech.

Useful charts may show organization structure, such as in a major corporation or in a university. The following chart shows how our university is organized on the academic side (another chart would show the structure of the business affairs of the university and the many administrative and staff positions involved).

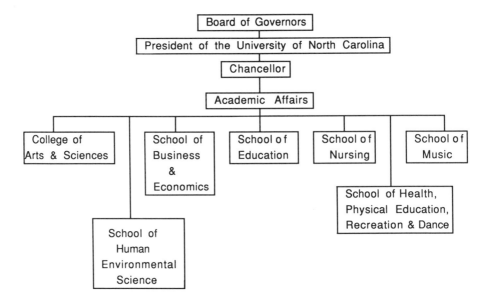

UNIVERSITY ORGANIZATIONAL CHART

A celestial chart, much like a map of the heavens, would enable the speaker to point out the location of the stars and planets. An astrological chart is helpful in understanding the signs of the zodiac.

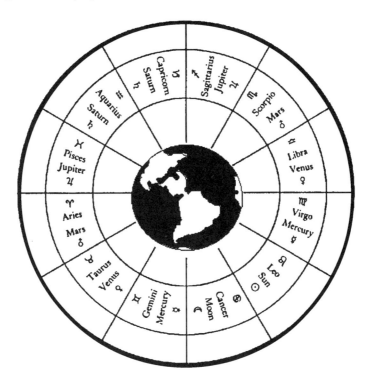

Diagrams might be house plans or floor plans for showing furniture arrangements. Tree diagrams illustrate modern linguistic generative grammar theory.

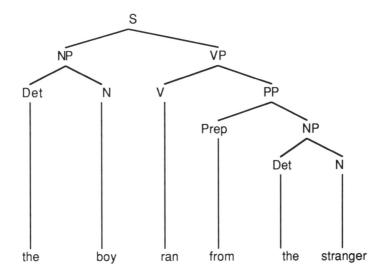

Linguistic Generative Grammar Theory

Latin squares could be displayed in a diagram.

$$\begin{bmatrix} 2 & 3 & 4 & 1 \\ 3 & 4 & 1 & 2 \\ 4 & 1 & 2 & 3 \\ 1 & 2 & 3 & 4 \end{bmatrix}$$

LATIN SQUARES

Cutaways can be used to show an essential interior or mechanism of an object.

Cross-Section of Human Heart

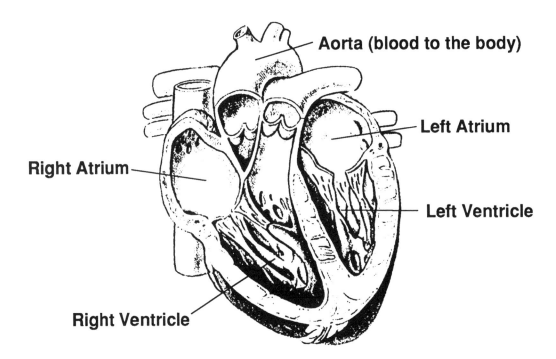

Graphs, such as bell-shaped curves to study student grades or line or bar graphs to demonstrate growth, help to show the relationship between two or more sets of facts such as time or productivity changes.

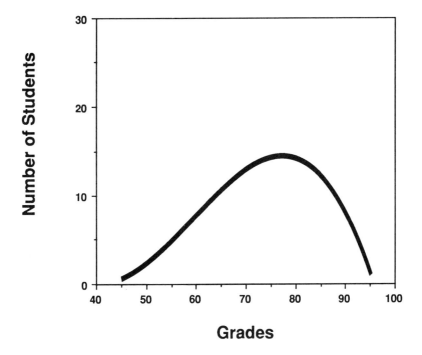

1989 Distribution of Freshman Grades

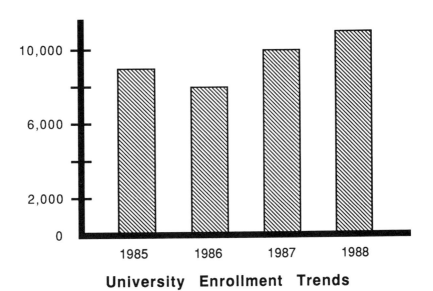

Pie graphs suggest relative size of one of several parts of a whole, such as the amount of student fees and tuition used for student government.

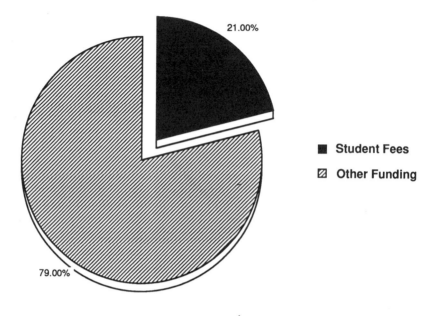

Student Government Budget

Illustrative posters depend upon your ability to draw or to find pictures that fill your need. Speeches dealing with such topics as the history of military uniforms in the United States, techniques for downhill skiing, and the process of stripping and refinishing furniture are but a few of the large number of subjects that could be enhanced with posters. Occasionally a prepared poster may be augmented with drawings done during the speech. For example, one student brought a poster with a large drawing of a woman's face, then used colored pastel chalk to show the principles of applying stage makeup. Another had done a poster with large musical staff segments, then added the symbols for notes, keys, and rests that showed how music is written down.

Several guidelines need to be observed for effective preparation and use of charts, diagrams, and posters. The first is size. If the drawing is not large enough to be seen easily from the back of the room it is worthless. Many beginning speakers have come in with a poster covered with dozens of small pictures cut from magazines. One had very small pictures of all the possible positions for the fingers on guitar frets in order to produce different notes and chords. Not only were we unable to see them but no audience could retain so much detailed information. The speaker would have been much better off to prepare one poster showing the neck of the guitar with the strings and frets, then explain how depressing them causes the changes in sound.

As a part of the problem of size, remember that any lettering must be readable at the back of the room. Label only major parts, not many small subparts. Study the two drawings shown below to see how you could simplify, yet still make effective use of, a drawing of the vocal mechanism.

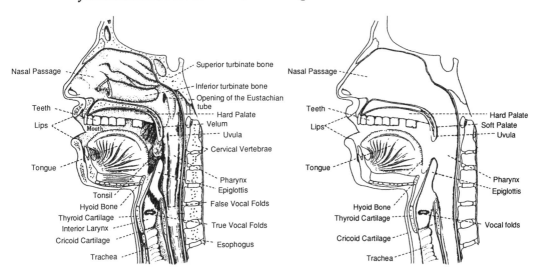

The level of artistry of your poster is important. Your drawing details must be precise and the overall appearance must be neat and clean. If you must roll up the poster board in order to get it to class, do so very loosely and in a large roll—many a tightly rolled poster has refused to straighten out when the time came to use it. Use a variety of colors—felt-tipped markers are especially good for drawing and lettering.

The same rule holds here about eye contact as with board drawings and objects—you must look at your listeners, not at your poster. You need to know it well enough that a quick glance can enable you to use a wooden or plastic pointer to identify key aspects. If you use a series of posters, have them stacked in order on the easel, discarding each as unobtrusively as possible when you have finished with it. Speakers who must dig through eight or ten poster boards to find the next one lose control of themselves and possibly of their audience.

Be sure the easel is positioned so that the audience can see it easily and so that you can stand to the side, moving toward it as needed, away when you are not making a specific reference. Paul LeRoux suggests that the information should be "to the presenter's left because our eyes are used to seeing information from left to right—like reading a page. So the presenter on the left is the anchor or focal point to which the listener's vision always returns."[2] State clearly what device you intend to show visually, pointing out the main features. Do not depend upon the visual aid to carry its own meaning. Reinforce that meaning through your explanation and by directing the audience's eyes toward the art to which you wish them to pay attention.

If the poster illustrates only one section of your total speech, you will be better to turn its plain white back toward the audience until you are ready to refer to it. This prevents audience members from studying the poster when you want them to be listening to you. Remove the poster when you are through with it. And never pass it around in the audience.

Always remember that the speech is primary, and any visual aid should be just that—an *aid*, not an event in itself. We have had a few students who spent so much time working on elaborate posters that they slighted the verbal dimensions of the speech. That is counterproductive, for visual aids are merely as "something extra" and must be kept in proper perspective.

ELECTRICAL VISUAL AND AUDIOVISUAL AIDS

Many electrical and electronic devices are available for speakers to use as aids to public speaking. Simplest among these are the overhead projector, the opaque projector, and slides. The overhead projector uses a plastic transparency to transfer a small image to a larger surface, such as a screen or blank wall. Most transparencies are made in advance, although it is possible to do some limited drawing while the audience watches. The overhead projector is especially useful if you have a number of charts that need to be included, and simple line drawings can work well. You can use a typewriter to letter directly onto the plastic transparencies.

The opaque projector enables you to transfer an image, such as a picture in a book, to a larger surface. No special preparation of the material to be projected is required. The opaque projector can be useful if pictures are a major focus; however, some fidelity of color and design may be lost as the enlargement is made. Proper adjustment of the page or book being projected is often difficult, and speakers struggle to get the image centered and upright.

Slides enable photographs to be projected to a screen. Slides are especially useful for geographic topics, such as overseas trips or tours of the campus. Slides are useful for taking pictures of pictures, such as a speech on costumes or the works of a famous artist. With a close-up lens you can take pictures of small items, even print, and have them come out well when projected.

Overhead, opaque, and slide projectors are usually used with some darkening of the room in order to have the image appear clearly on the screen. This darkening can be a serious problem to the speaker who may be unable to see the outline or note cards. It may also be difficult for the audience to see the speaker's face, thus losing eye contact and expression. Unlike the next group of audiovisual aids, these three projectors do allow the speaker to keep control over the aural (sound) dimension of the message, since transparencies and slides can be shown while the speaker continues to talk. They can also be handled one at a time, stopping and starting to fit the timing of the speech. And Paul LeRoux suggests that it is not even essential that you dim the lights: "True, slides will be brighter in the dark, but at what a price? Slides show up adequately in a fully lit room. Sometimes closing the blinds or curtains will be enough."[3]

Other equipment includes filmstrips, movies, and videocassettes. Filmstrips are much like slides, in that they are negatives of pictures that project to a positive image. With filmstrips, several pictures are put together to create a story or sequence of events. Many have accompanying sound tracks, and most are commercially produced.

Many wonderful films for education and for pure entertainment are available for both film projectors and videocassette recorders. Your teachers probably use films and tapes in class from time to time. Many business presentations are accompanied by, indeed even built around, a film. But for the student speaker in the classroom, films are of less potential value. Filmmaking is expensive and demands talent and experience to produce high-quality work. Finding good, short tapes and films that illustrate a point is a difficult job. The equipment for showing films and tapes is often cumbersome and time-consuming to set up and operate.

Even if you had access to the equipment and the films, we would not advocate this equipment for the classroom speaker. To begin with, they are not just visual aids, but are *audio*visual aids, for most have sound tracks of their own. We want to hear you, not some prerecorded speaker. All require almost total darkness for clear viewing. We want to see you, not the figures on the screen. And most films and tapes would not merely accompany a speech; rather, they would take its place since they are complete structures in themselves. And most take far too long when you have probably been limited to 6 or 7 minutes for your total speech.

We have made an occasional exception. One student gave an excellent 7-minute speech on the use of motive appeals in persuasion, using one 30-second television commercial as a single illustration for the entire speech. The audience needed to be able to see that commercial for the speech to make sense. But generally we steer away from electronic devices and ask our students to choose models, objects, and posters for visual aids. This enables them to keep the speech foremost, with the visual aid merely the adjunct that we have already suggested it should be. Discuss this with your instructor so that you will know the guidelines for your classroom. Be aware, also, that if you do tape something from commercial television to use in a speech, the law provides that you may use it for in-class purposes only and that you cannot keep it more than 30 days. Otherwise, you would be in violation of the copyright laws.

KEY POINTS

- A variety of visual materials can enable a speaker to clarify, substantiate, arouse interest, and dramatize the verbal material of the speech.

- Concurrent drawings are those done on chalkboards or flipcharts.
- Models or mock-ups are useful substitutes when real objects would be impractical to use.
- Many real objects can be helpful and totally appropriate for the classroom or business settings.
- Charts, diagrams, and posters can be prepared in advance to illustrate all sorts of topics and are especially useful to the student speaker with limited resources.
- Finally, many electric and electronic visual and audiovisual aids, such as slides, films, and video cassettes, are available, but may be of less use to the student speakers than in the professional world.

QUESTION FOR DISCUSSION

What kinds of visual aids might you prepare for this classroom? In your business or service organization some day? What visual aids have you seen other speakers use in the past year? Were they effective?

ACTIVITIES

1. What types of visual aids might you use to support the following speech topics:
   a) Donate Blood
   b) Organize for Taxes
   c) Tan Safely
   d) The Successful Interview
   e) Shelter the Homeless
   f) Stress Control through Exercise
2. Examine all of your textbooks for examples of various types of visual aids. Do they use charts, graphs, photographs? How do these help clarify and reinforce the text?
3. In your other classes, what types of visual aids do your instructors use? Again, how do these clarify or reinforce the material?
4. Investigate the sources on your campus for help in creating visual aids—for example, computer laboratories, learning resource centers, bookstores, photography laboratories, and so forth.
5. Following your instructor's guidelines and requirements, illustrate at least one of your speeches with a visual that you prepare—a poster, chart, or series of board or flipchart drawings.

REFERENCES

[1]Christopher O'Malley, "Making Quick Presentations: How to Get Better Visuals in Minutes," *Personal Computing,* December 1985, 76–77.

[2]Paul LeRoux, "Mastering the Art of the Winning Presentation," *Working Woman,* February 1985, 85.

[3]Ibid., p. 86.

Part IV

Development Patterns for Different Speech Purposes

In Chapter 5, you learned that much of the way that speeches are composed and delivered depends upon the purpose that the speaker has in his or her expectation of the response of the audience members. In Part IV, we will examine those purposes and how they help shape speeches in much more detail. The three chapters deal with the informative speech, the persuasive speech, and those several different speeches that are given on special occasions.

Chapter 10

Informative Speaking

The general purposes into which we divide speeches are derived from the basic needs that exist in listeners. One of those listener needs is to have facts and information about the world around us, to know what is going on, to know how to do things, to know what words and concepts mean, and in general to be informed individuals. Speakers can help meet that need by giving informative speeches, speeches that share and clarify information so that the audience members can increase their knowledge and understanding.

The sheer quantity of information is exploding around us all the time. Advances in technology in fields such as space and aeronautics, medicine, data processing, and communications bring new techniques and equipment each year. Changes in political systems and the realignment of nations leave us with a constant need to learn about government and international politics. Social and physical scientists are learning much more about human behavior and the human body. So many fascinating new discoveries challenge us to keep learning all the time, and one of the best ways we can keep up to date is by listening to and giving informative speeches.

The *purpose* of an informative speech is to get the audience to understand and to remember some particular piece of information. In order to retain any fact or idea, we must first understand what we have heard. As an informative speaker, your role is to make the presentation so clear and so interesting that your listeners can easily follow what you are saying and can remember the information at a later time.

TYPES OF INFORMATIVE SPEECHES

Several different types of speeches share the general purpose of informing. *Lectures*, such as in the classroom, at conferences, or by travel groups, are basically informative. *Demonstrations* of how objects are made or *instructions* on how they operate seek to inform. *Oral reports*—of books read or findings of a research team or an investigative committee—share information. Speeches of *explanation* or *definition* clarify objects, terms, or ideas to the listeners.

A useful distinction in identifying the types of informative speeches is to think of topics that are primarily *concrete* in nature as opposed to topics that are primarily *abstract*. Concrete subjects are those that can be closely related to real-life experiences. They can be seen, heard, touched, pictured, measured, or weighed in some tangible manner. Speech topics that are concrete would include "how to" make, do, or operate something; demonstrations of any kind; or explanations of material objects or processes. Abstract topics are those that deal with qualities further removed from the tangible or less specifically associated with real-life instances. They are more difficult to understand because we cannot see, hear, or in any way directly perceive them. Abstract speech topics would include definitions of abstract words—"liberty," "love," or "optimism," for example. Speeches that explain theories or concepts and speeches that deal with values and attitudes would be classified as abstract.

Your instructor will give you guidelines for the type of informative speech or speeches you will prepare for your class. Dividing into concrete and abstract topics is very helpful in understanding the nature of information. Remember that you do not have to build a line of argument, for your purpose is not to persuade but to help the audience clarify and comprehend anything from a simple, observable object to a highly abstract theory.

Structuring the Informative Speech

The informative speech should contain the same major divisions that you learned in Chapter 7—the introduction, the thesis statement, the body, and the conclusion. The introduction should arouse listener curiosity so that audience members will want to listen to what you have to say. This requires creating goodwill by tying the subject to the listeners' interests and by establishing a friendly, relaxed communication climate. There is less need to motivate the audience to change, as in persuasive speaking, than to attract and hold listener attention.

The thesis or specific purpose statement should be clear, making your goal completely obvious. Sometimes in persuasive speaking, you may wish to hold back on your exact purpose until you have laid a common ground of under-standing. But in informative speaking, you are better off to state a purpose overtly and near the beginning of the speech. Frame a direct statement, as in the following examples:

> I would like to tell you how Career Planning and Placement can help you find a job.
>
> Stress can be defined by the factors of environment, fatigue, and fear.
>
> Southern dialect differs from Standard English in several phonemic and semantic features.

Organizing the body of the speech follows the same guidelines that you learned in Chapter 7. The chronological, spatial, and topical patterns are espe-cially useful in informative speaking, whereas problem and solution, or cause and effect, are of more value in persuasive speaking. In the three thesis state-ments above, we would probably develop the first—on the Career Planning center—with a chronological pattern—when a student should first register, what is done next, and so on through a time sequence. The other two thesis statements would fall into the topical order suggested by the purpose state-ments—*environment, fatigue,* and *fear* for the speech on stress, and *phonemic* and *semantic* features for the speech on dialects. Remember that topics must be grouped for ease in handling and remembering.

In planning the main headings of the speech, try to group your materials so that you do not have too many main points. Although it is important to be thorough, listeners can follow and remember more easily if the number of main points is limited. Consider the difference in these two approaches to explaining the 15 plants placed in a garden:

> The gardener planted violets, roses, carnations, gardenias, daffodils, dillweed, marjoram, oregano, sage, thyme, chestnut, Chinaberry, elm, oak, and maple.

OR

> The gardener selected five types of flowers, five herbs, and five trees to plant in the garden. The five flowers were violets, roses, carnations, gardenias, and daffodils. The herbs included dillweed, marjoram, oregano, sage, and thyme. And the five kinds of trees were chestnut, Chinaberry, elm, oak, and maple.

We now have three main points to make about the planting, not a list of 15 items. Listeners are much more apt to remember because of this "clumping" of facts.

Some outlines for informative speeches seem almost to structure themselves because of the logical progression through the explanatory process. You would talk about a procedure in the same series of steps that the procedure itself follows. It would make no sense in a speech on house painting to talk about preparing the surface after you talked about applying the paint, for it is done in the opposite order. We put on socks before shoes and wash clothes before we dry them. This inherent sequencing guides the structure of many informative speeches, especially those with concrete topics. When the subject matter is abstract, the speaker will need to choose an appropriate structural pattern, as discussed in Chapter 7.

Finally, the conclusion should provide a summary of the key points. Possible applications may be suggested. There is no call for action, as in a persuasive speech, although it is difficult to avoid suggesting that the listeners do something with the information you have just given them. A closing story, example, or quotation helps bring a sense of closure to the speech and leaves the audience with a renewed level of interest.

Techniques for Informing

The techniques for developing verbal aids, discussed in Chapter 6, and for developing visual aids, covered in Chapter 9, will serve you as you begin to build your informative speech. Particularly useful of the many forms of supporting material are explanations, definitions, descriptions, and factual data.

Visual aids can be most useful, especially in speeches on concrete topics. Charts, graphs, models, or real objects help the listener to visualize your explanation. You need to remember the guidelines limiting the amount of physical activity while you speak, especially using your own body as an object of demonstration. Establishing eye contact and keeping a direct audience interaction is always far more important than a visual aid. With skillful planning and practice, however, you can maintain the contact while using the visual aid in an effective manner.

Language in the informative speech needs to be precise and correct. Make sure you can use an accurate term for every part of an object or process. Saying "this part over here" or "this thing" weakens your explanation. If you determine that your audience has little or no knowledge about your subject, you will need to find simple rather than technical language, avoiding excessive jargon. While most of us have some basic knowledge about computers, a recent classroom speech that was filled with "640 Kb of memory, 3.5-inch diskette drive, 20 MB fixed-disk drive, and Micro Channel architecture," with none of these terms defined, left most of the listeners somewhat confused.

The most important information in the speech must be emphasized as it is said the first time—make it somewhat slower and louder, with longer pauses before and after the new thought so that the audience has time to let it sink in. Information can be emphasized by repeating it, not just the same words over and over, but by finding new and different ways to say the same thing. In the following speech titled "Television Lighting," notice how many times the speaker repeats the names of the three major types of lights. Study this speech carefully to make sure you understand each step.

SAMPLE SPEECH

Television Lighting by Melissa Roy

(As visual aids to illustrate this speech, the student speaker used three large flashlights, stands to hold them, and a volunteer from the audience.)

1. I expect that at one time or another, everyone in here has watched bad lighting on television.	attention-getter relate to immediate audience
2. You might not have realized you were looking at it, but if you are a *Saturday Night Live* fan, for example, you've seen microphone shadows on the wall or only one side of a performer's face.	orienting—many college students watch *Saturday Night Live*
3. I'm going to show you the basic three-point lighting scheme that's used for television news production and sitcoms.	specific purpose statement
4. A three-point lighting system, while it can include other types of lighting, always consists of at least three basic types of lights—the key light, the fill light, and the back light.	preview of main headings
5. The most important of these lights in the three-point scheme is appropriately named the *key light* because it is the key to the entire lighting scheme.	first main head: also, a definition
6. Its most important use is to reveal the basic shape of the object that you are trying to light—today that's my volunteer, Brandie.	explanation; setup for first visual aid
7. It's used from a 45-degree angle, from either the left or right side of the person.	further explanation
8. It is hung from above, but since we're using flashlights today, I will be holding it above the eye level, and it's directed at the temple.	turns on first flashlight to demonstrate
9. It is used to reveal basic shape and can also be used for dramatic effect, as in the *Phantom of the Opera*, with the light on only one side of the person.	example

10. It emphasizes key features and highlights.	
11. The key light, even though it is the most important, is completely useless without the *fill light*.	transition; second main head
12. The fill light is used on the opposite side and from a 30-degree angle in front of the subject's face.	explanation; speaker attached second flashlight to a stand
13. Since the real world consists of both light and shadows, you don't want to get rid of all the shadows. That would not look realistic.	comparison—real world to TV lighting
14. So, you have to have less intensity so that you can still have shadows on one side of the face.	demonstrates with other flashlight
15. To do this, you can either move the fill light further back from the key, use less wattage, or—like I've done today—do something to diffuse the light.	as speaker explains, she demonstrates with flashlights
16. I've used tissue paper.	places tissue paper over one light
17. The light is not as bright.	comparison
18. So, if you turn the key light on, too, both sides of the face are illuminated, but one side is lit a bit more.	continues to illustrate
19. If you will notice, one side of a face is almost always a little lighter than the other.	example
20. Both the key light and fill light are useless without the back light.	transition; third main head
21. The *back light* is directly behind the subject's head.	explanation
22. It can be off to a 30-degree angle, but it is also on the same side as the key light.	
23. It is pointed at the top of the subject's head, so you can get highlights on the hair.	explanation by purpose
24. Its most important use is to create depth.	
25. If you noticed when the key and fill lights were on and the back light was not on, she looked flat.	comparison
26. This separates her from the background and also gives a halo effect where it puts light around her head.	demonstration with third flashlight; other two are turned off
27. If you ever watch *Moonlighting,* they consistently use this for Cybill Shepherd—she always has the halo around her head to make her look good.	example

28. The next time you watch television, notice the good lighting and remember what makes it good.	suggested application of the information; motivation to remember
29. You will notice some bad lighting also.	contrast
30. If you want to get an idea of really bad lighting, turn on Channel [local TV channel] and watch the six o'clock news.	illustration
31. For labor reasons and money reasons, these lights are set and stay the same all day long—from six in the morning, the noon news, and the six and eleven o'clock in the evening newscasts.	explanation and brief description
32. They don't change light intensities or focus or anything.	
33. Yet everything is different and that affects the lights they need to use—the clothes that people have on, the color of their skin, their hair, as it reflects different light intensities.	specific examples
34. A black person needs different lighting from a white person.	contrast
35. So on the six o'clock news, everyone looks good except [name of local newswoman], the black anchorwoman.	specific example
36. She looks really bad under that lighting. They need to do something about it.	
37. Remember that the three-point lighting scheme always consists of the key light, the fill light, and the back light.	conclusion begins with a summary
38. There are other lights that may be used, such as the *kicker* from the side—this highlights one side.	brief mention of two other lights to illustrate that others exist
39. Or the *background light* from the front to light up the background.	
40. But you always have to have the three—when you turn them all on, you have this effect.	turns on all three flashlights at the same time
41. I hope this has helped you to understand television lighting and that you will watch more closely the next time you turn on the TV.	closing thought directed to immediate audience; suggested application

KEY POINTS

- Informative speeches can help speakers and listeners to acquire new information and to clarify and remember facts, ideas, precedures, and processes.
- The different types of informative speeches include:
  lectures
  demonstrations
  instructions
  oral reports
  explantions
  definitions
- Topics for informative speeches can be divided into *concrete* and *abstract* categories, according to their closeness to a life experience.
- Some of the techniques for building an informative speech include:
  verbal aids
  visual aids
  limiting main points
  logical progression of ideas
  clear language
  emphasis of important information
  repetition
- The structure for an information speech should include:
  an introduction
  a specific purpose statement
  the body
  the conclusion

QUESTION FOR DISCUSSION

What are some of the informative speeches that people in your chosen profession give? In what settings do they give them?

ACTIVITIES

1. Analyze the instructors' lectures in your other classes by identifying the elements that are *concrete* and those that are *abstract*.
2. Analyze those same lectures for clear language and repetition (restatement) of main points.

3. Analyze those same lectures to determine whether they are primarily informative or whether they carry an element of persuasion.

4. List three topics that would be suitable for a demonstration. Three that would be suitable for giving instructions. And three speeches of definition.

5. Following your instructor's guidelines and assignments, prepare and deliver (a) an informative speech of a *concrete* nature, such as demonstrating or explaining a process; and (b) an informative speech of an *abstract* nature, such as exploring intangible ideas or defining terms.

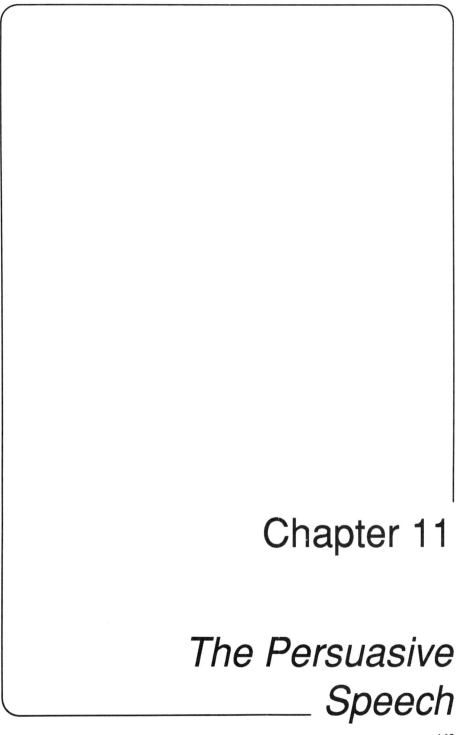

Chapter 11

The Persuasive Speech

Most of the tradition of public speaking instruction has been built on the study of persuasive speaking. The word *rhetoric* was historically defined as "discovering the available means of persuasion in a particular case."[1] Although today you will hear the word *rhetoric* used to mean speech that is mere words, devoid of any action, or to mean style in speech and writing, the classical definition is still used by speech teachers. The study of persuasion is a subspeciality of the study of human communication, and many universities offer advanced courses devoted solely to the study of persuasive speaking.

Persuasion can be defined as the efforts of one person or group of persons to effect some kind of change in another person or group of persons. Persuasive speaking is the open advocacy of the reasons the change is desirable. Dean Fadely and Ronald Greene summarize the process as follows: The present state of affairs, "things as they are," is called the *status quo*. We presume the status quo is satisfactory unless someone identifies a need to change or offers reasons for changing. We usually do not change the status quo without a reason. "The study of advocacy arose in response to the perceived need to know why people want to change and how it is possible to persuade them to do so."[2]

Although advocating change is the primary purpose of persuasive speaking, we also consider reinforcement of beliefs and attitudes to be a part of the persuasive process. Much political campaign speaking, for example, is designed to "inspire the convinced" rather than to change voters' minds. The United States traditionally has a fairly low voter turnout so a major job of candidates at various levels is to get the people who support them to go to the polls. Inspiring listeners and moving them to action is as much a part of persuasion as is effecting a change in listeners' beliefs. In either case, you aim toward getting listeners to deal with their own attitudes and opinions as they go through a process of change or reinforcement. Porter Crow tells us that "before and during a presentation, you move past a group's subjective posture, persuading them to (1) refeel, (2) re-think, and (3) re-new an opinion. You seek to replace one feeling with another and then engender a new commitment, a new direction."[3]

In general, then, we can say that persuasive speaking falls into one of two categories: that designed to alter either listeners' *beliefs* or their *behavior*. In the first, the speaker asks the listeners merely to accept a position as truth or to affirm an attitude or established belief. The listener is not asked to do anything as an immediate result of the change or reaffirmation. In the speech to influence behavior, the speaker hopes to *actuate* the listeners, to move them to *do* something as a result of the speech. This action may be to vote, to sign a petition, to buy something, to join an organization, or to begin a different pattern of personal behavior, such as a diet or exercise program. Note the difference in the following examples:

BELIEF: The United Way is beneficial to the community.
BEHAVIOR: Give to the United Way today.

BELIEF: Students have an obligation to vote in campus elections.
BEHAVIOR: Vote for Sue Smith next Tuesday.

BELIEF: Television keeps the college student informed.
BEHAVIOR: Buy a Motorola for your room.

Overlap exists between the two categories, for in order to get people to *do* something, the speaker must first alter their basic beliefs or move them from inactivity. And if we change a belief, somewhere down the line we will doubtless behave in a different manner. We should, however, have our purpose clearly framed in terms of desired listener response along a conviction/action continuum.

1	2	3	4	5	6	7	8
think about issue seriously	reinforce existing belief	consider possibility of changing belief	change belief	act on existing belief in the future	act on existing belief now	act on changed belief in the future	act on changed belief now

This continum moves from the least change, No. 1, to the most extreme change, No. 8. Know what you expect of your listeners before you begin your speech.

HOW TO MOTIVATE LISTENERS

Again we offer the directive that speakers must begin all planning with an analysis of the audience to whom they will speak. Review Chapter 2, especially the part that deals with determining audience attitudes. What needs might you tap in your listeners that would open them to the possibility of change or reinforcement? How can your information and materials be organized and phrased in a way that is most palatable to the audience? Where do you find the meeting point between your goals and the listeners' wants and needs so that your message can be adjusted to achieve maximum effectiveness? Those are the issues we will address in the remainder of this chapter.

Good Reasons

An axiom for the persuasive speaker is giving the audience "good reasons" for whatever it is he or she is trying to get listeners to believe or do. Good reasons are the heart of persuasion.[4] We make most of our decisions based on fulfilling personal motives. This means that we constantly ask "What's in it for me?" before we commit to active participation or a change in thinking. The effective speaker must answer that question by letting listeners know just how the proposition can benefit them. Politicians do not ask you to vote for them because they need a job and want to fulfill their own ambitions. Rather, they assure you that if they are elected they will keep your taxes down, offer your children better education, or make your streets safe from crime. Manufacturers do not ask you to buy their products because they operate on a profit motive and you can help them make money. Instead, they tell you how their product will make you feel and look better, live longer, or in some way improve your life. You need to find ways to discover and build the best possible reasons for listeners to go along with your proposal.

In building good reasons, a speaker must work from an understanding of the needs and wants of the audience. One effective way to study listener needs is through the needs hierarchy developed by Abraham Maslow. Maslow identified five major categories of human needs, ranking them according to their importance.

Self-actualization needs
Esteem needs
Belongingness needs
Safety needs
Physiological needs[5]

Beginning at the bottom of the ladder, Maslow suggested that we must satisfy the needs on each step before we can become concerned about the higher levels. Thus, physiological needs are the most basic, for they concern food, water, air, sleep, and sex. A person who is hungry and exhausted has little interest in the higher needs.

Moving up to the next higher level, safety needs include security, law and order, protection, stability, and freedom from fear. Belongingness needs are for love, friendship, family closeness, affection, and group acceptance. Esteem needs depend on recognition, status, prestige, competence, and the respect of others. Finally, self-actualization is the highest level, the level at which we live up to our self-expectations and become the best that we can be.

A speaker can structure an argument on any level of need and may often combine two or more categories. For example, if your speech is to urge environmental control, you may argue that the polluted air that is killing trees on mountain tops may soon reach the cities and kill us—without clean air to breathe, we cannot survive. You have appealed to a basic physiological need.

Or perhaps you are trying to convince a group of high-risk high school students not to drop out. Esteem needs might be the area in which to build—the additional status and potential for recognition that can come to educated people. Compare the Maslow hierarchy with the motive appeal list on the following pages. Either method can be an effective means of determining and utilizing audience needs to design the best line of argument for advocating your proposition.

SPEAKER APPEALS

Three forms of appeal by which a speaker can reach out to the audience are logical appeal, emotional appeal, and ethical appeal. Speakers should provide forms of proofs in all three areas, for it takes a balance to achieve maximum success in persuasion.

Logical Appeal

Logical appeal relates to the facts, the verifiable data that can be used to support one's proposition. Logical appeal is also the line of reasoning or argument built from those facts. Thoughtful listeners want accurate information on which to base their decisions. Much of the supporting material that we covered in Chapter 6 is factual—especially examples, statistics, and authoritative testimony. Visual aids with charts, graphs, or other illustrations can reinforce the logical appeal.

If I want to get you to give money to my favorite charity, I need to offer you the facts about what the charity will do with the money. This can be a dollars-and-cents breakdown of how much is spent on each of the projects sponsored by the charity, as well as the amount spent on fund raising and operation. I need to offer you several specific examples of the work the group has done. Testimony from those who have been helped would be useful. Charts and pictures would clarify and strengthen the argument.

Two major ways of reasoning from facts are the *inductive* and *deductive* methods. Inductive reasoning moves from a series of specific instances to a general conclusion. In my speech to get you to give to my charity, an inductive argument might begin with a series of specific examples about the good done by the charity, then move toward the conclusion that this is a worthwhile organization that justifies your support, just as charities in general are worthy of our support.

Deductive reasoning begins with a generalization and moves toward applying that general principle to a specific case. In the charity speech, I might begin by justifying charitable organizations in general, especially those that adhere to certain guidelines. By showing you that my particular charity follows those guidelines, I can lead to the conclusion that giving to this group is justifiable.

Either method can be equally effective. Your facts must be structured in some specific manner, however, for if they are presented randomly to the listeners, the value of the logical appeal will be lost. Factual matter should be interspersed with emotional appeal, for a lengthy recital of facts alone is not persuasive. Study the various methods of structuring a persuasive speech that are depicted on the following pages, then carefully plan a pattern that you believe will be most effective for your persuasive speech topic or topics.

Emotional Appeal

Emotional proof appeals to the psychological needs of the listeners, rather than the need for facts and information. We do not make our decisions solely on the basis of logic, but often we are influenced by our wants and desires. Television commercials make heavy use of emotional appeals—there is little logic in the proposition that using one after-shave instead of another will cause girls to chase men down the street or that one soft drink can promote world harmony while another leaves you dancing in the streets!

Much of the verbal supporting material you select will help you build your case on an emotional level. Especially useful are anecdotes, illustrations, and analogies, for they depend more heavily on pictorial and figurative images rather than bare facts. Visual aids can add emotional appeal. For example, pictures can describe more vividly than words, and attractive objects can make you want to buy and own them.

A word of caution: Do not confuse the term "emotional proof" with emotional speech *delivery*. Emotional delivery suggests dramatic use of the voice and body, ranting, pacing, or gesturing more than the average speech situation demands. Emotional appeal means supporting material that appeals to the listeners' wants and needs. Emotional delivery means intensity in the use of the voice and body. They are not synonymous.

Structuring emotional appeal in your speeches requires mixing facts with interpretations designed to motivate the listeners psychologically. The most useful *motive appeals* for speakers are:[6]

Acquisition and saving: We all enjoy owning things—clothes, cars, possessions of all sorts—and we enjoy it when we can get those things at bargain prices. We flock to sales, use "cents off" coupons, and shop at discount stores. Television commercials and newspaper and magazine ads make heavy use of this motive appeal.

Adventure. We would like to escape the boredom of the everyday world from time to time and find excitement to make life more lively and interesting. Cigarette ads that show the Marlboro man riding a horse across the desert or the Newport smoker on a sailboat, each with attractive women in the picture, are using primarily an appeal to adventure.

Companionship. Most of us want someone to be with—we do not want to be lonely. Propositions that show us how we can make friends and be with other people if we participate are appeals to the motive for companionship. Advertisers have used this appeal extensively in showing elderly people who are without friends and family.

Creativity. Most of us enjoy making things, doing crafts and art projects, building clubs and organizations, or in any number of ways creating something new and different. The vast do-it-yourself industry furnishes designs and instructions for those of us who would like to create something but lack the skill or talent to do so.

Curiosity. We are motivated by curiosity, by a desire to know what is going on around us. We are fascinated to learn about people—both those whom we know and those who have achieved fame. Arousing curiosity in listeners is a good way to prepare them to be persuaded.

Fear and *safety* are natural human motivators. We fear the unknown and the unexpected, and we do what we can to protect ourselves against harm. The insurance industry is built on our desire to make the future for both ourselves and our loved ones as safe as possible. Appeals to fear are especially effective when the speaker has a high level of credibility with the listeners, for it is then more difficult for listeners to discredit the source. However, if the speaker arouses too much strong fear, listeners may distort the message content or find other ways to rationalize their own rejection behavior.[7] A particularly good example is the campaign of the past two decades to get people to quit smoking cigarettes. Smokers find ways to discredit the source, the Surgeon General's office, or to rationalize their own behavior if the message is presented as a strong fear appeal. However, speeches that range from advocacy of the Rape Crisis Line to locking your car in the parking lot can make excellent use of an appeal to fear and proposed safe alternatives.

Imitation is another motive appeal that is used frequently by advertisers. By using famous people, especially sports and entertainment personalities, to endorse their products, advertisers hope we will follow by buying those products. Persuasive speakers may draw attention to community or campus leaders, using them as role models in the hope that listeners will imitate their outstanding behavior.

Loyalty to friends, family, and to the nation serves to motivate us on such various topics as becoming better empathic listeners, joining the Parent-Teachers Association, or rallying to defend the country if we are threatened by another nation. Calling upon the natural sense of loyalty held by most people is an effective strategy for persuasion.

Personal enjoyment motivates all of us to make decisions that affect our sense of comfort and luxury or our desire for recreation and freedom from restraint. We enjoy good tastes and aromas, pleasant household surroundings, and beauty in art and nature. Persuasive appeals can be designed that will show listeners how the proposition can bring more personal enjoyment into their lives.

Reverence or worship motivates us as we pay respect to our leaders, honor our heroes, or observe and revere our traditions. Worship of a deity, whether in a church or synagogue or in one's own personal meditation, is a strong motivator for many of us.

Sexual attraction moves us to buy perfumes, hair products, and clothes that we believe will appeal to the opposite sex. We join organizations to meet people so that we can find mates. Sexual attraction is far more than a basic sexual drive, for it has become a strong norm in our society to build much of our adult interaction on mating and marriage.

Sympathy moves us to act on behalf of other people, to give to charitable organizations, or to donate time to volunteer projects. A speaker who can arouse our genuine concern for others, even for animals, may be able to move us in the direction of support of a particular proposal.

Three motive appeals that may appear to be somewhat negative are also useful. *Destruction,* when we tear down the old in order to make way for the new, or when we destroy that which is evil, is a strong motivator. *Fighting* that arouses a sense of competition can also stimulate us. And *revulsion* that so sickens us with the status quo that we are ready to make a change can be a highly useful persuasive strategy. A garage dump, graphically described by the speaker with images that appeal to sight and smell, can be pictured as so repugnant that listeners are ready to vote for a new sanitary landfill project.

Other motive appeals include *independence, power and authority,* and *pride.* These appeals are the means by which a speaker moves the audience psychologically. When coupled with solid logical proof, they enable persuasion to take place.

Ethical Appeal

The third avenue by which a speaker reaches the audience is through ethical appeal. In many ways, this may be the most important of the three appeals, for ethical appeal hinges on the speaker himself (or herself)—who the speaker is, how the audience feels about the speaker, or the relationship between speaker and listeners. We use the term *source credibility* to describe this phenomenon.

Source credibility has both extrinsic and intrinsic factors. The extrinsic factors are those elements outside the immediate speech situation—who the speaker is, who he or she represents, or the general impression we may have of the speaker in advance. Well-known people come before an audience with prior reputations. Speakers who represent large corporations or have high government positions customarily have higher credibility than do everyday folks. Some professions carry a higher level of believability than do others—teachers and doctors, for example.

The principal elements of credibility are *competence* and *trustworthiness*. We believe people whom we perceive to be competent—that is, they know what they are talking about and have demonstrated their expertise. And we are more apt to believe people whom we feel we can trust because they have always been honest and straightforward in their dealings with us and with the public.

On a secondary level, but also very important, the qualities of *dynamism* and *sociality* affect credibility. Enthusiastic, dedicated people who seem to be genuinely friendly and interested in us are more persuasive than are those who seem cold, distant, and lifeless.

The *intrinsic* factors of source credibility are those things that a speaker does within the speech, as it is being delivered. *Fluency* is one factor, for those speakers who can deliver their message in a smooth, flowing manner are more believable than are those who stumble a great deal or vocalize their pauses with a series of "uhs." *Mispronunciation,* especially of key words central to the content of the speech, also impacts on believability. Repeated mispronunciation weakens the speaker's ethos. Finally, *disorganization* is an intrinsic factor that works against a speaker. If listeners cannot follow the train of thought in a clearly arranged pattern, they are much less likely to believe the speaker.

As a beginning speech student in a classroom setting, you have little control over the extrinsic factors in the early part of the semester. Unless you happen to be president of the student body, a star campus athlete, or have been in other classes with several of the same students, you probably have no prior reputation. But it is interesting to watch how the credibility level grows in a speech class as the term progresses. After about the second round of speeches, you will find yourself developing an expectation level toward your classmates—those who have appeared competent and dynamic in their first speeches will lead you to believe that you are about to hear another good speech when the next round comes up. Those who disappointed you in the first rounds may stir up a negative prospect about what you may hear in future speeches. Wayne Minnick suggests that the best way to reveal desirable traits to the audience is through the arguments, the facts, the feelings exhibited by the speaker, through the propositions defended, through the persons and things praised and deplored, through the sources used, through the way the speaker meets heckling and objections—in fact, through everything the speaker says and does.[8]

You can work on the intrinsic factors of credibility by preparing speeches that are clearly organized, learning to pronounce all the words accurately, and practising aloud until you are completely fluent. By building a good reputation through the intrinsic factors, you will earn source credibility as your classmates come to trust you to give them your best. And remember the importance of a dynamic, friendly manner as you speak. The word *charisma* is often used to describe leaders with a high level of personal magnetism or to talk about speakers with a special charm or magic quality that draws people to them. Charisma can also contribute to ethical appeal, for it relates closely to the factors of dynamism and sociality. You can increase your charisma by working to incorporate all the elements of source credibility.

STRUCTURING THE PERSUASIVE SPEECH

The persuasive speech should contain the same four parts that an informative speech contains—an introduction, a thesis statement, the body, and the conclusion. Some differences of focus and patterning, however, are more suited to persuasion.

The *introduction* needs to begin by capturing audience attention, with the same techniques discussed in Chapter 8. In the second step, where you seek to orient the audience and to let them know something about you, more time may be needed to build goodwill and establish your credibility. This may include a statement or two about why you are there, why you were chosen to speak on the particular topic, or what experiences you have had that give you personal expertise. This is not bragging about who you are or what you know, but a straightforward statement of past association that enables you to know the value of what you advocate. For example, a speech urging classmates to attend school football games in order to boost the morale of the team would be strengthened if the speaker can say, "I played football for three years in high school, and I know what it means to be behind in the score, to be so exhausted that you think you cannot go on, then to hear the cheering and applause from the stands—you feel you just have to keep trying so that you don't let your fans down."

The final step in the introduction, the statement of specific purpose, is sometimes given directly, so that listeners know just what you want them to believe or do. In other instances, you may wish to hold off on a specific statement until you have had a chance to do some explaining. If the audience is inclined to be hostile to either you or your proposition, it may be best not to tell too much too soon, lest the listeners close their minds to your proposition without giving you a fair hearing. As Walter Kiechel states, "the standard tell-'em-what-you're-gonna-tell-'em, tell-'em, and tell-'em-what-you-told-'em works fine if your goal is to inform. If you're out to persuade, though, you're probably better off laying out the problem, marshalling the evidence for your view, then ending with a call to action."[9]

To make sure that your speech contains enough "good reasons" for listeners to adopt your proposal, you would do well to remember the technique we discussed in Chapter 7 for using the word "because" to connect the specific purpose to the main heads of the speech body. This is not a word you would necessarily say aloud to the audience, but by having the word at the top of the first page of your outline, you are constantly reminded of the need to make the reasons come through clearly in your speech.

The *body* of the speech may be developed by any one of several different structural patterns. The cause-and-effect pattern is useful in persuasion, as is the problem-and-solution pattern. Both patterns could be designed to first discuss *need*, either by showing the causes and effects of the existing problem or by simply analyzing it as a problem, then move to a second step that would show a *plan* to solve the problem. The final main heading would press for the adoption of that plan, showing how it would solve the problem. This is called the *need/plan/solvency* pattern, and it is very effective in persuasive speaking.

Another useful method is the topical structure when the topics are designed to be the reasons for advocacy. For example, if your purpose is to persuade the listeners to buy health insurance, your three main heads might be:

I. It benefits you, the patient.
II. It benefits the hospital and the doctor.
III. It benefits the community.

These reasons, divided topically, are *assertions*. You are assuming that these statements are valid reasons for buying health insurance. They are your arguments. The supporting material under each main head will be the proof for that assertion—the facts, figures, explanations, and examples that build a case for the correctness of your assertion.

If you use the *good reasons* structure, you will need to decide how many reasons to include—one or even two is seldom enough, but more than four or five can overload listeners and make it hard for them to remember your line of reasoning. Another question concerns the placement of reasons, for usually you will have one or two best reasons, with perhaps one or two that are not as strong. Place your best reason first, so that you capture and hold the audience, then refer back to that best reason throughout the speech. Or, place your best reason last, leading up to it with a series of transitions that suggest that while reasons one and two are important, just wait until you hear number three! Placing the best reason either first or last is effective, but never place it in the middle. For reasons of emphasis and listener retention, the middle of the speech is the least useful placement.[10]

Another consideration in building your arguments is whether or not you should mention the opposing arguments, a technique called a *two-sided message.* One method of persuading is *refutation;* the speaker states the opponent's arguments, then shows them to be false or erroneous by the use of evidence and counterargument. If you determine that your audience is well informed about your topic, inclined to be opposed to your stance, or will later be exposed to the counterarguments, then you might be better off to anticipate the points on the opposite side and try to discredit them in your own speech. If, however, the audience is not especially well informed about the topic, or your analysis suggests that most audience members already favor your proposition, then a *one*-sided argument may work more effectively.[11]

One additional structural pattern that is highly effective was developed by Alan Monroe many years ago. He called it the "motivated sequence." While similar to the need/plan/solvency pattern, the motivated sequence is more specific and can be adapted to both informative and persuasive speaking. The five steps are:

1. Attention—you must get the audience to listen to you before you begin to explore the problem.
2. Need—show that the status quo is not satisfactory by describing a need or analyzing a problem.
3. Satisfaction—here you present a proposed solution, suggesting how your plan can meet the need.
4. Visualization—imaginatively "try on" your proposed solution—talk through how it might work. *See* your plan in word pictures.
5. Action—ask listeners to adopt your plan, to approve your proposal, to believe as you ask, or in some way bring closure to your speech with a call to action.[12]

The *conclusion* of a persuasive speech should offer a summary, connect the speaker and listeners with some direct remarks about their relationships, and end with a closing thought that asks for a commitment from the audience. Much as the good salesperson tries to get you to sign a contract before you leave the store, so too the good persuasive speaker asks listeners to commit to believe or to do—go buy, vote, join, participate, or whatever the speech has been about. If you have held off from a clear statement of purpose in the beginning of the speech because you believe the audience to be somewhat hostile or to lack interest in your proposal, the conclusion is the time to be specific. Having given them clear reasons, good evidence, and a careful analysis of the problem and your proposed solution, you hope that you have convinced them to give serious consideration. Let your conclusion reflect this desire on your part.

Carefully study the developmental pattern in the following examples. These two persuasive speeches both deal with sensitive issues, for they concern contraception and rape. Such subjects must be handled with tact and care. Notice that the first speech depends primarily on logical appeal—the speaker uses quotations, cites authorities, presents statistical support, and in general builds a logical case. Except for a brief emotional statement at the beginning, referred to only briefly in the conclusion, the approach is straightforward and factual.

The second speech, advocating a Rape Crisis Hotline, depends more heavily on emotional appeal, especially one long illustration, for its impact. Because listeners have been furnished the proposal in writing, the speaker does not need to dwell on the facts and figures. Rather, he needs to arouse listeners' motivation to commit.

Follow the analysis of each speech carefully to be sure you understand all the marginal comments.

PERSUASIVE SPEECH (NUMBER 1)

The Distribution of Contraceptives in High School
by Sheila Smith

(In this classroom speech, the speaker deals with a highly controversial issue by presenting reasons in support of her belief, but by also acknowledging the strength of the opponents' arguments.)

1. "My whole world is falling apart. I don't know where to turn. In one month I'll graduate from high school. And in August I'm going away to college. Everything was falling into place until now—I just found out I'm pregnant. My boyfriend wants to get married, but I don't. I need a husband and a baby? If I had someone I could turn to, someone I could talk to. I can't tell my parents—my mother would go crazy, and my dad would try to kill my boyfriend. If only I had somewhere to turn."

    opening illustration is told in the first person for dramatic effect

2. This scene, repeated many times ever day in this country, could have been avoided through the distribution of contraceptives in high school clinics.

    first statement of purpose

3. I wonder how many of you had such a clinic in your own high school? I know I did not, but in looking back, I wish we had. I was fortunate that I never got in trouble, but several of my friends did. And I am sure most of you know at least one or two girls who suffered through an unwanted pregnancy.

    orienting material, involves immediate audience

    need is suggested

4. The New York Board of Education has supported a state-funded program that dispenses contraceptives in nine city high schools.

example in favor of the proposition

5. On the other hand, a group of black clergymen has sued a school-based clinic in Chicago because they feel that the distribution of contraceptives is, and I quote, "a calculated effort to destroy the very fabric of family life."

speaker admits from beginning that there is strong opposing opinion; uses quotation

6. The programs that dispense contraceptives are being attacked with a number of strong arguments. I believe, however, that the advantages far outweigh the disadvantages. These programs are an asset to our society because they are preventing teenage pregnancies, they are prompting teenagers to wait later to have sex, and they are preventing the spread of sexually transmitted diseases.

statement of personal belief

7. The main reason to provide high school students with contraceptives is to reduce pregnancy. The *Statistical Abstract* for the United States reports that in 1985, the latest year for which figures are available, that out of every 1,000 births to unmarried women, 280 of the mothers were 19 years old or younger. That's 28 percent of the total that were teenage girls.

first main head

startling statistic

8. Since the first clinic opened in St. Paul, Minnesota, teen pregnancies have been reduced by 66 percent in the St. Paul area, according to the Center for Population Options. Of the 61 clinics now open in the area, 10 directly dispense contraceptives and 40 have physicians on staff who will write prescriptions.

one example of a solution, backed by strong percentage number from an authoritative source

9. Another reason to support high school clinics is that the help and the information prompts teens to wait until later to have sex. Teens who learn about sex and realize that contraceptives are available have more choice about when they will become sexually active. No longer driven by fear and ignorance, the students are more inclined to wait. Professor Laurie Zalin of Johns Hopkins School of Public Health reported that in two schools in Baltimore, students have postponed their first intercourse by an average of seven months as a result of the services provided by the school-based clinics.

transition into second main head

authority helps to support assertion

10. Not only are the clinics helping to prevent teen-age pregnancies and prompting teens to wait later to become sexually active, but they are also helping to prevent sexually transmitted diseases. The Surgeon General has stated that condoms reduce the risk of contracting AIDS. AIDS has made having sex not just a moral question, but a question of life and death.

transition with summary leading to third main head

authority helps to support assertion

11. According to Lopata's book *Marriage and Families*, one in 30 men between the ages of 20 and 50 may already be infected with AIDS, but many do not realize it. That is a lot of men. Many women are going to contract this disease if we don't do something. The prevention of AIDS should begin in high schools. By providing contraceptives to high school students, we are taking an important step toward controlling this dread disease.

citation and startling statistic emphasize the urgency

12. There are two main arguments that have been made against the distribution of contraceptives. The first is that it encourages abortion, and the second is that it promotes premarital sex.

fourth main head presents opponent's arguments

13. The spokesman for the National Right to Life Commission argues that school clinics promote abortion because they are affiliated with the Population Institution in Washington, D.C., an organization that favors legalized abortion. This is simply not true. The clinics provide students with facts, with the information about birth control and counseling on the various options for dealing with unwanted pregnancies. Abortion is presented as one of those options, but no one tries to convince the young woman that abortion is a better choice than parenthood or adoption—she is simply given accurate information about the alternatives. And isn't it much better to prevent pregnancy altogether than to have to come to grips with the wrenching decision to have an abortion?

quotes authority for opposing viewpoint

refutation and explanation

14. School clinics do not deal with the morality of premarital sex. It is not their place to do so. As a part of an educational institution, their purpose is to teach, not to mold morals. Not one piece of solid evidence supports the claim that having contraceptives available increases sexual activity—just the opposite seems to be the case.

refutation of second opposing argument

15. And the opponents of school clinics need to face one unarguable fact—teenagers are having sex, whether we like it or not. They do not need clinics to encourage them. Having contraceptives available simply ensures that the sex is less likely to produce babies and diseases.

another argument in favor of speaker's proposition

16. The distribution of contraceptives through high school clinics benefits our society. Fewer young mothers have babies they are not equipped to care for. Teenagers may wait longer to become sexually active. And the spread of sexually transmitted diseases is being slowed.

conclusion begins with summary of main assertions

17. Some say ignorance is bliss, but ignorance about the facts of life can destroy a young person. Ignorance of the facts of life can lead to the facts of misery and even the facts of death—learned the hard way.

challenging thought

18. If you are one of those who has opposed public school contraceptive clinics, I hope you will re-think your position. That girl whom I quoted in the beginning of my speech could be your own daughter some day—would you want her to suffer so? I think not—none of us would.

restate purpose, appeal to family love and loyalty

19. So, I urge you to support all efforts of our public schools to establish school-based clinics for the distribution of contraceptives to high school students. Through them, our teenagers can find help and direction instead of heartbreak and disaster.

closing call for belief

PERSUASIVE SPEECH (NUMBER 2)

Vote YES for the Rape Crisis Center
by Jonathan Ross

(Since the group is fairly small and the speaker is there for a previously identified purpose, the introduction is kept quite short.)

1. Ladies and gentlemen, I would like to speak to you tonight about a Rape Crisis Hotline. You, as the members of the Haleyville City Council, will be asked to vote next week on committing the funds for this center. I would like to tell you something about the proposed Hotline and urge you to support it with a unanimous endorsement.

purpose statement

2. To begin with, the Hotline will require only minimal funding—the details of the proposal are on the handout in front of you. You will note that with the exception of one paid director, all of the work is to be done by volunteers—unpaid volunteers—who are willing to help out. The Haleyville First National Bank has agreed to give us an office with no cost to us at all. We need only a single room, two desks, and two telephone lines. Skillman's Furniture is giving us the desks and chairs. All that the city will have to pay for will be the director's salary and the phone bills—a very small price for a very important service, for we will offer an around-the-clock trained staff to talk to victims of rape, most of whom have no place to turn.

first main head; speaker reassures listeners of minimal cost

3. But perhaps you are saying to yourself, rape is not that frequent in Haleyville—we have no problem here—right? Wrong! Let me give you some statistics based on a national survey, but that are completely applicable right here in our hometown. Out of 100 reported rapes, 15 are not true—these are the reports that receive so much publicity—when some young woman says she has been raped in order to attract attention or make trouble for a man. But at most, this happens only 15 out of every 100 times. That means that 85 out of the 100 reports are true. Out of that 85, only 43 of those rapists are apprehended—42 are never caught. Of the 43 who are caught, 33 of them are prosecuted. Of those 33, 16 are released on legal loopholes. That means that only 17 of the 85 rapists are sent to jail—68 of them are back on the streets, ready to rape again!

main head two; begins to personalize the issue

statistics dramatize the importance of the issue

4. Until the law finds a better way to deal with apprehending and punishing rapists, especially keeping them away from other victims, we must do the best we can by providing help to those victims after the rape has occurred. And that is the purpose of the Rape Crisis Hotline.

transition into third main head

5. I want to tell you a true story of one 12-year-old boy, for his story vividly illustrates the need for this Hotline. This boy was raped—but he could not tell his friends—after all, he was only 12 years

third man head is not an assertion—it becomes a reason by virtue of the in-

old. His friends lacked the maturity to understand, and he feared they would make fun of him
and ostracize him. He could not tell his parents,
for he believed they would blame him for what
had happened and would think that he was a bad
boy. He had no one to talk to, and held this awful
story inside him for over three years. His school
work suffered, he lost his zest and enthusiasm, he
had nightmares, he stayed away from his
friends—and if he had not happened to find a
school counselor who persisted in trying to help
him, he might never have straightened out his life.

*tensity of the illus-
tration*

6. Let me tell you what happened. This 12-year-old
boy walked into the mall, went to the ice cream
store, and bought himself an ice cream cone. He
spilled some of it on his hands, so he went into
the restroom to wash it off. He had just dried his
hands and was throwing away the paper towel
when a stall door behind him was kicked open.
There was a man standing there, naked, with a
knife in his hand. He grabbed that boy, pulled
him back into the stall, stood up on the toilet seat,
put the knife to the back of the boy's neck, and
forced him to engage in oral sex. When he was
through he pressed the knife in further, then said,
"You're nothing but a little faggot—get out." Ladies and gentlemen, this awful experience did not
happen in some remote, larger inner city—it happened just two blocks from here in our own mall.
I know, because I am the counselor to whom this
poor boy poured out his story—over three years
after he had lived with the shame of it night and
day. He is still in therapy and is struggling hard
to remake his own sense of worth and self-iden-
tity, and to answer his own doubts and fears
about his sexuality.

*several motive ap-
peals—fear, sympa-
thy, anger, disgust*

7. Now, how could a Rape Crisis Hotline have
helped this boy? It could not have prevented the
attack, obviously. But had there been a place the
boy could have called, he might have begun to
work through his feelings much quicker. Had he
been willing to come forward and identify himself, perhaps the rapist could have been apprehended. As it was, since the rape was never re-

*transition into sum-
mary; wrapup of il-
lustration*

ported, the boy lived in constant fear that he
would see that man again.

8. Having a Rape Crisis Hotline in a community   conclusion begins
   dramatizes the ever-threatening reality of rape.
   With proper encouragement, after an initial publicity campaign, victims can gain confidence that
   help is available for them. Far too many rape
   victims suffer in silence. With a trained Hotline
   staff, victims can be steered to report the crimes to
   the police and to carry through with prosecution
   when the rapist is caught.

9. Haleyville needs this Hotline. No more 12-year-   closing call to action
   old boys should ever have to suffer because they
   have no one to talk to. Vote "yes" when the proposition is presented to you next week.

KEY POINTS

- Persuasive speaking seeks to discover the available means by which to effect some kind of change in another person or group of persons. Reinforcement of existent beliefs is also a part of the persuasive process.
- Persuasion aims to alter and reinforce either *belief* or *behavior*.
- Listeners are most inclined to be persuaded by offering them *good reasons* for the change.
- Good reasons must have the potential to fulfill listeners' needs, such as those delineated by Maslow in his needs hierarchy.
- Speakers reach out to audiences in three areas of appeal: logical, emotional, and ethical.
- Logical appeal is factual matter and the reasoning from those facts. Reasoning patterns are usually either inductively or deductively arranged.
- Emotional appeal reaches the listeners in their *wants and needs*, showing how the speaker's proposition can satisfy those needs. Motive appeals are the areas of psychological needs from which we make decisions.
- Ethical appeal is source credibility, the reputation of the speaker, his or her perceived competence, trustworthiness, and dynamism. Intrinsic factors of source credibility are fluency, pronunciation, and organization.
- Persuasive speeches need the same four section that all speeches have—the introduction, thesis statement, body, and conclusion. Some special techniques work better with persuasion.

QUESTION FOR DISCUSSION

What are some of the persuasive speeches that people in your chosen profession give? In what settings do they give them?

ACTIVITIES

1. When Aristotle defined rhetoric as "The discovery of all of the means of persuasion," he implied that a speaker must find as much evidence as possible. But this does not mean that a speaker uses all the evidence that he or she discovers. Discuss this in light of your own research and preparation for giving speeches.

2. Take the list of topics that you developed at the beginning of the semester (Chapter 1, Activity 3). How could each be designed to reinforce beliefs, alter beliefs, or alter behavior of the listeners?

3. Go through a magazine and examine the ads to determine which motive appeals are employed in each. Watch several television commercials to determine whether they use primarily logical or emotional appeal. Do any *products* have an ethos of their own? (BMWs, Perrier, Chanel, Tiffany's, Prudential, Alpo?)

4. Match the motive appeal to the following examples:

____ A. Somewhere a child is crying. Give to the Children's Fund.	1. companionship
	2. personal enjoyment
____ B. Get a $600 rebate when you buy a new Cadillac between now and May 1.	3. authority/power
	4. independence
____ C. Come to a place where you can explore beaches and mountains.	5. sympathy
	6. acquisition/saving
____ D. Reach out, reach out and touch someone.	7. fear
____ E. Put a tiger in your tank!	8. adventure
____ F. When it's time to relax, we've got the beer. It's Miller time!	9. loyalty
	10. imitation
____ G. Bill Cosby: "JELL-O pudding is the very best!	
____ H. You've come a long way, baby!	
____ I. Last year handguns killed 48 people in Japan, 8 in Great Britain . . . 10,728 in the United States. Stop handguns before they stop you.	
____ J. I'd rather fight than switch.	

(See page 220 at the end of the book for answers to matching quiz.)

5. Following your instructor's guidelines and assignments, prepare and deliver a persuasive speech to CONVINCE your audience to think or believe as you do. Deliver a second persuasion speech with the specific purpose being to ACTUATE.

REFERENCES

[1]Lane Cooper, trans.; *The Rhetoric of Aristotle* (New York: Appleton-Century-Crofts, 1932), 7.

[2]Dean Fadely and Ronald Greene, "A Man, A Prophet, A Dream," in *The God Pumpers: Religion in the Electronic Age*, eds. Marshall Fishwick and Ray B. Browne (Bowling Green, Oh: Bowling Green State University Popular Press, 1987), 75–76. The authors wish to acknowledge the help of Dr. Fadely in the preparation of the chapter.

[3]Porter J. Crow, "How to Change Their Minds," *Vital Speeches of the Day* 51 (May 1, 1985), 441–442.

[4]Karl R. Wallace, "The Substance of Rhetoric: Good Reasons," *Quarterly Journal of Speech* 49 (October 1963): 239–249.

[5]Abraham H. Maslow, "A Theory of Human Motivation," *Motivation and Personality*, 2nd ed. (New York: Harper & Row, 1970).

[6]Douglas Ehninger, Bruce E. Gronbeck, Ray E. McKerrow, and Alan H. Monroe, *Principles and Types of Speech Communication*, 9th ed. (Glenview, Ill.: Scott, Foresman, 1982), 104–109.

[7]Carl Hovland, Irving L. Janis, and Harold H. Kelley, *Communication and Persuasion* (New Haven: Yale University Press, 1953); Lyle Sussman, "Ancients and Moderns on Fear and Fear Appeals: A Comparative Analysis," *The Central States Speech Journal* 24 (Fall 1973): 206–211; Mary John Smith, "Extreme Disagreement and the Expression of Attitudinal Freedom," *Communication Monographs* 46 (June 1979): 112–118.

[8]Wayne C. Minnick, *The Art of Persuasion* (Boston: Houghton Mifflin, 1957), 121.

[9]Walter Kiechel III, "How to Give a Speech," *Fortune*, June 8, 1987, 179.

[10]Carl I. Hovland, and others, *The Order of Presentation in Persuasion* (New Haven: Yale University Press, 1966), 13–75; Anthony J. Clark, "An Exploratory Study of Order Effects in Persuasive Communication," *The Southern Speech Communication Journal* 39 (Summer 1974): 322–332.

[11]Erwin P. Bettinghaus, *Persuasive Communication* (New York: Holt, Rinehart & Winston, 1968), 154–157.

[12]The Motivated Sequence was first introduced by Alan H. Monroe in *Principles and Types of Speech* (New York: Scott, Foresman, 1935) and has been refined and expanded through 10 subsequent editions of the book, as well as used by a number of different authors.

Chapter 12

The Special Occasion Speech

Speech making is a part of many traditional gatherings. We expect speeches at banquets where employees or club members are recognized and rewarded; we expect speeches at political rallies and meetings where organizational officers are elected; and we expect speeches of eulogy at funerals and memorial services. These special-occasion speeches fill a need for ritual that we all hold in common. They enable us to participate in time-honored ceremonies that bond us together as family, friends, and members of a society.

Ceremonial speaking is widespread in the United States; we estimate that a majority of the speeches made each day across the nation fall into this category. You have probably heard many of them—in fact, you may not have been aware that what you heard would be classified as a speech. Placing a friend's name in nomination, presenting an award, or dedicating a new building are but some of the many occasions where a short speech is appropriate. In Classical Greece, speaking of this type was called *epidectic*. Today we use either the term *ceremonial speaking* or more informal *special occasion speech*.

TYPES OF CEREMONIAL SPEECHES

Introducing Speakers

Customarily, when a speaker is to present a major speech in public, another speaker paves the way by introducing the featured guest to the audience. The purpose is to give the listeners more information about the speaker, to get them to like and respect him or her, and to stimulate them to listen by arousing curiosity about the speaker, the topic, or some special relationship to the audience.

The first rule for preparing a speech of introduction governs all special occasion speeches—be brief! Seldom is there any reason for a special occasion speech to exceed three minutes. Far more guest speakers have suffered from an overly long introduction than from one that was too short. By the time the introducer was finished, the audience was already tired! You cannot tell everything about the speaker, especially older people who have long résumés of accomplishments. Choose those aspects that are the most important, especially those that relate to the speech the person is about to give or to his or her relationship to the occasion. This information may include educational background, professional experience, volunteer participation, special honors, unusual accomplishments, or contributions such as books, inventions, theories, or programs for which the individual has received recognition.

Do not overly praise the speaker—lavishing excessive compliments can be embarrassing. Stay away from unnecessary comments about the person's speaking ability—"He is the funniest speaker I've ever heard" or "I know she will hold you spellbound for the next thirty minutes" are difficult statements for speakers to follow. Let the audience members discover for themselves that the person is a good speaker—you stick to background information.

How do you obtain information about the speaker to prepare your introduction? You can ask the speaker; many have fact sheets ready for just such occasions. Secretaries can be helpful, even spouses if you are unable to contact the speaker personally. If it is a famous person, you may be able to find information in the library in one of several "Who's Who" books that give brief biographies of famous people. As a rule, the more famous the speaker, the less you need to develop a lengthy introduction, for listeners will already know the background facts. The most widely heard introduction is also the shortest, for when the President gives a televised address or holds a press conference, he is introduced with one phrase: "Ladies and gentlemen, the President of the United States." Nothing else is necessary.

Give the title of the speech, if the speaker has chosen one. Be sure to state it clearly. You may comment on the appropriateness of the topic for the occasion or on its significance, but do not give any of your own opinions about the subject matter. Your views on the topic have no place in your introduction of the speaker.

The style of a speech of introduction should be straightforward and direct.

Overly elegant and flowery language is out of place. Finding words to fulfill the required conventions without a trite repetition of overworked phrases is difficult. Such beginnings as "Today I have the honor of presenting to you . . . " or "It is my distinct privilege to introduce to you . . . " have been heard so many times that they lack originality. We hope you will never be guilty of the most hackneyed of all phrases associated with the speech of introduction: "I bring you a man who needs no introduction." If he needs no introduction, why are you there?

While you seek to avoid the overly stilted style, you need also to stay away from the opposite—the style that is too conversational. Because this is a formal speech, you need to treat it with dignity. Slang or street-corner vocabulary is out of place here. You may be tempted to convey familiarity if the speaker is a close friend. Mentioning the relationship is fine, but do not try to overly personalize it with anecdotes about when you drank beer together!

As you conclude the speech, turn to the speaker, then back to the audience, so that you help establish the eye contact between speaker and listeners. Look directly at the speaker as you turn the platform over to him or her, smile, and add all the nonverbal dimensions of the gracious host ushering in a very important guest.

Guest speakers are introduced at all kinds of club meetings. Organizations such as the Lions Club, Rotary International, or Kiwanis often have outsiders speak to their groups. The PTA, book or study clubs, or professional associations commonly have someone speak at their weekly or monthly meetings. Meetings that take place at luncheons, dinners, and banquets usually have formal speakers. Many university campuses hold symposia or have special guest lectures for faculty and students. The list of possible situations for guest speakers is almost endless, and for each guest speaker, someone will usually prepare a speech of introduction. Remember the guidelines above when you are called on to do the introducing.

Presenting and Accepting Awards

Another well-established tradition that calls for a short speech is honoring a person by presenting some sort of an award for outstanding achievement. The entertainment industry has made the honoring of its own a national media event, with televised presentations of Oscars, Emmies, Tonys, Obies, and Grammies drawing large viewing audiences each year. Schools from elementary through college give awards for scholarship, service, and athletic achievement, while clubs and professional organizations typically give plaques, certificates, or gifts to those members whose service is meritorious.

Guidelines that govern the preparation and delivery of the speech accompanying the presentation of an award begin with this warning—*keep it short!* You need to be as sincere as possible, commending the recipient and his or her accomplishments, but do not use such excessive praise that you embarrass the person. Specifically, list and explain the accomplishments that led to the award and how they came to be recognized. Your analysis of the audience's prior knowledge of the event is most important, for if there are listeners who may not know the history of the award, you need to include a brief summary. This might be a short explanation about the person an award is named for, the event that the award commemorates, the history of the award, other notable winners, or the criteria for winning the award.

Avoid the temptation, however, to use this as a time to speak on your favorite subject. One negative example was an overzealous presenter who was giving an award for the outstanding volunteer of the year for a local humane society. The speaker went on for over 10 minutes arguing against the use of animals in laboratory research. This was neither the time nor the place for the presenter's personal views.

As the presenter, downplay the importance of the award, especially if it is cash. Do not predict what that cash will enable the recipient to do—the recipient will discuss this if he or she feels it is appropriate. Focus instead on the honor that the award signifies and the accomplishments of the honoree.

Finally, awards are often presented with a surprise element, for neither the winner nor the audience may know in advance who the recipient will be. If such a surprise is planned, then you will need to withhold the person's name until the end of your speech, thus adding to the suspense. Occasionally we have seen awards presented where both presenter and recipient pretended a surprise element, but it was most obvious that both knew in advance. We would have preferred that they did not fake surprise, for it is not necessary. Recipients often need to know in advance so that they can be sure to attend the meeting, and perhaps can even prepare a few remarks in response.

If you are the recipient, your primary task is to convey a sincere expression of appreciation. Find a balance between excessive modesty and bragging. Never apologize for winning, and do not disclaim your worth with statements such as, "I didn't deserve to win." The selection committee obviously thought you did deserve to win or it would not have chosen you. Include thanks to other people who have been significant factors in your accomplishment, but avoid trying to thank everyone from your first-grade teacher forward.

Talk about your plans for the future—how will the award change or influence the days and years ahead. If the award is cash or a scholarship, stress the importance of the money toward your goal fulfillment. If the award is one that has been given to a number of other people in the past, mention the honor of joining their ranks.

Finally, just as with presenting an award, we think it is better if you do not feign surprise if you are not truly surprised. Many occasions for awards are arranged so that several finalists will appear at the big event, without knowing in advance who the winner is to be. If you are a finalist, surely you will spend a little time thinking what you might say if you received the award. It is possible, however, for the speech in receipt of an award to be totally impromptu, as happened recently to one of your authors when an organization gave her a special recognition award that she was not expecting. At those moments, we all must call upon the best of our impromptu speaking skills to help us acknowledge the award with some graciousness and composure.

Welcoming and Responding

The welcome address is often called a speech of courtesy, for its primary aim is to make a group or an individual feel welcome in a new situation. When professional associations hold conventions in a large city, often some person from the mayor's office will come and extend an official welcome to the group. When a church choir goes on tour and a choir in a neighboring city hosts a dinner to launch the visit in the guest city, someone may give a speech welcoming the entire group. When a minister moves to a new church, when a manager is transferred to another corporate office, or a new administrative official is hired at a university, some formal opening event is often given to make the new arrival feel at home and wanted. The welcome speech is a part of these events. Although not as common as speeches that introduce speakers and present awards, welcome speeches are still important parts of many traditional occasions.

If you are giving the welcome, your task is to extend greetings and promote feelings of friendships between the two groups or the group and the new individual. You need to make the group or individual feel sincerely wanted and at home. Share such information as you feel the listeners do not have—either the home group or the visiting group. For the visitors, this may include mention of special events planned for them, things to do and see in the community, parking or babysitting facilities, or anything that will make their stay more pleasant and comfortable. For the home group, you may need to share some information about the visitors, who they are, where they are from, and something about their organizations.

If you are welcoming an individual, tell the person something about the group—its history, accomplishments, or interesting characteristics. If the audience does not know your new arrival, you have much the same task as introducing a speaker, for you need to let the audience know the pertinent background facts about the newcomer.

As with all special occasion speeches, be brief, keep it simple, and convey sincerity and genuineness, not gushiness or excessive flattery.

If you are the one being welcomed, you may sometimes be called on to give a *response to a welcome*. This is not always necessary, especially when an entire group is being welcomed. This could also be an impromptu speech, for you may not know in advance that someone is planning a formal welcoming speech, leaving you on the spot to respond.

Express appreciation, both to the host speaker and the entire group, for any extended hospitality. If extra courtesies have been mentioned, acknowledge them. If you speak for a group, extend greetings from your organization. Suggest how this event can be mutually advantageous. If the welcomer has not explained something about your group or about you as an individual that you feel is important, talk about it yourself in the response. End with a prediction of pleasant future associations between the host group and yourself, or all the members of your group if you are a representative.

Dedicating New Facilities

Another familiar special occasion speech is given when a group officially recognizes the opening of a new facility, such as a building, bridge, or highway. This may include naming the new facility as well as launching it. The tradition of dedication is another of the ceremonies that we have come to expect and to enjoy. Sometimes the dedicated item may be smaller than a major facility, for objects such as paintings, statues, or new furnishings for a room may be recognized by a formal unveiling. Closely related to the speech of dedication is the speech sometimes given at groundbreakings—the intent is similar, but the ceremony is held when construction of the building starts, not when it is completed.

The guidelines for preparing a speech of dedication include the same warning to be brief and sincere that goes with all special-occasion speaking. You would need to begin by stating the purpose of the occasion, even though you assume that your listeners know why they have come together. If the event has some special significance to a particular group or organization, briefly discuss that significance. For example, state how a new YMCA will enable the staff to bring more extensive programming to the community, or tell how the new bridge will enable the people who live in an isolated area to get their children to and from school without long travel times.

Give the pertinent facts about the facility, such as its history from conception to completion. If you are unveiling a statue, give a brief biography of the person immortalized. A university senior class once gave a much needed new light board to its theatre as a final gift. The delightful dedication speech was full of anecdotes about the inadequacy of the old board with its many foibles and failures. If the facility is to be named for someone, then you need to tell something about that person—who he or she was (or is), and why this honor has been awarded.

If any individuals or groups have been especially helpful in seeing the accomplishment through, from the beginning idea to the final completion, they should be recognized. Finally, end on a note of inspiration for the future—how this new library or park or bank will offer opportunities for personal or public growth and development.

Saying Goodbye

When someone leaves a company, either to go to another position or to retire, some organizations will have formal ceremonies honoring the departure. Whether or not such an occasion takes place depends upon the rank and position the person has held, the length of time the person has been with the organization, and the customs and traditions that have been established in the past within that organization.

A speech given at one of these gatherings is called a *farewell address*, a short message designed to honor the departing member and to create in the listeners a desire to emulate the exemplary behavior of the honoree. Just as with the speech of introduction, you cannot tell everything about the person in your brief tribute, so you will need to pick out the most outstanding achievements, the most admirable personal traits, and cite examples of the departee's influence on others.

If the person is going on to another position or moving away, tell your listeners about the honoree's future plans. Be optimistic about his or her future. The effective farewell speech combines just enough "we will miss you" with "you are going on to greater things." You want the audience to feel some regret over the departure, but not to become maudlin. The individual has not died, but is merely moving away or retiring. (The *eulogy* is another form of special occasion speech, one that is given in honor of a person who has died recently or sometime in the past. The eulogy follows many of the same guidelines as the farewell speech. We find the eulogy to be more difficult for beginning college student speakers, and since the likelihood that you would have to deliver a eulogy some day is small, we do not focus on it as a separate type of ceremonial speech.)

Sometimes a gift is associated with a farewell and may be anything from a gold watch to a trip to Bermuda. If, as the speaker, you are called upon to present the gift, follow the same guidelines as you would for presenting an award—focus on the achievement, not the material value of the gift, yet let the audience know just what the gift is.

If you are the person honored by a goodbye party or banquet, you will need to be able to say a few words of appreciation—for the years of good associations with your colleagues, for the opportunity to have served with the organization, and for the tribute this special occasion symbolized. You will need to comment briefly on your plans, elaborating if the presenter has not done so. Finally, thank the group for any tangible gift, saying what it will mean to you or how you will use it.

A special note: The term *Farewell Address* is also used to refer to a major speech given by a leader when he severs connections from his followers. Two well-known examples are George Washington's "Farewell to the Troops" and Douglas MacArthur's "Address Before Congress."

Nominating Candidates

While many organizations use a nominating committee to select persons who will run for office, others have floor nominations. A combination of the two processes sometimes occurs, with floor nominations added to the slate brought in by the nominating committee. While some groups ask only that a name be offered, other organizations include a formal speech of nomination for each candidate. This tradition has evolved into a major ritual at the national political party conventions held every four years to select the presidential and vice-presidential candidates. Being chosen to give the nominating speech is an honor that is often extended to rising young politicians, for it gives them wide media coverage.

The nominating speeches that you may give to your clubs or professional organizations will be short when compared to political conventions. You need to think of your speech as persuasive rather than merely informative, for you hope to get your candidate elected. You will need to list his or her qualifications for the job and tell why your candidate is the best person for the office. If your candidate has a platform, which is a list of goals and objectives for the organization, you need to cite and explain the major points. Let the listeners know what your candidate can do for the group and how the group stands to benefit.

A nominating speech should be delivered in an enthusiastic and energetic manner. You need to convey your sense of excitement about the candidate so that the audience will become enthusiastic also. You need not be overly formal or serious; tactful humor is perfectly acceptable. A dynamic and confident attitude on the part of the speaker is a help in convincing listeners to support the candidate.

Making Announcements

The last type of special occasion speech may not seem to you to be a speech at all, for it is merely an *announcement.* We call it a speech, however, because the individual making the announcement usually stands before a group of people and presents information that has been planned in advance. We have attended many meetings where announcements went unheeded because the speaker failed to follow the brief guidelines that ensure a clearly made announcement. An announcement is persuasive in nature, for in addition to sharing information about the upcoming event or activity, you hope to encourage listeners to attend or participate.

Be sure that you have accurate information in advance and that you have arranged it in a logical order. Include the name or description of the event, the place it is to be held and how to get there, the day and date, the beginning and ending times, and the admission charge if there is one. Make the event sound exciting if it is social or recreational; this will inspire audience members to attend. If your announcement is for a less fun-filled activity, such as a committee meeting, stress the importance of what the meeting must accomplish.

Key facts in an announcement should be repeated at least three times. Give an overview of these key facts in a short introduction by saying, for example, "Next Saturday is the big event you've all waited for—the senior class picnic at Mountain Lake." Then, take each part of the announcement and explain it in detail—what the annual picnic is; where Mountain Lake is and how to get there; the date and hours; and how reservations can be made. Talk about the many games and activities that have been planned, the good food that will be served, and the wonderful opportunity to be with friends and classmates. Conclude your announcement with a summary that is a restatement of the key facts. If you wish, pause for a moment and ask your listeners to take out a pencil and paper, then go slowly over the precise details, asking that they write them down. Make the event sound exciting and fun, and be sure you state the time, place, and method of making reservations two or three times.

As with the nomination speech, your enthusiasm in delivering the announcement helps persuade audience members that what you are promoting is worthy of their attention.

KEY POINTS

- Several types of ceremonies provide opportunities for special-occasion speeches. These are relatively formal speeches, following guidelines that have developed as the ritual and the traditions of the event evolved.
- Among the types of ceremonial speeches are:
  introducing a speaker
  presenting and accepting awards
  welcoming and responding
  dedicating new facilities
  saying goodbye
  nominating candidates
  making announcements
- Each type of speech has certain rules and guidelines; all should be kept fairly short and should be delivered in a sincere, honest, and energetic manner.

QUESTION FOR DISCUSSION

What kinds of special-occasion speeches might the people in your chosen profession give? In what settings do they give them?

ACTIVITIES

1. In any special occasion speeches that you might have heard recently, did the speaker seem to follow the guidelines we have suggested in this chapter? If not, do you think the speech would have been better if he or she had known what you now know about speeches of this type?

2. Watch the Academy Awards, Emmies, or other televised awards show. What special restrictions make these presentations different from the giving and receiving of awards in clubs and businesses?

3. Compare television commercials and newspaper advertisements to the guidelines for making an announcement. Do they follow the same principle of repetition? How do they combine informing and persuading?

4. Write a short speech of "introduction" about yourself as if someone else were going to introduce you before your next speech in this classroom.

5. If you were to be nominated for president of the student government, what major points might the speaker make to convince your fellow students to vote for you?

Part V

The Speaker and the Delivery Process

Since we have left the chapters on delivering the speech until the final section of the book, you may think that "how you say it" is less important than "what you say." This is not the case, for many a well-planned speech has fallen flat because the speaker could not be heard or was so lifeless that the listeners could not stay focused.

We place it last because it occurs last in the process—speeches are fully prepared before they are given to an audience. Ideally, you should read Part V before you give your second or third speech so that you can begin to improve your delivery as you polish the content of your speeches.

You must learn that as a speaker, you can exert much control over the speaking situation. As Russell Lynes humorously tells us,

The platform, however one gets to it, is a perilous and unpredictable place. There are gremlins that persecute lecturers. They put slides in the projector upside down and out of order; they swipe the light from the lectern; they hide the glass of water or put it out of reach. They make the microphone squeal. They laugh at the wrong times. They mix up the pages of the manuscript. They turn the lights up before the last slide and start clapping before the lecture is over. They are not always there, but their threat certainly is.[1]

Mastering the principles of delivery can help you control those gremlins and take charge of the speaking situation.

Chapter 13

Delivery Styles

If five different speakers were each to deliver the same speech, you would have five different experiences, for each would bring to the presentation his or her own unique style of delivery. We all have different voices and bodies, and we all develop preferences about the spaces and equipment we use as we speak. What follows are some of the variables over which you have some choice.

THE SPEAKER AND THE MANUSCRIPT

Speakers and speech teachers differ in their preferences for the degree to which a speech is written out and referred to during the presentation. Four styles permit flexibility in choice.

The *manuscript* speech is one that is written out word for word in advance. The fully developed manuscript allows speakers to polish their language and sentence structure to its fullest. It also permits speakers to time their presentation precisely, which is essential in radio and television where time is paid for by the minute and even by the second. The manuscript can offer a form of support to the speaker who suffers from severe anxiety, for it eliminates the fear of forgetting.

A manuscript speaker is less likely to make a mistake, which is why most political candidates stick mainly to their scripts. With radio and television ready to broadcast any mistake to the entire world in a matter of seconds, political speakers must be cautious. Business executives often work from manuscripts, sometimes written for them by someone else. Many ministers prefer a full manuscript, although others will speak from an outline only.

The major disadvantages of the manuscript speech is that it is usually read, not spoken. And few speakers can read aloud as well as they can speak in their own conversational style. If the speaker feels she or he must adhere strictly to the manuscript, then any opportunity for inserting appropriate spontaneous comments is lost. Keeping eye contact with the audience is more difficult. Not only eye contact, but the sense of direct outreach to the listeners, the sense of talking *to* people instead of *at* them, is weakened when the speaker must read from a manuscript.

The *memorized speech* is the manuscript speech entirely committed to memory. With the speech memorized, you are freed from the problems connected with reading—seeing the print clearly, turning pages, or possibly losing your place. You can maintain eye contact and move around more freely.

The disadvantages, however, outweigh those advantages. Few people can deliver a memorized speech without sounding as if it is memorized. A noticeable difference exists in the facial expression of a person who is thinking up what to say next and the one who is trying to remember previously memorized lines. The first is natural and fits our image of spontaneous speech; the second often seems to search for the words on the ceiling as the speaker's face goes blank. Experienced actors and speakers learn to make memorized speech sound natural, but for most people memorization is stiff and uncomfortable. Forgetting is another disadvantage. If you have learned ideas, as in an outline, rather than precise words, you are much less likely to forget. Memorizing key ideas, a few primary facts, or an occasional interesting phrase may be helpful, but memorizing every word, including the articles and prepositions, weakens delivery for the average classroom or inexperienced business speaker.

The *extemporaneous speech* is one delivered from an outline or notes. The speech is carefully planned in advance, following all the steps we have covered in earlier chapters. The final draft, however, is not put on paper in complete sentence and paragraph form. Exact composition of sentences is done as you give the speech. When you are using flipcharts or posters, you can have your main headings on the charts themselves, thereby reinforcing the structure for the audience and also helping you remember the main points.[2]

The primary advantage of extemporaneous style is the fresh, spontaneous quality of the delivery. When you are generating your own sentences as you go along—based on solid advanced preparation of the topic, supporting material, and organizational structure—your speech will have a conversational manner that is more natural and pleasing to audiences than the stiffness that often accompanies a manuscript or memorized delivery. The focus is on thoughts and ideas rather than precise language or remembering certain words.

Many speech teachers prefer extemporaneous style for the classroom because it trains students to think on their feet. You may fear that you cannot create the language of the speech as you go along, but you surely can. This is what you do many times every day as you speak to friends, family, or your teachers. You have an idea of what you want to say—as you begin to talk, the choice of words and the syntax of the sentence (order of words) come naturally and easily. Spontaneous sentence generation is one of the marvels of the language center in the brain.

The *impromptu speech* is one delivered on the spur of the moment with no advanced preparation. These are usually shorter speeches, such as might be heard at a club meeting when members did not know an issue was to be discussed and could not prepare formal remarks. When you speak out in class, sharing your thoughts about the subject under discussion, you are giving a form of impromptu speech. If a board member speaks out against a newly introduced concept in a corporate meeting, he or she is giving an impromptu speech. Many times throughout life you may be called on to speak when you have not had time to research or prepare in advance. Impromptu speeches are excellent practice for thinking on your feet and for making you feel more comfortable in the classroom.

If you are asked to give an impromptu speech, the topic will be something with which you are familiar. You will already have ideas on the subject. As you walk to the front of the room, run the topic quickly through your mind, making sure you have a clear point of view and a specific purpose. Then try to find two or three major points of explanation of arguments to support a viewpoint. You will be surprised how much you can plan in the 20 to 30 seconds that you have walking forward and settling yourself at the front of the room. Use that time to plan, not to panic with worry that you cannot make it through. Use brief pauses to think through the next sentence. Beginning speakers tend to fear pauses and to think the pause lasts longer than it actually does. Listeners need pauses to catch up and sort what is being said. Use the pauses as opportunities to think ahead.

THE SPEAKER AND THE SPACE

In Chapter 4 we talked about the size and layout of the place where the speech is to be given as a factor that, when possible, should be considered as the topic is chosen. Certain subjects can be handled in intimate spaces that might be out of keeping in a large auditorium. Topics that require considerable formality might be difficult in small, informal spaces. But often you will not have the luxury of knowing well in advance where you will speak. Also, you may be asked to give the same or a smiliar speech on different occasions. Adjustment is then more a matter of delivery style than of topic choice and speech preparation.

You need to enlarge your delivery for a large space. This means more volume in your voice, a slightly slower rate of speech, and stronger emphasis on key words and phrases. For your body, it means larger gesture, bigger facial expression, and a more formal posture. Occasionally we might condone sitting as a part of a circle if the speech is given in a living room, but as a general rule, and especially in large spaces, we advocate that, regardless of the size of layout of the space, you plan to stand up while you talk. Standing says something to your listeners—it says, "I am in charge, I am confident, I am your focal point for the next few minutes." Standing also can help you as the speaker, for you can use more natural action and movement to help free physical tension, you can breathe deeper and with more support for your voice, and you can bring all of your body into play, not just your hands and face. Finally, research suggests that you think faster on your feet. "A person's information-processing speed accelerates 5 percent to 20 percent . . . when he's standing as compared with when he's sitting."[3]

If you give a speech in a large auditorium, chances are that you will need to use a *microphone*. Microphones are an accepted part of today's electronic society, and they enable us to share face-to-face messages with far larger groups of people. They also enable us to record the speaker's words for any number of future purposes. You need to think through four areas of concern if you are deciding about the use of a microphone.

To begin with, in large auditoriums or outdoor spaces, the speaker has little or no choice about using a microphone, for without it, the audience could not hear. But many speakers in much smaller areas request amplification when they do not really need it. The space does not require it, but somehow they feel the microphone gives them authority. This is not the case; all the microphone gives you is amplification and a series of restrictions on your physical and vocal mobility. Second, some speakers use unneeded mikes to substitute for lack of adequate projection. A small number of people may have serious problems in being heard, but the vast majority are simply overly shy, are holding back, or in some cases are too lazy to use the extra physical energy required to project and articulate carefully. Do not let microphone availability give you an excuse for lack of vocal effort.

A third concern connected with microphone use is that the instrument may become a barrier between you and the listener. "If you can be heard comfortably by all the people in the room without amplification, by all means, talk without a microphone. Relying on a sound system for a few dozen people, or in a room with excellent acoustics, distances you from your audience."[4] In your ongoing effort to keep performance anxiety under control, you need to break down physical and psychic barriers between you and the audience. If you can use your own voice clearly and fully, without electronic interference, one barrier may be removed.

A final concern is with skillful use of the microphone when the space dictates that you must use one. Depending upon the quality of the microphone, the amplifier, and the speakers, you will need to stand somewhere between 8 inches and 2 feet away from it. Too close will cause static and distortion; too far away, it will not pick up your voice. When you are testing a microphone in advance, never thump it or blow into it, for this could damage it. Just speak normally and have someone listen to check the volume level.

Talk fairly directly into the mike, although quality equipment allows you to move your head freely from side to side as you shift eye contact from one side of the auditorium to the other. You must speak distinctly and with forward placement, for a microphone will not offset poor enunciation. Make sure the mike is positioned properly—high enough that you do not have to lean over, but low enough so that it does not cover your face. The lavaliere microphone, or one made to clip on the lapel, allows a speaker more freedom to move around the platform and may be preferable in many situations.

Lecterns present some of the same problem as do microphones, especially the psychological distance created by a physical barrier between speaker and audience. Beginning speakers often hide behind lecterns or large podiums. Again, remember that the best way to reduce your anxiety is to become closer to your listeners, not more distant. Closeness is established by eliminating barriers.

The primary purpose of a lectern is to hold notes and papers—the speech manuscript or outline, or the note cards with quotations and statistics to be used during the speech. This frees your hands to gesture and add visual expression to your speech. In large, darkened auditoriums, the lectern frequently has a light so that the speaker can see the notes. Often the microphone is attached to the lectern.

The lectern is for your notes, not you. Do not lean on it or clutch it as if it were going to run away. Speakers who "white knuckle" the sides of the lectern often also sway back and forth, a distracting physical movement. Do not be afraid to step to the side of the podium from time to time if no microphone is involved. In small auditoriums, the speaker can move away from the lectern, as he or she continues talking, then walk back at a change of thought or in transition to the next ideas in the speech.

You should always check out in advance the room in which you are going to speak. If the lectern is not the right height for you, plan to stay away from it unless the hosts can provide a different one. It should allow you to be seen from just above your waistline upward. Any higher would block your face; much lower and you probably could not see your notes.

Microphones and lecterns are useful devices to help the speaker fill large auditoriums and hold speech notes. But they should not become barriers, either by creating a psychological divider between the speaker and the audience or through poor usage.

In our survey, we were surprised to discover that 50 of the 87 speaking occasions that we examined served some sort of *food or drink* as part of the meeting. This ranged from a simple cup of coffee to full dinners. Speakers sometimes spoke from a tabletop lectern placed at a head banquet table, sometimes at the front of a room with people tiptoeing back and forth to a snack table at the rear of the room. Some listeners held plates and cups of punch while they listened; others ate and drank either before or after the presentation.

Regardless of the exact arrangement, chances are high that your listeners will have food and drink at the speaking event. This can be advantageous, for refreshments usually tend to put people in a good mood. It can be disadvantageous if listener attention strays to the food rather than you. Speaking before or after the serving of food or refreshments is obviously preferable to having food handled while you speak. Yet conference and board room meetings during which coffee cups are frequently refilled offer no real barrier to a speaker. When people can sip along on some liquid, they are less likely to cough and clear their throats—a distraction that bothers many speakers.

You should limit your own intake of food and drink prior to your speech. Too much food can make you feel bloated; carbonated beverages may cause you to belch; caffeine increases natural nervousness. Be moderate in eating and drinking when you are the guest speaker.

As the speaker for the event, you have the right to exert some control over these and other physical features that might interfere with your delivery of the message you have prepared. If chairs in a lounge or living room area are poorly arranged so that listeners cannot see you, ask them to move into a more advantageous arrangement. If the light is so poor that you cannot comfortably see your notes, ask for a lamp or move the speaker's stand to another area with better lighting. If waiters and waitresses continue to clear dishes when you are about to begin, ask them to wait until you have finished.

You do not have to feel trapped and helpless when you believe the setting variables may work against you. Take control—after all, you are the "main event" for this program or meeting. Both you and your listeners will profit if you show yourself in the best possible surroundings.

QUESTION-AND-ANSWER SESSIONS

Time in speech classrooms is usually too limited to allow extensive discussion of the topics of the various speeches, which is unfortunate, for we often have questions about the speech subject that we would like to ask. In those speeches that you will give someday in your careers, however, the question-and-answer session might be the most important part of the occasion. Robert Lehrman asks, "What, after all, is the advantage of being face-to-face with an audience? It is the chance to interact with them . . . . Q & A eliminates the need for long speeches. It flatters the audience, by asking it to take part. It also shows off the speaker as someone who can think quickly."[5]

Radio and TV interviews and talk shows have made the question-and-answer format a familiar form of public communication. Our own observation of 93 speeches found that 73 of them were followed by question-and-answer sessions. Obviously this is a popular part of a speaking event. View it as a good opportunity to restate your main points, thus helping the audience to remember what you have said.

When you are faced with questions from an audience, remember a few simple guidelines. To begin with, you do not have to know everything about your subject. As Lehrman observes, "An occasional 'I don't know' is not only acceptable to audiences, it is attractive because it shows humility."[6] Restating the question before you begin to answer ensures that you have heard it correctly, rephrases the question for the rest of the audience, and gives you a few seconds to formulate your reply.

Try to answer only the question that has been asked. Do not wander off on tangents that may be related, but not absolutely germane, to the question as it was asked. Keep your answers as short as possible; many questions can be fielded in one or two sentences. Encourage questions from different members of the audience rather than letting one person dominate the floor.

Finally, keep your temper under control and your sense of humor active. Some questioners may try to trap you by pointing out contradictions or omissions in your presentation. Some may merely want to heckle. Others want to impress the audience with their own brilliance. Most, of course, simply seek a point of information. If you will remain calm and unafraid, knowing that you cannot answer every possible question but that you will do the best you can, you can handle the session with ease.

KEY POINTS

- Four possible styles of using notes or complete text are:
  the manuscript speech
  the memorized speech
  the extemporaneous speech
  the impromtu speech
- Extemporaneous style has many advantages for the classroom speaker.
- Speakers choose whether or not to use a lectern to hold their outline or speech notes.
- When a microphone is required, the speaker must use it carefully for maximum advantage.
- If food and drink are served at the occasion, they may provide some difficulties for the speaker.
- Question-and-answer sessions give speakers a good opportunity to restate their main points and to have a more personal interaction with the audience.

QUESTION FOR DISCUSSION

As you observe speakers outside the classroom, what delivery style do they most often use? Do most speakers use microphones? Lecterns? In thinking of the situations in which you might give speeches someday, what do you imagine the physical surroundings would be?

ACTIVITIES

1. Listen to a question-and-answer program on television, such as *Face the Nation* or *Meet the Press* or a talk show, such as *Oprah Winfrey* or *Donahue.* How do the speakers handle difficult questions? Do you feel that the questioners are friendly or do you sense some hostility? Discuss the impact of questioner style on speaker responses.

2. If you have never used a microphone, arrange with your instructor to let you and some of your classmates practice using one. Take turns speaking into the mike, with the other students monitoring you. Become accustomed to the correct distance and direction that you need to be heard clearly.

3. "To hold the manuscript" is obviously not the only reason that speakers use lecterns or podiums. Discuss the possible reasons for and implications of
   a) the minister's pulpit
   b) the judge's bench
   c) the jury's box
   d) the teacher's desk

4. How can you, as a listener, tell whether and speaker is reading a manuscript or speaking extemporaneously? What differences do you see and hear?

REFERENCES

[1] Russell Lynes, "Perils of the Platform" *Architectural Digest* 44, (Dec. 87) 47–48.

[2] Marilyn Moats Kennedy, "10 Surefire Ways to Give a Successful Speech" *Glamour,* February 1984, 172.

[3] Max Vercruyssen, as cited in "Study: People Think Faster on Their Feet," *Greensboro News and Record* 10 Nov., 1988, A4.

[4] John Stoltenberg, "How to Use a Microphone Well," *Working Woman,* February 1986, 79.

[5] Robert Lehrman, "Lessons from Campaign '84," *Public Relations Journal* 40 (December 12, 1984): 14.

[6] Ibid., p. 14.

Chapter 14

Voice and Body

Effective delivery depends to a large extent on skillful use of the speaker's voice and body. A speaker is much like a musician who must select a high-quality composition, then play it with proficiency on a well-cared-for instrument. For the speaker, the instrument is the voice and the body. This chapter gives you information for personal improvement.

VOICE

We customarily characterize voice by identifying its three major components—volume, pitch, and quality. A fourth component, rate, relates mainly to speech sounds. *Volume* is the loudness or softness of voice, the result of the intensity of the initial vibration and the *overtones*. You have a great deal of control over the volume of your voice, with the ability to produce anything from a whisper to a shout.

Voice placement works in conjunction with volume, for it relates to the speaker's ability to *project*, a process that combines increased volume with focusing the voice on the front of the mouth. Think of the term *projection* as it is used with movies; the projector is the instrument by which an image is moved from one position to another, enlarging the image as it travels. If the instrument is not in focus, the image will be fuzzy and unclear. You can project your voice by using a stronger column of outgoing air to initiate and reinforce the vibration process, but you must also focus your voice by funneling the emphasis of the resonance to the front of your mouth, rather than allowing it to remain in the back of the mouth or the throat. Such forward placement is the secret of a voice that "carries," one that can be heard easily in a large auditorium.

Many beginning speech students have problems with sufficient projection. Often they believe they are talking loud enough, but others in the class cannot hear them. If you have such a problem, practice the exercises at the end of this chapter, concentrating on improving breath control and forward placement.

The second characteristic of your voice is *pitch*, which is determined by the frequency of the vibration of the vocal folds. We hear pitch as the highness or lowness of both the overall voice and of the inflections and changes that occur in words and sentences as we talk. A few speakers have voice pitches that are so high that listeners find them annoying; we would recommend a speech therapist, for this can contribute to problems of speaker credibility, especially if the voice also has a whiny or squeaky quality.

The most common problem with pitch is lack of sufficient variation. Natural human speech tends to be filled with inflections and changes of pitch key. We know that excitement and heightened emotions are often conveyed with higher pitches, whereas despair or physical weakness may be reflected in lower pitches. The formality of the public speaking situation causes some speakers, especially beginners, to lose this natural variation and to speak in a restricted pitch range, called a *monotone voice.* This is especially true when the speaker is reading from a manuscript rather than producing spontaneous sentences.

A monotone speaker can be boring and may lose audience attention. Enthusiastic voices that are varied in pitch and volume make the listener's task much simpler. If you feel your voice lacks sufficient variety, or if your teacher or classmates suggest that you are speaking a monotone, practice the exercises at the end of the chapter that will help develop pitch flexibility.

The third characteristic of voice is *quality*, the result of the combination of overtones and the focal point of resonation. Desirable voice qualities are described by words such as *rich, resonant, pleasing, melodious, sonorous,* or *silver or golden toned.* Undesirable voice qualities may be called *harsh, husky, hoarse, nasal, breathy, weak,* or *unpleasant.* Undesirable voice qualities usually result from inadequate breath support, lack of balanced resonance, or improper placement. If you feel you have an unpleasant voice quality, find a speech therapist or take a voice and diction course. It is possible to change your voice quality, just as it is possible to alter your pitch level and improve your projection. It will take concentrated hard work to make a major change, for voice production is a deep-seated habit pattern; to change it, you must first break old habits, then acquire new ones. But it can be done. We offer a few exercises at the end of the chapter. These can help you if your problems are minimal and if you will practice daily.

As you prepare to deliver your classroom speeches, or in later years those speeches you will make in a business or volunteer setting, our best advice is to make an effort to expend a high level of vocal and physical energy. Chicago voice consultant William Rush says, "Projecting power doesn't just mean wearing a good suit or preparing a good speech. Your voice gives out a wealth of information."[1] Jeffrey Jacobi, of Jacobi Voice Development of the firm "Manhattan," agrees: "The ideal is to have a strong voice, speak in a wide range of tones, and use more inflection."[2] A clear, expressive voice adds interest to the speech, enabling the audience to keep its attention on the speaker with less effort. Because the speaker conveys enthusiasm and excitement vocally, listeners are more inclined to believe that the speaker has a genuine enthusiasm for the topic. As Walter Kiechel says, "If you're not excited about your subject, you won't be able to excite your audience about it either."[3] It is not enough for you to be enthusiastic about the topic; you must also convey that eagerness to the audience. Your voice is your principal tool in communicating your zest and fervor.

SPEECH: ENUNCIATION AND PRONUNCIATION

We identified the fourth division of the vocal mechanism as the articulation system, the part of the process by which outgoing vibrations are shaped into specific, individual speech sounds. The word *speech*, used to mean this utterance of language, may be a bit confusing because we also use the word to mean a total product of public discourse, as in the phrase "give a speech." To avoid confusion, we will use the term *pronunciation* to suggest the correct choice of sounds for a given word, and the word *enunciation* to discuss the clarity with which those sounds are uttered. Rate of articulation is also a factor in speaker clarity.

Pronunciation

Speech teachers disagree on the importance to be placed on standard pronunciation. Indeed, some argue that there is no such thing as "correct" and "incorrect" pronunciation, but rather imply different versions of the same word. Varying pronunciations, along with rate, inflection patterns, and some vocabulary changes, create the different dialects of American English. Some of these dialects come from regional differences, such as Southern or Brooklyn or Boston dialects. Ethnic background may determine a dialect, such as black English, or the Scandinavian influence in Wisconsin and Minnesota. Social and educational experiences also may shape pronunciation habits. Dialects are unique and important, for they give identity and a cultural character to their speakers.

In the past three decades, we have had three Presidents of the United States with distinct dialects—John Kennedy with a New England speech pattern, Lyndon Johnson with a Texas dialect, and Jimmy Carter whose Georgia background had shaped a Southern dialect. While journalists and cartoonists poked fun at their dialects (Kennedy was pictured saying "Cuber" and "Hawaiier," Johnson with "Mah fellow Amuricans," and Carter referring to himself as "Cahtuh"), this was mostly good-humored teasing and certainly did not prevent these three men from reaching the most powerful elected office in the United States.

Although we accept the validity of dialects, most of us still think of certain pronunciations as "accurate" or "correct." The horseback unit of the military is the *cavalry*, not the *calvary*, and an off-the-point comment is *irrelevant*, not *irrevelant*. In general, we accept those pronunciations listed in dictionaries, either regular dictionaries such as *Webster's* or *Funk and Wagnalls*, or in special pronouncing dictionaries, such as Kenyon and Knott's *A Pronouncing Dictionary of American English* (Springfield, Mass.: Merriam, 1953), Abraham and Betty Lass's *Dictionary of Pronunciation* (New York: Quandrangle/The N.Y. Times, 1976), and *A Concise Pronouncing Dictionary of British and American English* (London: Oxford University Press, 1972). The editors of dictionaries make choices based on what language-scholars determine to be the current preference of educated people. This suggests that standard pronunciations will change from time to time, which they do. But for now, when we want to know how a word is pronounced, we consult our dictionaries.

We hope you will follow the model that we believe Kennedy, Johnson, and Carter set for you—retain your native dialect if you wish, but know the correct pronunciation for all topic-related words that you use. This is your professional vocabulary, and it needs to be standardized. One of our students failed to heed this warning when he gave a speech comparing the Soviet Union today and under Stalin (a topic about which he had little firsthand experience). He included four important words: *bourgeois, proletariat, glasnost,* and *peristroika*—and seriously mispronounced all four of them, saying, for example, "ber-jeese" for the first one! His credibility suffered as a result.

The degree to which your instructor wants you to try to standardize your pronunciation will vary from one classroom to another. We know that extreme mispronunciation causes a speaker to lose credibility. Mulac and Rudd found that dialect speakers were rated lower than General American speakers in the audience's assessment of the socio-intellectual status and aesthetic quality of the speaker.[4] If your own pronunciation is such that listeners seem to hear *how* you say words more than *what* you say, then your pronunciation is interfering with your communication. You should make a serious effort to change your dialect pattern.

Some of the nonstandard pronunciations that are likely to call attention to themselves are:

WORD SPELLED	NONSTANDARD PRONUNCIATION
asked	axed
can't	cayhnt
escape	ekscape
fifth	fif/fit
get	git
idea	idier
iron	arn
library	liberry
secretary	sekuterry
strength	strenth
theatre	the-a-ter
thing	thang
through	thu
wash	warsh
you all (all of you)	yawl

A few of the professional words in the study of voice and speech production that are often mispronounced are:

WORD SPELLED	NONSTANDARD PRONUNCIATION
diphthong	dipthong (*p* for *f*)
larynx	lar-ninks
pharynx	far-ninks
pronunciation	pro-nounce-iation
vowels	vouls

Enunciation

Enunciation refers to the clarity with which you articulate your speech sounds. The emphasis is on the distinctness of production rather than a choice between sound variants. Well-enunciated speech is easy to understand, for the words come across plainly to the listener. The opposite of clear enunciation is mumbling, a muffled production that may leave the hearer wondering just what the speaker said.

Clear enunciation depends upon an active use of the organs of articulation, especially the lips and tongue. Again, forward placement is important, for it helps prevent mouthing and swallowing the words. Focus on the front of your mouth, make sure you are using your lips carefully to complete each sound, let your jaw be relaxed and flexible, and think about sending the words out to the listener "loud and clear."

One problem of producing clear enunciation is the degree to which you assimilate sounds, one into the other, as you move from word to word in a sequence. Conversational quality requires that we use connected speech, but the blending must be between the slurring of words together at one extreme and speaking one word at a time at the other extreme. Say the extremes in the following examples:

Howdjaliketugotthushow?
or
How///would///you///like///to///go///to///the///show?

The second example would obviously sound very stiff and unnatural. But the first is so jumbled together that we probably could not understand it. Clear assimilation is smooth, but permits a crispness of speech, so that meaning is unmistakable. Practice the exercises at the end of the chapter to help you improve your enunciation.

Speech Rate

Over-assimilated, slurred speech often results from a speaking rate that is too fast. The speed of human speech is quite flexible, varying from as slow as 100 words a minute up to around 400 words a minute. Either extreme would be difficult for listeners to follow. You need to establish a rate that is comfortable to listen to—slow enough to be completely clear, yet rapid enough to convey energy and enthusiasm. Listeners have a difficult time maintaining attention when a speaker drones on at a dragging pace, but listeners also will become discouraged and may quit listening if they must struggle to keep up with fast speech.

Many beginning student speakers talk too rapidly. They do this because they are nervous and feel insecure. Or they may fear pausing or slowing down because they suspect that we, the listeners, might think they had forgotten something. Some are rapid speakers by habit, using a fast pace even in a conversational setting. Overly rapid speech can make it difficult to enunciate clearly and may increase the tendency to slur words together. Try to maintain a comfortable pace, using your pauses as times to think ahead and as time for listeners to catch up.

USE OF THE BODY

From the study of nonverbal communication, researchers report that much of the message we convey is sent through the three primary nonverbal modes—kinesics, proxemics, and paralinguistics. *Kinesics* is the study of the body, especially facial expression and gesture. *Proxemics* deals with space and spatial relationships. *Paralinguistics* covers those vocal elements that accompany language, such as pitch, inflection, and tone quality, or sounds that have meaning without language—grunts, screams, or laughs. Estimates of the amount of any message that is conveyed nonverbally range from 65 to 90 percent.[5] While experts do not agree on an exact number, and we suspect that some of the estimates err on the high side, we nonetheless know that much is added to the clarity, expressiveness, and impact of a speech by skillful use of the speaker's body and voice.

We have already discussed the vocal elements in the first part of this chapter, and we touched upon proxemics in Chapter 13. The remainder of this chapter focuses on the specifics of the speaker's body, namely the kinesic elements of nonverbal communication.

Posture

Good posture helps both the speaker and the listeners. If you stand straight and tall, rather than hunching your shoulders and bending over, your breathing passages are open and the chest can expand more fully to support your voice. As you work to stand straight, do not get stiff and rigid in your posture, for that can make you tense and uncomfortable. Good posture is aided by finding a firm position for your feet—just a bit apart, one slightly ahead of the other, so that you do not sway back and forth.

Listeners enjoy watching a speaker with good posture, for it conveys confidence and self-control. With good posture it is easier for the speaker's head to remain erect so that the face is visible from the audience.

Gesture

Your arms and hands can add meaning and emphasis to what you say. Gestures can help describe and enumerate, as in suggesting size, shape, or number. They can aid the speaker in stressing certain key points and ideas, from a simple extended palm to the extreme of a fist hitting into an open other hand. Some gestures are specific symbols or emblems, like a *V* for victory, a circled thumb and index finger for A-OK, or the overused first two fingers tapping against the thumb while the arms are held high in the air to indicate that the speaker is quoting someone. "Gestures give rhythm to sentences, creating pauses so that everything isn't run together. Hands can display the ease and competence that persuade even difficult audiences to pay attention."[6]

Many beginning speakers are afraid to use their hands and arms. They may feel awkward and often express a confusion about what they should do. Our best advice is to follow your natural impulse—if you notice what you are doing, you may find yourself making small hand movements while your hands hang at your sides. These are your impulses to gesture. Go ahead and follow through—raise your hands up higher, get the gesture out where the audience can see it. Generally, gestures are more effective when the hands are kept above the waistline and in front of the body. Putting your hands behind your back is a very weak, ineffective position. Moving away from a podium makes it much easier for you to use your arms in broad movements. If you do not have to hold a manuscript, your hands are free to gesture.

You should not impose gestures artificially, but you should follow the natural instinct that we all have to use our hands and arms as we speak. Watch your friends in animated conversations and you will become aware of just how much we use gestures all the time.

Facial Expression

The face is the most expressive part of the body. By watching facial expression we know if a person is happy, sad, angry, or just lost in thought. As with many elements of voice and body, most people are far more animated in conversational settings than when they stand in front of a group of people to give a speech. Fear, discomfort, and a lack of information about what makes good speech delivery cause some speakers, especially beginners, to freeze up, and they fail to make use of nature's effective tools of communication.

A smile conveys not only good humor but also a confident attitude. Brows knit together in a frown may telegraph concern or resentment. Facial animation suggests that you have a true interest in your topic and your listeners, a significant factor in their becoming interested in you and your topic. Like gestures, facial expressions cannot be superimposed or faked—they must come from your own natural impulses. Few of us have blank, cold stares when we talk with our close friends, yet will become wooden-faced and expressionless when we give a formal speech. As you rehearse and develop confidence in your speaking ability, practice getting more animation and meaning in your facial expressions.

Eye Contact

Of all the parts of your face, your eyes say the most to your listeners. When we are able to contact another person with a direct gaze, a message goes between us that adds an extra layer of meaning to the words we speak. Audiences appreciate good eye contact, for it makes them feel that you are truly interested in them, and this enhances your credibility.[7] Effective public speakers learn to find several individuals in the audience on whom they may focus eye contact. These are the listeners who are looking at the speaker, often nodding approval or frowning concern, and from them the speaker gains feedback about how the speech is getting across.

Obviously you cannot look at the audience as easily if you are reading from a manuscript as you can when you speak extemporaneously. You cannot make eye contact if you look over the heads of your listeners, nor if you are looking down at the floor. Even in a large, darkened auditorium, with lights on the stage area only, an effective speaker can find eyes to engage. Vary your gaze across the audience—a few seconds toward one area, then catch the eyes of another listener in another area.

Learning to establish eye contact is useful not only for the two reasons already suggested—conveying interest in the audience and receiving feedback—but it is one of the best strategies for controlling stage fright. Instead of averting the gaze and turning away from the listeners, an action that pulls us back into ourselves, making direct eye contact is an outreach that helps break down barriers of separation. Good eye contact conveys frankness, openness, and an outgoing interest in sharing a message with the listeners.

Clothing and Grooming

One final element of body communication that increases speaker effectiveness is the choice of clothing and careful personal grooming. Books such as John T. Molloy's *Dress for Success* and *The Woman's Dress for Success Book*[8] stress the importance of personal appearance and the impression it makes on a viewer/listener. Clean, neat clothing, appropriate for the setting, adds credibility to the speaker, for it says that he or she is one who cares enough to put a best foot forward. In the business world, appropriate clothing usually includes a suit and tie for men, and a suit or tailored dress for women. In the college classroom, we are often less formal, permitting customary school clothes to be worn on speech days. Acceptable classroom clothing, however, may vary widely from slacks and sports shirts to ragged blue jean cutoffs and sweatshirts for the men; the women may attend in dresses, wearing hose and heels, or they may come in shorts, T-shirts, and sneakers. Your campus has its own norms.

In addition to the impression a speaker makes on an audience by his or her appearance, we believe that appearance also affects the way a speaker feels about himself or herself. We all self-monitor our appearance frequently, glancing in mirrors whenever we pass by them. We know the feeling of being all dressed up and knowing we look our best. That is a satisfying feeling. For beginning speakers struggling to gain self-confidence, we suggest that dressing on the more formal side of the classroom norm will help you feel better on speech days. Obviously if no one ever wears a coat and tie to class, then a male speaker would feel out of place and overdressed in such attire. But showing up barefooted in your cutoffs does little to help you feel better about yourself.

The same advice holds true for general grooming. Men look better, hence feel better about themselves, if they take the time to shave and comb their hair. Women usually have certain hair styles that they feel look best on them. Plan that style for speech day, and if you are accustomed to wearing makeup, apply it carefully when it is your turn to give a speech.

Look your best, both to convey a message of caring to your audience and to help you feel good about yourself. It is worth the extra time and effort.

KEY POINTS

- Effective delivery depends on the skillful use of the voice and body.
- The human voice is produced through the functioning of four physical mechanisms:
    respiration system
    phonation system
    resonation system
    articulation system
- The human voice is characterized by three elements:
    volume
    pitch
    quality
- Projection involves voice placement, energy, and enthusiasm.
- Pronunciation is the choice of sounds in a given word, whereas enunciation is the clarity with which the sounds are produced.
- Effective speech is characterized by:
    1. correct pronunciation of words
    2. enunciation that is clear and crisp
    3. a rate that is neither too fast nor too slow.
- The study of the human body is a part of the study of nonverbal communication, which includes:
    1. kinesics—individual body movements
    2. proxemics—the use of space
    3. paralinguistics—vocal elements that accompany language but are not language itself.
- Speakers need to improve bodily communication in the areas of:
    1. posture
    2. gesture
    3. facial expression
    4. eye contact
    5. clothing and grooming

QUESTION FOR DISCUSSION

Listen to the voices and speech patterns of all the speakers you hear—inside this class and outside in other situations. How do they affect your understanding and receptivity of the speaker's ideas? How might you continue to work to improve your voice and the use of your body for future speech making?

ACTIVITIES

The exercises in this chapter are from Ethel C. Glenn, Phillip C. Glenn, and
Sandra H. Forman, *Your Voice and Articulation*, 2nd ed. (Englewood Cliffs, N.J.:
Prentice-Hall, 1989).

1. Discuss with your classmates what you think your primary problem might be with
   either your voice or your speech. Extend the discussion to include speakers you have
   heard outside the classroom, particular dialects, and voice qualities, and how they
   do or do not interfere with the message.

2. *Breath Control*
   a) Place your fingertips lightly halfway between your navel and your breastbone, in
      the triangle formed by the lower, floating ribs and the waistline. Gently but
      firmly inhale so that the air seems to travel all the way down to the area where
      your fingers are resting. The area should move outward as you inhale, then
      gently flatten back inward as you exhale.
   b) Inhale deeply, then see how far you can count on one breath. Speak in a clear,
      projected tone as rapidly as you can but enunciating each word distinctly. Make
      sure you do not unconsciously take an additional breath by gasping in air while
      you continue to count. It is possible to produce a distorted speech sound on
      inhaled air, but this is not a desirable method of phonation. *Note:* In counting,
      women should work toward an ultimate goal of 45 to 50. Men, who generally
      have larger chest cavities than women, should aim for 55 to 60.

3. *Placement*
   a) Place your fingers on your pharynx or upper throat, just under your chin. Pull
      your voice downward in this area. Think of it as being down and far back. Say:
      In learning voice placement I surely must note
      How cloudy and weak is this sound from my throat.
   b) Puff your cheeks out with air. Place your fingers gently on the puffs. Using a
      somewhat higher pitch, read the following, pushing the tones into your fattened
      cheeks:
      Voice tones and words that are trapped in the cheek
      Will sound dimpy and wimpy and puny and weak.
   c) Concentrate on completely relaxing and lowering your soft palate so that you let
      all the air go through your nose. *Whine* as you say:
      One of the worst of a listener's woes
      Is a voice that exudes from the speaker's nose.

4. *Pitch variation*
   a) Starting with the lowest tone you can produce with a clear, controlled voice, say
      "one, two, three, four," and so on up the scale. How many notes can you include?
      Twelve? Fourteen? Then begin on the highest note and count down. If you are
      not making at least nine or ten distinct tones, try pushing a half step more at each
      end of the scale until you can stretch your range.
   b) Repeat the following sentences with the different moods and emotions sug-
      gested. Note the changes in your pitch.
      (1) Go away and leave me alone. (sad, angry, frustrated)
      (2) It's all mine now. (elated, greedy, defensive)

(3) I can't stand this. (laughing hysterically, depressed, in pain)
(4) Let me go with you. (pleading, suggesting, demanding)
(5) He won the contest. (jealous, incredulous, excitedly happy)

5. *Voice Quality*
   a) To ensure that the throat is fully open and relaxed, yawn deeply, emitting a big sigh as you exhale. Your throat is now relaxed. With your head tilted back, place your fingers gently on the front of your throat in the pharynx area, on either side of the passageway. Now ease your fingers down two or three inches so that you pass the larynx, then stop at the sides of the upper trachea. Move your fingers up and down several times until you are sure you have identified the passageway and the muscles on either side of it. Return your head to its natural position, keeping your fingers on your throat. Now pantomime screaming—make no sound, but act it out. What do you observe about the muscles of the throat? You should have felt a great deal of tension. Such tension prevents the pharynx from resonating fully and should be avoided.
   b) Pinch your nose and say "ah." Let go of your nose and say "ah." Alternate opening and closing the nostrils, repeatedly saying "ah." Try to eliminate any stress on nasal resonance by keeping the two sounds as much alike as possible. Concentrate on vibration in the cheeks.
   c) Try to keep the throat open and free as you practice the following sentences:
      (1) Fight the good fight fearlessly.
      (2) She freely spiced the rice with herbs.
      (3) Hopping, jumping, leaping and running are good exercises.
      (4) Wet your whistle with the water in the wicker wok.
      (5) Babies creep with legs and feet before they walk.

6. *Clear enunciation*
   a) Ifyourunallyourwordstogetherlikethisyourspeechratewillsoundawful. This is the opposite of "I/see/the/dog,/the/dog/sees/the/cat" style of speaking, where words are presented almost in isolation. Try to achieve a balance in the following phrases between overly deliberate articulation and slurring that alters pronunciation:
      Did you?
      How do you do?
      Right now.
      Watch out!
      I wish you would.
      Up and down.
      Did you eat?
      Cats and dogs.
   b) To sensitize yourself to assimilation, try timing word pickup with others. Go around the class with a series of telescoped sentences. Telescoping is a process in which the second speaker says the first word of his phrase or sentence at exactly the same time that the first speaker says the last word of her phrase; and so forth. Transcribed, it would look like this:
      (1) Apples are *red*.
      (2)   *Trees* are *green*.
      (3)   *Clouds* are *white*.
      (4)   *Daisies* are *yellow*.

Continue practicing until group members are always timing the first and last words exactly together:

(5) *Dirt* is *brown.*

(6) *Cheeks* are *pink.*

(7) *Royal* robes are *purple.*

(8) *Fresh* carrots are *orange.*

(9) *Celery* is *green.*

(10) *Pale* purple is *lavender.*

(11) *Summer* skies are *blue.*

(12) *Winter* skies are *gray.*

(13) *Some* cars are *beige.*

(14) *Spades* and clubs are *black.*

(15) *Coins* and candlesticks are *silver.*

(16) *Deep,* rolling seas are *azure.*

(17) *Crowns* and curls are *golden.*

(18) *Red* and purple make *fuchsia.*

(19) *Dark* red is *magenta.*

(20) *Nothing* I know is *puce.*

REFERENCES

[1]Suzanne Wooley, "Putting More Power in Your Voice," *Business Week* (April 4, 1988), 112.

[2]Wooley, 112.

[3]Walter Kiechel III, "How to Give a Speech," *Fortune,* June 8, 1987, 179.

[4]Anthony Mulac and Mary Jo Rudd, "Effects of Selected American Regional Dialects Upon Regional Audience Members," *Communication Monographs* 44 (1977): 193–194.

[5]Albert Mehrabian, *Silent Messages* (Belmont, Calif.: Wadsworth, 1971).

[6]Jack Franchette and George McCartney, "How to Wow 'em When You Speak" *Changing Times,* August 1988, 31.

[7]Steven A. Beebe, "Eye Contact: A Nonverbal Determinant of Speaker Credibility," *The Speech Teacher* 23 (1974): 21–25. Martin Cobin, "Response to Eye Contact," *Quarterly Journal of Speech* 48 (1962): 415–418.

[8]John T. Molloy, *Dress for Success* (New York: P.H. Wyden, 1975); *The Woman's Dress for Success Book* (New York: Warner Books, 1978).

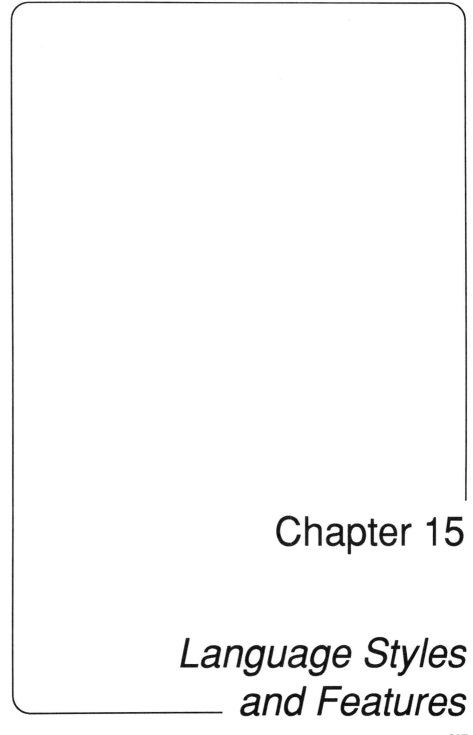

Chapter 15

*Language Styles
and Features*

The English language offers infinitely creative opportunities to speakers to find new, interesting, and effective ways of expressing ideas. The study of language is customarily divided into four major subdivisions; phonemics, syntactics, semantics, and pragmatics. *Phonemics* concerns the vocal sounds we produce and combine into syllables, words, and longer passages of speech. *Syntactics* deals with sentence structure, the order in which we place words in a sentence to create form and meaning. *Semantics* is the study of vocabulary, the meaning we assign to words, and how we use shared meanings to communicate with other speakers of English. *Pragmatics* examines the usefulness of language, the rules of social interaction, and the ways in which patterns and customs of language usage shape our relationships.

The guidelines for using language in public speaking spring from these four areas. Speakers can choose words that create oral pictures through their *phonemic* features, such as onomatopoetic words like *crash, zap, buzz,* or *babble,* where the word sounds something like the action it represents. Or we encourage stressing words whose rate and duration aspects allow us to reinforce meaning, such as *far, tall,* or *quick.*

We examine *syntactic* features in order to identify the differences in written and spoken English and between formal and informal style. Those differences are also found in *semantic* features, the actual words chosen by the speaker. This is the element that offers the speaker the widest range of choices, for almost every major noun and verb in our language has many synonyms and closely related words that can add variety, clarity, and exactness to the speaker's meaning.

Finally, *pragmatics* governs to a large degree the kind of language that we consider appropriate for the public speaking setting, language that is tasteful, adapted to the listener, and in keeping with the accepted norms and social amenities. The following brief discussion of language styles and features of language usage can help you improve and polish your own speeches.

FORMALITY/INFORMALITY

As far back as ancient Greece and Rome, speech scholars have recognized that language operates on a number of different levels of style. Cicero recognized grand style, moderate style, and plain style.[1] Although we no longer use those descriptive terms, we know that some situations demand a more formal style than do others. A major address at a convocation or founder's day dinner, or a somber gathering such as a funeral or memorial service, require a formal style. The least formal language style would be found in a casual conversation, while in a public speaking setting, talking before a close group of colleagues at work, or to a club whose members are all close friends would suggest informality.

The semantic features of informal speech include the use of colloquialisms, slang expressions, and simple words that we would call "plain, matter-of-fact English." Formal style demands a higher level of correctness, words with a national rather than regional meaning, and dignified words rather than slang. Formal style stays away from homey or folksy terms and seldom uses language in a playful way, such as puns and wordplays.

As we have emphasized throughout this book, every aspect of speech preparation and delivery should begin with an analysis of the audience and the occasion. And so must your choice of language style. By knowing when and where you will speak, the nature of the gathering, and the membership of the audience, you will be able to choose the appropriate style.

WRITTEN/ORAL STYLE

In Chapter 13, we urged you to use extemporaneous delivery of your speech—working from an outline or brief notes, but choosing the words and creating the sentences as you went along. Another reason for this preference comes from the differences in written and oral style. Originally—many, many centuries ago—written language developed as a means of putting spoken language down so that it could be preserved or could be transmitted to a receiver who was not in earshot at the time the message was sent. But written language has long since moved in a different direction from its spoken ancestor, and it now has its own set of norms, rules, and conventions.

The speaker who writes a speech as if it were a formal essay fails to recognize the differences in the two sender modes. He or she also runs the risk of forcing listeners to receive the message as if the listeners were *reading* rather than *hearing* the thoughts and ideas. A good speechwriter knows and utilizes spoken English rather than written English style, thereby keeping the end product in the appropriate mode. As Walter Kiechel observed:

> In putting it [the speech] together, bear in mind that this is an oral, not a written, communication. This means you should use short, simple words, go long on personal pronouns—I, me, you, we—and repeat your main points, since the listener won't be able to go back and reread what was puzzling. To achieve the right effect, try composing initially with a Dictaphone or cassette recorder . . . .[2]

In the syntactical aspects of style, written English is created in full sentences, often with a complex arrangement of subordinate clauses and phrases. Sentence fragments are not acceptable, nor are "run-on" sentences. Oral English, on the other hand, is often characterized by a failure to complete sentences—fragments are commonplace, and speakers will substitute connecting words, especially "and" for the end-of-the-sentence period that we see in written English. The degree to which this grammatical difference is unobjectionable is closely related to the previous discussion of formal and informal styles. The more formal the occasion, the more the speaker's style will move toward the written standard. In your classroom speeches, your instructors will urge you to formalize your style to the extent that you use pauses rather than conjunctions to separate sentences, and that you complete each thought rather than leave an idea dangling.

One interesting specific difference in written and spoken style comes in the grammatical order present in a sentence. Speakers tend to use more "right-branching" construction, where most of the message is placed "to the right" of the subject and verb. Authors, however, often "left-branch" their sentences, giving much of the meaning before the noun and verb are offered. For example, an author might write

> In choosing the President of the United States, issues such as the economy, foreign policy, and civil rights will be examined by Republican and Democratic voters.

A speaker would be more inclined to say

> Republican and Democratic voters will be examining issues such as the economy, foreign policy, and civil rights as they choose the next President of the United States.

This illustrates another difference—the use of the active instead of the passive voice. Speakers, when they are not misled into believing that they must "write" speeches, will most often use phrases such as "The fraternity paid its debt" or "The committee has planned an interesting program" as opposed to the passively stated, "The debt was paid by the fraternity" or "An interesting program has been planned by the committee."

In the area of semantics, speakers usually use simpler words than do writers. Speakers' words tend to be more concrete and commonplace. Writers often deal with abstract terms and may seek out less familiar words when those words have fine shades of subtle meaning, thereby choosing precision over familiarity.

Speakers use many more personal pronouns than do writers. In many types of formal writing such as essays or journal articles, personal pronouns are virtually taboo. Speakers, however, use "you," "we," and "us" to identify themselves and gain closeness with the listeners. And, finally, speakers use contractions, such as *don't* for *do not*, *I'm* for *I am*, and *that's* for *that is*, while writers more often avoid them.

FACTORS OF ATTENTION

Some features of language are closely aligned with the psychological factors of attention, since the primary purpose of improving speaker style is to capture and hold audience attention. An attentive audience is more likely to be a responsive audience.

The factors of attention include the following:

1. *Activity or motion.* That which stands still and remains motionless is less likely to attract attention than that which moves forward. Speeches must make progress toward a recognizable end.

2. *Reality.* Listeners prefer concrete, specific language to vague, abstract ideas, especially in building examples. Talking of "Tom Johnson and Tim Brown" is more attention-getting than mentioning "some guys I know."

3. *Proximity.* That which is nearby and close to us is more commanding than descriptions or examples of distant objects or people. Use what is near you—people in your audience, events in your school, or places in your city.

4. *Familiarity.* We identify with what we already know, and we may feel more comfortable than with totally new information. Metaphors and analogies make use of the familiar to help us move from what we know to what we do not know.

5. *Novelty.* Something that is new and exciting can capture listener attention, especially if it is rooted in a contrast to the familiar. Novelty wears off quickly, as evidenced by the many fads that sweep the country, only to die out soon afterwards. But when first heard, new ideas can be a source of attention.

6. *Suspense.* Holding out an element of the plot is the key to the attention created by mystery stories. We keep reading or listening because we are curious about the outcome. Speakers who are presenting an exciting new proposal may

withhold its description until near the end of their presentation, just as speakers who present awards often keep the name of the recipient secret until the end of their speech. Some suspense created by speakers helps listeners remain alert.

7. *Conflict.* Most of us find a challenge in being presented two sides of an issue when the parties under discussion are in conflict. Many people thrive on the publicized marital conflicts of movie stars and politicians, and we may follow lurid court cases with great interest. The speaker who can describe a conflict clearly can attract attention; for example, you might present the viewpoints of both the students and the administration in the campus unrest of the late 1960s and early 1970s.

8. *Humor.* That which is funny can capture our interest and cause us to pay heed to the speaker. Humor suggests not only joke telling but also witty descriptions and comments as part of the development of the speech. As we discussed in Chapter 8, the humor must be tasteful and pertinent to the speech topic.

9. *Vitalness.* We are most attentive to those issues that directly affect our daily lives. Topics that are developed to appeal to the immediate concerns of the listeners help keep listeners alert. For example, illustrations in a classroom speech on crime prevention would be better drawn from campus crimes than from large inner-city examples, especially if your college is not in a large city.

These factors of attention will help you as you work on your language style and polish the illustrative material of your speech.

LANGUAGE FEATURES

Many features of language can help speakers develop a more effective style. The following discussion focuses on three of the more important features: language that is accurate and clear, language that is colorful and varied, and language that is creative.

Accurate language is clear language, with the speaker choosing the words that most closely convey his or her intended meaning. Accurate language is precise, not vague. Rather than saying "I had a lot of stuff in my closet," it is more accurate to say "My closet was full of old clothes and boxes of books." "They planted lots of things in the yard" is not nearly as specific as "They planted trees, shrubs, and flowers in the yard."

Although *abstract* language is not inaccurate, listeners may find *concrete* language more useful. Concrete words are those that have a close association with a real-life referent, such as object words (table, chair) or place or person words (New York City, Abraham Lincoln). As we move away from the concrete, concepts become more general and nonspecific. For example, rather than table and chair, we might talk about *furniture, housewares,* or *interior decor.* Terms such as *East Coast metropolitan areas* or *nineteenth century U.S. Presidents* are more abstract than *New York City* and *Abraham Lincoln.* In Chapter 10, we talked about an informative speech in which you try to clarify an abstract concept, a difficult task for any speaker. The more you can deal with concrete terminology and specific rather than generalized verbal description, the more clear you become to your listeners.

Clear and accurate language is mature language used by speakers who learn proper adult words rather than depend upon juvenile substitutes. "Stomach hurts" is a more mature choice than "tummy aches," just as "soft drink" is more mature than "soda pop," and "rest room" than "potty." Mature language excludes adolescent dependence on a single word, repeated to excess, to serve as the adjective to almost any noun— "super," "fantastic," or "cool," for example. Mature language is also contemporary language, avoiding outdated words such as "gee whiz," "young whippersnapper," or "queer" meaning odd or peculiar.

Accurate language today demands a consideration of sexist terms. English lacks a third person singular pronoun that can be used for either sex, causing difficulty when we want to talk about a group by using one person as an example. Throughout this text we have often written a sentence such as "A speaker needs to be able . . . as he or she prepares . . . his or her speech." The concern over avoiding sexist pronouns has caused many people to use "they" or "theirs," even when the noun is singular. This violates a basic rule that pronouns must agree with their antecedents. While an awkwardness exists in constantly repeating "he or she," we believe this is preferable to consistent use of the generic "he" or using nothing but plural nouns to avoid the problem.

Other sexist terms include *chairman* (chairperson, chairwoman, Madame chairman?), *mankind* (womankind, humankind, and human race?) and *manmade* (manufactured, crafted, machine-made?). Speakers need to be sensitive to ways in which language can be used to exclude women and try to find terms that will be more universally acceptable.

Finally, for language to be accurate and clear, we must assume that the speaker will follow the rules of English grammar that govern subject-verb agreement, verb tense, and negation. "They goes to church," "She's eated her breakfast," or "He don't got none" may be interesting dialect constructions, but for the business world, speakers need to standardize their grammar.

Colorful and varied language is the second feature that can help your speech style. Some words are more vivid than others, for they enable the listener to paint mental pictures. This ties closely to your ability to describe, as explained in Chapter 6, which grows from creating visual images in your head, then finding the right words to convey those images. Especially useful are adjectives to suggest descriptive detail and synonyms to keep your word choice from becoming overly repetitious.

In a speech on housing for the homeless, for example, you could talk about people living together in an abandoned barn. To add color, you could describe the barn as *decaying* or *tumbledown;* it might be *forlorn* or *desolated;* or the winter winds might *bluster* through *open cracks, piercing* or *penetrating* the inhabitants. Any of these words would add color and enable the listener to picture the scene.

Consider the following use of synonyms that add variety to a speech on crowded conditions in a neighboring hospital that needs funds for a new wing:

The patient in the ward lives constantly surrounded by loud noise. The other patients are often loud, and attendants make noises as they bring bedpans or meal trays. Visitors make loud noises as they come and go, and one particular intern has an extremely loud voice. Even the keys on a chain are noisy as the nurses come in and out.

> speaker uses word "noise" to excess

The patient in the ward lives constantly surrounded by noise. Attendants rattle bed pans, and the clamor of trays from the kitchen begins at 5 a.m. One disoriented patient shrieks in pain, and the big-voiced intern roars in to give medication. During the day, the constant hubbub of visitors resounds in the corridors, and when the visitors leave, even the jangle of keys hanging on the nurse's belt seems loud to the ear-weary patients.

> speaker uses several synonyms for "noise"

Look for novel ways to make your ideas come alive with brightness and intensity that colorful language can bring to them. Much of the richness of the English language derives from the extensive vocabulary that offers many choices to express ideas. Successful speakers constantly seek out new words, always expanding their vocabulary and making a conscious effort to use these words until they become familiar and comfortable. We are limited only by our imaginations or by lack of effort in vocabulary building.

The third feature of language is *creativity*, which, much like color and variety, suggests that speakers need to work on language usage, not rely repeatedly on the same limited vocabulary. Creativity is found in using the factors of attention as we search for novelty, humor, reality, or words that make our thoughts vital. Creativity is achieved by avoiding clichés, those trite, overworked words and expressions that become monotonous when used to excess. Creativity develops through the use of a number of figures of speech, specific stylistic devices that have been identified and classified. We have already mentioned onomatopoetic words, those words that sound like or echo their meaning. We have also mentioned using the active rather than the passive voice. While we know that in a beginning public speaking course you are limited in just how much time can be devoted to developing an unusual speech style, we suggest that you study the following list of figures of speech, drawn from speech making and literature with further examples taken from popular music, to become aware of the rich opportunities our language offer us.

1. ALLEGORY—extended metaphor. Represents one thing in the guise of another, as an abstraction in the guise of a concrete image.
   Examples: *Everyman; Pilgrim's Progress;* extended comparisons of heads of state as captains of ships or football teams.
   Popular Music: "I Made It Through the Rain" (Barry Manilow), "Come On

Baby, Light My Fire" (The Doors), "Raindrops Keep Fallin' on My Head"
(B.J. Thomas)

2. ALLITERATION—repeated initial sound in several words of a sentence.
Examples: "The great gray ghost gallops ghoulishly over the green gar-
den."
Popular Music: "Betty's Bein' Bad" (Sawyer Brown); "She Sells Sanctuary"
(The Cult)

3. ANALOGY—a relationship or likeness between things that are otherwise
unlike. More extended than a metaphor or simile.
Examples: "The United States, like a great raisin pie, may not only be cut
into pieces, but may be examined by looking at each raisin."
Popular Music: "The Knife Feels Like Justice" (Brian Setzer)—also a simile;
"Baby When Your Heart Breaks Down" (The Osmond Brothers)

4. ANTITHESIS—contrast of ideas, direct opposites; opposite of parallelism.
Examples: "Ask not what your country can do for you, but ask what you
can do for your country."
Popular Music: "To Live and Die in L.A." (Wang Chung); "Pleasure and
Pain" (Divinyls)

5. APOSTROPHE—words addressed to an absent person as if the person
were present, or to a thing or idea as if it could appreciate them.
Examples: "Milton! thou shouldst be living at this hour" (Wordsworth);
"Oh moon, I thank thee for thy sunny beam" (Shakespeare)
Popular Music: "Rock Me, Amadeus" (Falco); "Oh Lord, Won't You Buy
Me a Mercedes Benz?" (Janis Joplin)

6. EPIGRAM—brief, witty statement, usually with an unexpected turn.
Examples: "It is not disgrace t' be poor, but it might as well be" (F.M.
Hubbard); "A cynic is a man who knows the price of everything, and the
value of nothing" (Oscar Wilde)
Popular Music: "I Can't Live Without My Radio" (L.L. Cool J); "The Sun
Always Shines on TV" (A-Ha)

7. EPITHET—adjective or noun expressing some quality or attribute.
Examples: Richard the Lion Hearted; " . . . drowsy tinklings lull the distant
folds" (Thomas Gray)
Popular Music: "When You Were Blue and I Was Green" (Joe Stampley);
"Manic Monday" (Bangles); "Moon River" (Andy Williams)

8. HYPERBOLE—exaggeration beyond line of truth done for special effect.
Examples: deaf as a rock; lovers in Elizabethan poetry who burn, freeze, or
fry.
Popular Music: "Party All the Time" (Eddie Murphy); "How to Be a
Zillionaire" (ABC)

9. LITOTES or MEIOSIS—frugality or understatement for effect; use of negative opposite.
Examples: Not bad, huh? This is some war!

Popular Music: "Oh, What a Lovely War" (Musical Review title song); "Sound of Silence" (Simon and Garfunkel)

10. METAPHOR—comparison between two things that changes our understanding and appreciation of either or both.
    Examples: "to take arms against a sea of troubles . . . " (Shakespeare); She's a doll. It's raining pitchforks.
    Popular Music: "You Are My Music, You Are My Song" (Charly McClain and Wayne Massey); "You Are the Rock, and I Am the Rolling Stone" (Carl Jackson)

11. METONOMY—name change, use of one word for another, such as specific word for abstract word.
    Examples: "The White House decided . . . "; "Cradle to grave . . . "; "He lent a hand . . . "
    Popular Music: "Sex as a Weapon" (Pat Benatar); "We've Got a Good Fire Going'" (Don Williams)

12. ONOMATOPOEIA—sound conveys sense; word imitates sound.
    Examples: splash, flip, gurgle.
    Popular Music: "Who's Zoomin' Who" (Aretha Franklin); "The Superbowl Shuffle" (Chicago Bears Shufflin' Crew)

13. OXYMORON—combination of contradictory words.
    Examples: cruel kindness, peaceful war, thundering silence.
    Popular Music: "Dueling Bicycles" (Ray Parker, Jr. and Helen Terry); "The Sweetest Taboo" (Sade)

14. PERSONIFICATION—attributing human qualities to inanimate objects or ideas.
    Examples: "There was a star danced . . . " (Shakespeare); "Till like a clock worn out with eating time/The wheels of weary life at last stood still" (Dryden)
    Popular Music: "The Heart Is Not So Smart" (El Debarge with Debarge); "While the Moon's in Town" (The Shoppe)

15. RHETORICAL QUESTION—question asked only for effect, not information; answer is implied.
    Examples: "This little life, from here to there—/Who lives it safely anywhere?" (Edna St. Vincent Millay); "Hath not a Jew eyes? hath not a Jew hands, organs, dimensions, senses, affections, passions?" (Shakespeare)
    Popular Music: "What's a Memory Like You Doing in a Love Like This?" (John Schneider); "How Will I Know" (Whitney Houston); "Who Needs Love Like That?" (Erasure)

MAKING THE ORAL STYLE YOUR OWN

While all of the foregoing elements of language—formality and informality; oral rather than written style; factors of attention; the features of accuracy, colorfulness, and creativity; and figures of speech—are important in building an effective style, the most important element of all is making that style your own. This can be an especially difficult problem for beginning speech students, for you are trying to find a balance between your own ideas and the research needed to support and develop those ideas. You are trying to find a balance between the way you talk naturally and the more formal, polished style required of the public speaker.

Another difference between oral and written language that we did not mention earlier concerns the style in which supporting material found in books and articles is restated. In most written materials, quotes are given directly, either indented and single-spaced or placed in quotation marks just as you do in the papers that you write. The original quote is repeated exactly. But for the speaker, repeating lengthy verbatim quotes would create the problem of mixing oral and written styles. Your language suddenly changes to be the language of the quoted author in the more formal written style.

For this reason we believe it is better for speakers to restate in their own words whenever possible. You can still give credit to the author but without feeling that you must quote exactly. Certainly some short quotations or passages from poetry or novels will always be appropriate in their exact original form. But they should be kept short so that they do not cause an abrupt shift in speech style. They should also be delivered in the speaker's natural rate, rhythm, and pitch—few people can deliver written material in the same personal style in which they speak their own words.

The most effective speakers are those who convey a sense of "ownership"—of their ideas, of their language, and of the vocal and physical elements of delivery. Although they cite many sources to give authority to the speech, they incorporate those citations into their own style so that the references are made naturally and easily. While they work to find fresh and interesting words and language devices, they integrate and internalize the language so completely that it becomes a part of them. And they practice for improved use of the voice and body, then absorb the new behaviors so that they sound and appear relaxed and comfortable. They are in command of their thoughts, their words, their voices, and their bodies. This is your ultimate goal as you strive to become a better speaker—both today and for tomorrow.

KEY POINTS

- Language is studied from four perspectives:
  phonemics
  syntactics
  semantics
  pragmatics

- Language styles include the formal versus the informal and written versus oral.
- Language features are closely aligned with the factors of attention, which include:
  activity
  reality
  proximity
  familiarity
  novelty
  suspense
  conflict
  humor
  vitalness
- The three most important language features are:
  accuracy and clarity
  colorfulness
  creativity
- Clear and accurate language is concrete rather than abstract, is mature, contemporary, and free from sexist terms.
- Colorful and varied language uses adjectives for descriptive detail, builds mental pictures, and finds novel constructions.
- Creative language avoids cliches and utilizes figures of speech to find new ways to express thoughts.

QUESTION FOR DISCUSSION

Listen to the language used by speakers you hear—inside this class and outside in other situations. How does the speaker's word choice affect your understanding and receptivity of the message? How might you continue to work to improve your language usage for future speech making?

ACTIVITIES

1. The following paragraph is in *formal* language. How could you restate the content in a more *informal*, conversational style?

   The unitary comprehension process theory argues that the same linguistic and cognitive skills are required for the written modes of reading and writing that are central to the oral modes of speaking and listening. In contrast, others argue that significant processing differences exist between speaking and listening, skills acquired with relative ease by physically normal children, and reading and writing, language skills that must be taught rather than acquired naturally. Low skill readers not only comprehend more slowly when the stimulus is presented in print rather than orally, but accuracy levels also suffer. A general acoustic-phonetic memory story process may allow a sequential retrieval of oral stimuli that may not occur in visual memory.

2. Take a copy of the daily newspaper and examine several stories to see if you can find examples of *reality, proximity,* and *familarity.*

3. Examine those same stories for any figures of speech. How effective are the figures as an aid to writing style?

4. For your next speech, make sure that you include at least one piece of supporting material that is *humorous* and at least one that would be attention-getting because of its *vitalness.* Make a conscious effort to include one or two figures of speech.

5. If your instructor has you critique speeches of other students in your class, make at least one of your comments on the language style—words that were accurate, colorful, or creatively used should be noted. If you should find an example of the unclear or inaccurate use of a word, note that too, suggesting that the speaker might seek out more effective synonyms.

REFERENCES

[1]J.S. Watson, trans., *Cicero on Oratory and Orators* (Carbondale; Southern Illinois University Press, 1970).

[2]Walter Kiechel III, "How to Give a Speech" *Fortune,* June 8, 1987, 180.

ADDITIONAL REFERENCES

Ayres, Joe, and Janice Miller. *Effective Public Speaking,* 2nd ed. Dubuque, Ia: Wm. C. Brown, 1986.

Banville, Thomas G. *How to Listen, How to Be Heard.* Chicago: Nelson-Hall, 1978.

Bostrom, Robert N. *Communicating in Public: Speaking and Listening.* Santa Rosa, Calif.: Burgess, 1988.

Bostrom, Robert N. *Persuasion.* Englewood Cliffs, N.J.: Prentice-Hall, 1983.

Bryant, Donald C., and Karl R. Wallace. *Fundamentals of Public Speaking,* 5th ed. Englewood Cliffs, N.J.: Prentice-Hall, 1976.

Burley-Allen, Madelyn. *Listening: The Forgotten Skill.* New York: John Wiley & Sons, 1982.

Byrns, James H. *Speak for Yourself: An Introduction to Public Speaking.* New York: Random House, 1985.

Cialdini, Robert B. *Influence: the New Psychology of Modern Persuasion.* New York: Quill, 1985.

Cragan, John N., and Donald C. Shields. *Applied Communication Research: A Dramatistic Approach.* Prospect Heights, Ill.: Waveland Press, 1981.

Daly, John A., and James C. McCroskey, eds. *Avoiding Communication: Shyness, Reticence, and Communication Apprehension.* Beverly Hills, Calif.: Sage Publications, Inc., 1984.

Ernst, Franklin H. *Who's Listening?* Vallejo, Calif.: Wheeler Printing, Inc., 1973.

Feingold, Alan. "Correlates of Public Speaking Attitude." *The Journal of Social Psychology* 120 (1983): 285–286.

Floyd, James J. *Listening: A Practical Approach.* Glenview, Ill: Scott, Foresman, 1985.

Gibson, James W., and Clifton Cornwell. *Creative Speech Communication.* New York: Macmillan, 1979.

Gibson, James W., and Michael S. Hanna. *Audience Analysis: A Programmed Approach to Receiver Behavior.* Englewood Cliffs, N.J.: Prentice-Hall, 1976.

Gronbeck, Bruce E. *The Articulate Person: A Guide to Everyday Public Speaking.* Glenview, Ill.: Scott, Foresman, 1979.

Harper, Nancy. *Human Communication Theory: The History of a Paradigm.* Rochelle Park, N.J.: Hayden, 1979 (chapters 4–6).

Hasling, John. *The Message, the Speaker, the Audience.* New York: McGraw-Hill, 1988.

Holtzman, Paul D. *The Psychology of Speakers' Audiences.* Glenview, Ill.: Scott, Foresman, 1970.

Hopper, Robert, and Jack L. Whitehead. *Communication Concepts and Skills.* New York: Harper & Row, 1979.

Johannesen, Richard L. *Ethics in Human Communication.* Prospect Heights, Ill.: Waveland Press, 1981, 1975.

McCroskey, James C. "Oral Communication Apprehension: A Summary of Recent Theory and Research." *Human Communication Research* 4 (1977): 78–96.

Montgomery, Robert L. *Listening Made Easy.* New York: AMACOM, 1981.

Morley, Joan. *Improving Aural Comprehension.* Ann Arbor: The University of Michigan Press, 1983.

Nirenberg, Jesse S. *Breaking Through to Each Other: Creating Persuasion on the Job and in the Home.* New York: Harper & Row, 1976.

Osborn, Michael, and Suzanne Osborn. *Public Speaking.* Boston: Houghton Mifflin, 1988.

Phillips, Gerald M., Kathleen M. Dough, and Lynne Kelly. *Speaking in Public and Private.* Indianapolis: Bobbs-Merrill Educational Publishing, 1985 (chapter 5).

Peterson, Brent D., Noel D. White, and Eric G. Stephan. *Speak Easy: An Introduction to Public Speaking,* 2nd ed. St. Paul, Minn.: West Publishing Co., 1984 (chapter 3).

Verderber, Rudolph F. *The Challenge of Effective Speaking,* 5th ed. Belmont, Calif.: Wadsworth Publishing Co., 1982 (chapter 12).

Walter, Otis M. *Speaking to Inform and Persuade.* New York: Macmillan, 1982, 1966.

Weissberg, Michael, and Douglas Lamb. "Comparative Effects of Cognitive Modification, Systematic Desensitization, and Speech Preparation in the Reduction of Speech and General Anxiety." *Communication Monographs* 44 (1977): 27–36.

Answers to Matching Quiz
(p. 168)

| A = 5 | C = 8 | E = 3 | G = 10 | I = 7 |
| B = 6 | D = 1 | F = 2 | H = 4 | J = 9 |

Index

A

Actuate (*see* Persuasive speaking)
Alston, Maude, 73
Analogy, 80–81
  figurative, 80–81
  literal, 80
Anecdotes, 73–75
  definition of, 73
  used in conclusions, 117
  used in introductions, 112
  used to support ideas, 74–75
Anxiety (*see also* Performance anxiety, stage
    fright)
Assertions, 103
  in persuasion, 159
Association of Communication Administration,
    3
Audience:
  adaptation, 16–27
  adjustive strategy, 27
  composition of, 17–23
  friendly, 24–25
  hostile, 24–25, 158

  passive, 24–5
  relational/attitudinal, 17, 23–26
Audiovisual aids (*see* Electrical visual aids)

B

Bandwagon effect, 76
Bartlett, John
  Familiar Quotations, 77
Blue, Richard, 83
Body, uses of
  clothing and grooming, 202
  kinesics, 199
  paralinguistics, 199
  proxemics, 199
Boone, Kitty, 70
Bradley, Bert, 16
Britt, Ginny, 81
Brown, William, 56
Bruce, Katharine, 17
Burns, Robert, 80